America as an
Ordinary Country

America as an Ordinary Country

U.S. FOREIGN POLICY AND THE FUTURE

Edited by
RICHARD ROSECRANCE

Cornell University Press | ITHACA AND LONDON

First published 1976 by Cornell University Press.
Published in the United Kingdom by Cornell University Press Ltd.,
2-4 Brook Street, London W1Y 1AA.

International Standard Book Number 0-8014-1010-X
Library of Congress Catalog Card Number 75-38427
Printed in the United States of America by LithoCrafters, Inc.
Librarians: Library of Congress cataloging information
appears on the last page of the book.

Contents

Contributors

CORAL BELL, formerly a member of the Australian diplomatic corps, held a Readership at the London School of Economics and Political Science before becoming Professor of International Relations at the University of Sussex. She has written extensively on American foreign policy and British-American relations. Her most recent books are entitled *The Conventions of Crisis: A Study in Diplomatic Management* and *The Politics of Détente.*

C. FRED BERGSTEN is a Senior Fellow at the Brookings Institution and formerly Assistant for International Economic Affairs to the National Security Council. He is the author of *The Dilemmas of the Dollar: The Economics and Politics of United States International Monetary Policy* and *Toward a New International Economic Order: Selected Papers of C. Fred Bergsten, 1972–1974,* and co-editor of *World Politics and International Economics.*

ALASTAIR BUCHAN, until his death in February 1976, was Montague Burton Professor of International Relations at Oxford University. He was Director of the International Institute for Strategic Studies (London) from 1958 until 1969, when he became Commandant of the Royal College of Defense Studies. His works include *Europe's Futures/Europe's Choices, The End of the Postwar Era,* and *Power and Equilibrium in the 1970s.*

FRANÇOIS DUCHÊNE, formerly *Economist* correspondent in Paris, was Director of the International Institute for Strategic Studies

(London) from 1969 to 1974. He is now Director of the Centre for Contemporary European Studies, the University of Sussex. In addition to a book on Auden's poetry he has written extensively on economic and strategic matters.

ROBERT GILPIN is Professor of Politics and International Affairs, Princeton University. He is the author of *France in the Age of the Scientific State* and *U.S. Power and the Multinational Corporation: The Political Economy of Foreign Direct Investment*.

PIERRE HASSNER, Senior Research Associate at the National Foundation for Political Science (Paris), is a long-time commentator on European-American relations. He is author of *Change and Security in Europe* and *Europe in the Age of Negotiation.*

KENNETH HUNT, formerly a Brigadier in the British Army, is Deputy Director of the International Institute for Strategic Studies (London). He was Visiting Professor at the Fletcher School of Law and Diplomacy in 1975. He has written frequently on arms control and strategic topics, including most recently an Adelphi Paper, *The Alliance and Europe: Part II, Defense with Fewer Men.*

PETER KATZENSTEIN is Assistant Professor of Government, Cornell University. His book *Disjoined Partners: Austria and Germany since 1815* has recently been published.

RICHARD ROSECRANCE is the Walter S. Carpenter, Jr., Professor of International and Comparative Politics at Cornell University. He taught formerly at the University of California and served as a member of the Policy Planning Council, U.S. Department of State. He has written *International Relations: Peace or War?* and edited *The Future of the International Strategic System.*

LEONARD SILK, leading financial writer, is now a member of the Editorial Board of the *New York Times*. He has written several books including *Nixonomics, Capitalism: The Moving Target*, and *Contemporary Economics.*

America as an
Ordinary Country

Introduction

RICHARD ROSECRANCE

Once so dominant in the international arena, America has become an ordinary country in foreign relations. The trauma over Vietnam, the radical reduction of American economic influence, the greatly increased independence of traditional allies in Europe and East Asia—all these have brought about an end to distinctively American leadership of the international system. The *Pax Americana* is over. These evolutions do not suggest that America does not still enjoy a margin of power over all other states. What they mean is that the United States is now only first among equals, *primus inter pares* among nations. She is an "ordinary" or "average" nation in that she cannot be expected to take on special responsibilities for world peacekeeping, to use her military forces where others do not wish to become involved, to support the world economy and sustain an international financial structure organized around the dollar. Her role as maintainer of the system is at an end.

America's "ordinariness" contrasts markedly to her world primacy of the past thirty years. Her position during this period was, if anything, even more dominant than the combined world roles of Germany and Britain in the 1870s and 1880s. Britain was the founder and operator of the international financial system. The pound sterling governed and set the standard for currency relationships. At the same time,

Britain was also the arbiter of empire. She not only obtained the (British) lion's share of colonial territory, but with her fleets also largely determined colonial opportunities for others. As late as 1910, Germany, a stronger power industrially and economically, had only limited access to colonies because of British superiority on the seas. British primacy overseas was paralleled by German power on the continent. At least until 1890, neither Britain, France, nor any other power was in a position to pursue a matter of national advantage in continental Europe without the consent of Bismarck. Thus the international system of 1870–1890 rested on the twin pillars of British financial and imperial hegemony and German domination of affairs on the continent. *Pax Britannica* in one sphere was supplemented by *Pax Germanica* in another. And since the British and Germans worked effectively together during this period, the system remained coherent.

For the post–World War II era and despite the rivalry with the USSR and the Soviet bloc, the United States amalgamated the functions previously performed individually by Germany and Great Britain. As Bismarck had forsworn specific national advantage in his regulation of the continental balance, so the United States conceived its role in a manner that transcended a narrow definition of U.S. national interests. American diplomats did not think of the nation as contending with a series of rivals: European, Soviet, Chinese and Japanese. They conceived its position as leader of a "free world" coalition of nations, and more or less identified U.S. national interests with the general success of coalition enterprises in all parts of the world. Thus, the Marshall Plan, economic and military aid, and assistance to the developing world did not appear to be a derogation from the American pattern of interest, but rather a reinforcement of it. The American conception of interest was limited and naive in that Americans could perceive no basic conflict between their own interests and those of their European and Japanese allies. The strengthening of Europe and Japan, economically, politically, and militarily—it was thought—could only redound to the benefit of the American position, for it would buttress the coalition of non-Communist nations in their struggle with ideological opponents.

In addition, because Americans erroneously conceived of a worldwide Communist "conspiracy," they tended to identify their national interests with resistance to Communism, internally and externally, wherever it might appear. This represented an analytical extension of U.S. geographic and functional interests that could not ultimately be sustained. Whatever the limitations of this position, however, it had benefits as well as disadvantages. It meant that the United States was at least initially prepared (and to some extent indefinitely prepared) to shoulder a far larger portion of the military burden of defending its coalition partners than would have been done if its position had been conceived simply as that of another nation-state. This support allowed Europe and Japan to devote the major fraction of their monies to internal economic development; it provided a political and security framework in which effective government could be reestablished.

Whatever the benefits for America's allies of such a policy, the U.S. analytical and doctrinal involvement against Communism in every sphere of the world—Asian, African and Middle Eastern—could not ultimately be borne. This fact became ever more clear and was particularly underscored by American doctrines obliging the United States to intervene within the domestic spheres of developing states to prevent (as American leaders thought) a "Communist take-over." As the limits of American power and influence were made dramatically clear in the denouement in Vietnam in the late 1960s, two possibilities emerged: either (1) the United States had correctly conceived the international struggle and had lost the battle; or (2) it had entirely misconceived the nature of the conflict and had failed to see that the triumph of Communism in certain states did not adversely affect either American or coalition interests. This second alternative required the United States to differentiate between domestic Communism in individual nation-states and Communist international policy. The triumph of domestic Communisms did not generally lead to international cohesion among Communist parties and leaders. Indeed, "national Communism" seemed more and more the result of domestic transformations that added to the difficulties of maintaining or even achieving a united Communist camp internationally. It was no longer crucial to think in terms of a free world coalition directed against Moscow's leadership of the Communist camp, for there was no coherent Communist camp to oppose.

With time, this second view came to seem more persuasive than the first. A new conception of American interests arose and new options appeared. Friendship with Eastern European regimes could be used to open their societies progressively to Western influence and economic penetration. The United States began to forge new relationships with smaller Communist powers, particularly Yugoslavia and Rumania. The opening to China and eventually to North Vietnam became possible, and one motive for a new policy was the estimate that China might be used as a lever to win concessions from Moscow. Chinese military strength on the Russian frontier could be added to European defense efforts to deter Soviet expansion.

This line of reasoning had a dynamic impact upon relations with America's erstwhile allies. It meant, first, that U.S. leadership in Europe and the Far East was no longer as necessary. The contradictions within the Communist bloc itself could be used to check Soviet ambitions. This greatly reduced pressure upon Europe; consequently, European states were enabled to formulate individual foreign policy stances vis à vis the USSR and also to move toward greater European unity. Strangely enough, the change in American policy even led Western nations such as Britain and France to take a harder line toward Moscow. The European demand for American troops in Europe has, if anything, intensified as the prospect of their removal has increased. The new American posture in foreign policy has liberated European and Japanese initiative.

But more important, the change has liberated the United States and restored maneuverability in foreign policy decision making. When Western Europe and Japan were the only supporters of American policies in world affairs, Washington could do little without consulting her allies. A series of Western European governments had vetoes over American nuclear sharing proposals like the Multilateral Force (MLF). The European Defense Community project failed. European states never devoted as large a portion of the GNP to arms as did the United States. In financial terms the United States suffered persistent balance of payments deficits that related to foreign military and economic spending, not to its balance of trade. An integrated defense organization under NATO never emerged, and the French went their separate way.

If, on the other hand, there were means of putting pressure on Moscow besides using a fulcrum based in Europe or Japan, what the Europeans did was less important. European weakness and dissension could be tolerated. The Japanese "low posture" did not present a major problem. Thus, for perhaps the first time the United States can afford to differ from an established European consensus. It can do so in economic as well as military fields. It gains bargaining leverage as a result. On some issues, even, it becomes possible to use *détente* with Moscow as a substitute for the traditional policy of firming up alliances. If Russia is partly checked by its own erstwhile allies, the United States can reach agreement with the USSR on strategic arms, the problem of the spread of nuclear weapons and superpower crisis control. The carrot may have its uses as well as the stick.

The United States did not develop its new foreign policy

stance simply as a result of the Sino-Soviet split or general disunion in the Communist camp. Even if these new and advantageous opportunities had not emerged, the United States would have been forced to find new policies in international relations. With the progressive weakening of the dollar, it became clear that America could no longer afford to run "foreign policy deficits" in the balance of payments unless she had a very strong surplus in the balance of trade. By August 1971, even the American balance of trade (the relationship between exports and imports) was in record deficit. The import surcharge, the cutting of the tie with gold and formal devaluation of the dollar were directed at America's European and Japanese competitors. In economics America's national interest had to take preference over coalition interests. It became increasingly clear that the United States had to find a new international monetary order in which adjustment processes were as available to the key currency as they were to other members of the system. This conclusion was endorsed at the Rambouillet and Kingston meetings of major industrial countries and the International Monetary Fund in late 1975.

Because of all the crucial economic and political changes in the international system, America must now find a means of acting on the world stage that does not pose the dilemmas of the Vietnam era. The long drawn out, indecisive and draining struggle in Vietnam clearly sapped the domestic support needed to carry on a vigorous and coherent foreign policy. In April 1971, a Gallup poll showed that only 45 percent of Americans questioned would send U.S. troops to help Mexico in the event she were attacked by Communist-backed forces. In the case of all other countries but England a substantial plurality preferred to send supplies or simply not to get involved, rather than to send U.S. troops.[1] For West Germany,

1. *Source:* A. H. Cantril and C. W. Roll, Jr., *Hopes and Fears of the American People* (Washington, D.C.: Potomac Associates, 1971), p. 47.

Israel and India the preferred option was sending supplies. For countries like Turkey, Japan, Taiwan and Yugoslavia, a plurality of Americans preferred not to get involved at all. It is apparent that unless U.S. forces are directly attacked, the most that can be expected of the American electorate and Congress is a decision to send military or economic assistance to the victim. This appears to be the course chosen in regard to Angola—although even here it is becoming clear that the Congress is increasingly unlikely to support aid for so dubious a cause.

If American forces are engaged in any conflict, the general lesson appears to be that the encounter must be short and decisive. Reacting to the draining stalemate in Korea, John Foster Dulles adhered to this maxim in the Quemoy-Matsu and Lebanon crises of 1958, but the lesson was forgotten during the Kennedy and Johnson administrations. It was again a presupposition of the American involvement in the *Mayaguez* incident in 1975. The use of American forces in counterinsurgency operations, however, is practically ruled out. U.S. forces in Japan, the Phillipines, or Western Europe are not likely to be strengthened by new ground troops in any significant way. While American forces will remain in some, though perhaps not all of those locations, U.S. commitments over time seem likely to be further reduced. The American physical presence in world politics will decline.

It is thus an appropriate time to reassess American foreign policy and to outline new directions for the future. At minimum, with a much smaller margin of economic and military resources over her competitors than she enjoyed in the past, America will have to pursue a more efficient international policy, husbanding her resources and diplomatic influence for those issues that are critical. What tack should she take? To answer this question a number of foreign and American scholars were invited to participate in the Carpenter Fund's lecture series "United States Foreign Policy and the Future" at Cornell University in 1975. Revised versions of these treatments appear in this book. Other experts were asked to contribute essays on political, economic and military policy in Europe and the Far East.

Alastair Buchan views American policy from the most comprehensive perspective, speculating on the need for new world "coalition" relationships. Coral Bell considers the worth of *détente* to the United States. Pierre Hassner notes the contradictions in American policy toward Europe and proposes specific remedies. François Duchêne asks whether the European Community is ultimately viable and examines its relationship to the United States. Peter Katzenstein speculates on one possible alternative to U.S. reliance on the European Community—choice of a German option. Kenneth Hunt considers the longer term defense and foreign policy problems of the American position in the Far East. Three well-known writers analyze the American role in the world economy. Leonard Silk examines the problems of inflation, energy and the threat posed by the Organization of Petroleum Exporting Countries (OPEC). C. Fred Bergsten discusses the problems that the United States will face if the Third World captures an increasing share of U.S. investment funds. Robert Gilpin notes that the multinational corporation has acted as a prime agent of the transfer of funds and recommends restraints on both MNCs and investment abroad. Richard Rosecrance asks whether the changed U.S. diplomatic position will lead to a drastic collapse of American influence in world politics and offers new directions for future American foreign policy.

The contributors agree that the overriding need is to fashion a strategy in which the United States is only first among equals, where the autonomy and strength of other major nations serve as checks and balances in the international system. Adaptation to a more limited role should offer America time and opportunity to put her own house in order; to bargain more effectively with OPEC; to limit the operations of multinational corporations; to cope with the growing challenge of the Third World. This volume does not, however, prescribe a nationalistic stance; rather, America's relations with erstwhile enemies and military allies should take the form of multiple coalitions in which U.S.-Soviet *détente,* the relationship with China and the traditional ties with Europe and Japan are held in dynamic equilibrium. The result could be a network of ties in which American efforts might be minimized and yet contribute to a new structure of peaceful relations in world politics.

2

United States Foreign Policy and the Future

ALASTAIR BUCHAN

The title is a daunting one, for it implies not only an ability to foresee how the interplay of domestic interests within this great country will materialize, but also the making of judgments about the whole future course of the international system. I have tried my hand at futurology in recent years, but I have made as many mistakes as my companions in that field, and I find this a particularly difficult time at which to write with any assurance about the future. The course of superpower relations, for instance, has been different from what one might have predicted after the summits of 1972 and 1973. Western Europe has been in travail since the collapse of monetary union, though not in the total disarray that is sometimes ascribed to it. The events of the past few years have illustrated the continuing strength of the United States at certain levels of international relations, in energy relationships for instance, and its weakness in others, the inability to affect the course of events in Southeast Asia or in the Middle East. In particular, this is a difficult moment to discuss American foreign policy, because an abnormal situation of a nonelected president, coupled with a dynamic secretary of state, both in a semiadversary relationship with Congress, exists; and even if this will be resolved by early 1977, I still find it difficult to find anyone who can give me a firm judgment as to what kind of leadership representing what predominance of views and interests will emerge to govern the United States in the last part of this decade.

Since I have recently been working on the early stages of a book on American foreign policy over the quarter century that followed Yalta and have been buried in the debates and decisions of the 1940s and 1950s, one contribution I can make is to try to approach the American future by way of the American past, offering as least a foreigner's assessment of what is permanent and what is transient in the behavior of the United States as a state.

I think it worth making the point that the stereotype which many non-Americans have, namely, of a United States that was completely isolationist until forced into world politics by the Axis powers some thirty-five years ago, bears little relation to the truth. Anyone who has studied the interwar years can trace a gradually rising American sense of strength in relation to the European powers, who still bore the primary responsibility for world order, and an increasing concern that the U.S. government should take a more active part in controlling the nation's international environment. Isolationism was as much a policy as an attitude and even so did not govern American relations with, say, Latin America or the countries of the Pacific littoral. It was a policy based on false premises, and because it was discredited by events, I see few signs and little likelihood of its revival, just as models like the Klingberg Cycle have lost any useful predictive value. True, it has never been clear to me how or if the United States would have become involved in the war against the Axis if she had not been attacked in December 1941. But once she was involved, there occurred a fabulous process of mobilization, military, industrial, intellectual, which has affected the whole social and economic fabric of the country ever since; and with this sense of confidence in American strength went Franklin Roosevelt's determination to play a determining if not *the* determining role in shaping the post-war order. We know the blind spots in his vision: his over-confidence in his ability to manipulate and dominate the United Nations in a close-working *entente* with the Soviet Union. We know that he somewhat misled the American public into thinking that the United Nations was an embryo system of world government and an instrument for the imposition of the rule of law. But it is, I think, relevant to our purpose to recall the the very marked enthusiasm that the American people displayed for assuming responsibility for the postwar order rested in part on a belief that understandings had been reached that would control and institutionalize the balance of power and the role of force in world politics in general.

We also know the sequel: the decline in American mobilized military power and the frustration of the American desire for an open world order; the challenge, as it appeared, both to American values and to American interests, of Stalin's action in Eastern Europe; the alarm, overlaid with ideological hostility, caused by the Berlin and Czechoslovak crises; the challenge to American values, interests, and responsibilities (though the latter were largely self-imposed) occasioned by the outcome of the Chinese civil war. These led, on the one hand, to the Marshall Plan and to the Atlantic Alliance in Europe, and to the hardening of the American definition of American security interests in East Asia, which in my view was one of the direct causes of the Korean War. And we know the sequel to that in turn: the conversion of what was originally conceived as a collective security system in Europe into a collective defense system, largely at European insistence; the militarization of what had originally been an adversary political relationship between the West and the Communist world; and the beginnings of a strategic arms race which is still with us.

I am not at all hostile to revisionism, although I find many explanations of why the Cold War took the form it did or how it could have been avoided, whether they fasten upon economic motivation or military ambition or the overconfidence of the foreign policy establishment, too simplistic. But I do think it is worth looking back at the debates of the 1940s, for the decisions that altered the course of American foreign policy did not go unchallenged, and certain of them may have relevance to the period ahead, when equally difficult decisions may have to be confronted. Some threads have perhaps become completely frayed by time; the dignified protests of Senator Robert Taft, for instance, that the United States was a special society and should be true to its tradition of avoiding entangling commitments in the external world. But others have relevance. One, for instance, was the protest of Senator Claude Pepper that the United States, in enunciating the Truman Doctrine and in entering into particular or ad hoc security agreements, was abandoning the Wilson-Roosevelt tradition and the support for the United Nations in which the United States had invested so much political and intellectual capital. A different variant was the protest of Henry Wallace in his famous Madison Square Garden speech in 1946, in which he argued that the first priority in American interests was to reach an accommodation and an understanding with the Soviet Union, and that to listen to Churchill's plea for a special American relationship with Britain and Western Europe was simply playing into the hands of the old imperialists. A third strand was represented by the views of George Kennan, who, though a public servant in the 1940s, was a severe critic of American public attitudes. He argued both in his cables and in the famous *X* article that the Soviet Union was an ideologically expansive power who would take advantage of every situation of Western weakness and whose ambitions must be contained by an adroit and watchful American diplomacy around the world until such time as the Soviet definition of its interests changed. And a fourth strand of criticism was that of Walter Lippmann in his book *The Cold War*, published in 1947, in which he in turn attacked Kennan's concept. Some of that criticism was misdirected because Kennan in his prescription of containment had used the unfortunate word "counterforce," to which he gave a diplomatic meaning, but which others, including Lippmann, took to mean military pressure. Lippmann, like Hans Morgenthau, and indeed like Kennan, argued that the United States had a group of national interests that were not necessarily those of the world as a whole, that it must sustain a balance of power with the Soviet Union. But what is still relevant is his argument that the United States had a special kind of constitution as well as special strength which made it impossible for her to conduct the kind of crafty and mobile diplomacy which, say William Cecil had conducted against Spain. Richelieu against Austria or England, or Bismarck in the furtherance of German interests.

"How, for example," Lippmann argued, "under the Constitution of the United States is Mr. X going to work out an arrangement by which the Department of State has the money and military power always available in sufficient amounts to apply 'counterforce' at constantly shifting points all over the world? Is he going to ask Congress for a blank check on the Treasury and for a blank authorization to use the armed forces? Not if the American constitutional system is to be maintained. Or is he going to ask for an appropriation and for authority each time the Russians 'show signs of encroaching on the interests of a peaceful and stable world'? If that is his plan for dealing with the maneuvers of a dictatorship, he is going to arrive at the points of encroachment with too little and he is going to arrive too late."

Again, though he mistook Kennan's diplomatic strategy for a military one, Lippmann put his finger on a valid point. "The United States cannot by its own military power contain the expansive pressure of the Russians 'at every point where they show signs of encroaching.' The United States cannot have ready 'unalterable counterforce' consisting of American troops. Therefore, the counterforces which Mr. X requires have to be composed of Chinese, Afghans, Iranians, Turks, Kurds, Arabs, Greeks, Italians, Austrians, of anti-Soviet Poles, Czechoslovaks, Bulgars, Yugoslavs, Albanians, Hungarian, Finns, and Germans. The policy can be implemented only by recruiting, subsidizing and supporting a heterogeneous array of satellites, clients, dependents, and puppets. The instrument of the policy of containment is, therefore, a coalition of disorganized, disunited, feeble or disorderly nations, tribes and factions around the perimeter of the Soviet Union. To organize a coalition among powerful modern states is, even in time of war and under dire necessity, an enormously difficult thing to do well. To organize a coalition of disunited, feeble, and immature states, and to hold it together for a prolonged diplomatic siege . . . is, I submit, impossibly difficult. . . . Even if we assume, which we ought not, that our diplomatic agents will know how to intervene shrewdly and skillfully all over Asia, the Middle East, and Europe, and even if we assume, which the Department of State cannot, that the American people will back them with a drawing account of blank checks both in money and in military power, still it is not a good prospect. For we must not forget that the Soviet Union, against which this coalition would be directed, will resist and react."

As we know, this was a somewhat unfair criticism of Kennan, but it was a not unfair critique of what eventually transpired. Lippmann, and Kennan too, believed that the United States had a limited group of natural allies around the Atlantic perimeter and that to extend American commitment beyond those countries, where there was a shared basis of values and economic interests, would be a source of trouble, of weakness rather than strength. However, the concept of containment did become militarized and enormously extended over the next decade. The United Nations slipped in the priority of American diplomatic instruments as it became less manageable. The United States did acquire a heterogeneous group of allies, though not precisely the ones that Lippmann named, and her alliances became proconsulates rather than coalitions. Soviet power was contained in Europe, but only at the cost of escalating the military strength of both coalitions. The extension of American power and commitments led to an increasing emphasis on the ideological role or interests of the United States as the upholder of freedom everywhere, and to the equation of non-Communist states with free states, of which Vietnam was one of the consequences. It has only been in the past five or six years that a measure of stability has been restored to Great Power relations, and then ironically by men who regarded Henry Wallace as a parlor pink, if not worse, but who nonetheless followed his advice that the United States should give high priority to its relations with the Soviet Union, and that China, whatever happened to its government, should not be treated as a Soviet dependency.

I do not mean to give the impression that I think the contemporary international system is entirely of American making. Despite the warning of Denis Brogan, against "the illusion of American omnipotence" after the Korean War, there still is a tendency in debates within the United States to credit the country with greater ability to control its international environment than I believe it possesses. Quite apart from the fact that neither China nor the Soviet Union has been a passive actor on the scene at any point in the last thirty years, I think it worth recalling that the United States was only one actor among several in creating the feud between Israel and her Arab neighbors. The process of decolonization which has swelled the ranks of the United Nations and contributed to American disillusion with it proceeded much faster than either the United States or the colonial powers envisaged

twenty years ago. The Sino-Soviet rift was not engineered by
the CIA. The ethos of the Third World was not of American
or Western devising, despite the entertaining attempt of
Patrick Moynihan in the March 1975 issue of *Commentary* to
ascribe it to what he calls the British revolution, namely, the
establishment of Fabian socialism as the dominant political
and economic philosophy of new states. I would note, however, in passing that we could make the mistake of perpetu-
ating the mystique of the Third World, both in the United
Nations and elsewhere, by treating all the seventy-seven nations who think they belong to it as if they were an adversary
coalition, long after its original unity of interest has disappeared.

Moreover, though the course of recent events has empha-
sized the fact that the United States still possesses greater
freedom of action than Western Europe or Japan, the uni-
polar world which writers like George Liska were discussing
a decade ago has now completely disappeared; the Soviet
Union has achieved in a real sense a position of strategic
parity with her fellow superpower; the United States has
suffered a tragic political reverse in Southeast Asia which,
though it does not necessarily affect her credibility as a guarantor power in relation to her major allies, has diminished her
influence by exhibiting the fallibility of her decision making
process; the dollar is no longer the world's basic currency and
the United States has lost the high measure of economic
autonomy which it possessed well into the postwar period.
The troubles that have beset the American political and social
system, though some of them are common to all industrial
states, have also circumscribed her influence. Above all, new
problems are rising to the surface of international debate
which are not capable of national solution even by a power
with the inherent economic and geographic advantages of the
United States: energy relationships; the control of the ecol-
ogy; the evolution of a new code of behavior on and beneath

the seas; transnational economic relations and the need to evolve a similar code of behavior for the multinational company; population pressures; food shortages; the disarray of the international monetary system; the risk that the proliferation of nuclear weapons may become a real danger again. These are all problems to which there is no obvious solution, let alone an agreed one, and which can be controlled only by forms of multilateral convention and diplomacy and the evolution of consensus.

Nevertheless, the United States retains its ability to exercise an enormous influence upon the character of the international system of the late twentieth century. Even though the dollar may no longer be the basis of the international monetary system, and even though the American economy has been in difficulties, external and internal, it remains the world's most powerful one. Even though the Soviet Union may have attained strategic parity, she does not possess a technological base comparable to that of the United States, and would fall behind should a failure to stabilize the strategic balance impose on both powers the need for fresh innovation in the design or protection of long-range weapon systems. I see, moreover, few signs that the vitality of American innovation in other fields, social, political or cultural, is ebbing. Even with a lame-duck president and a marked shift in the balance of power in Washington between Congress and the executive, no other country, adversary or friendly, is prepared to base its policy on any assumption that the United States is immobilized. The mistake that was made by Americans and non-Americans about Harry Truman and the Eightieth Congress is not likely to be repeated.

Moreover, responses have been made to some of the strands of criticism that emerged in the late 1940s. The arguments of the Left that the United States was drifting into a needlessly hostile relationship with the Soviet Union, and later with Communist China, have been answered by the policies of men of the Right. Kennan's contention that the United States must develop an adroit diplomacy to contain the thrust of Soviet ideological expansion has met with several answers. First, China has taken on the task of containing Soviet power in certain parts of Asia; second, this development has been encouraged by a greater flexibility in the conduct of American foreign policy, which is rightly associated with the name of Henry Kissinger; third, the problem of containment itself has changed since the Soviet Union has acquired the characteristics, not of a revolutionary power, but of an orthodox great power—ambitious, it is true, for the extension of its influence, somewhat old-fashioned in its equation of military power with influence, but no longer necessarily interested in the subversion and overthrow of non-Communist regimes. It is by no means certain how the Soviet Union would react to a Communist triumph in Portugal or Communist participation in the government of Italy.

Two strands of postwar criticism do, however, seem to remain unanswered. One is that, in becoming increasingly preoccupied with the traditional diplomacy of balance, the United States is neglecting the forms and forums of multilateral diplomacy at a time when their importance is increasing. Even if the United Nations is an unsatisfactory diplomatic market place, the Security Council still has an important function in the management of crises, and to pay a little heed to its resolutions, particularly on the rare occasions when they are mandatory (as occurred with Resolution 338 after the October 1973 Middle Eastern war), unnecessarily undermines its value. By the same token, the functional agencies of the United Nations are becoming increasingly central to the domestic interests of the United States as much as to those of other countries. Equally valid is Lippmann's criticism of 1947 —not only his point that to collect heterogeneous allies simply because they happen to be enemies of the Soviet Union leads to weakness rather than strength, but also his emphasis on the limitations which the American constitutional system places upon the practical exercise of American diplomacy. It does not become a foreigner to criticize the American secretary of state, but I do not think that either he or his admirers can do any service to American interests by equating him with figures such as Metternich or Bismarck, men who served absolute monarchs for periods of many decades, rather than having to participate in a turbulent system of democratic scrutiny and control. Tocqueville argued that if the United States became deeply involved in world politics the executive would inevitably acquire power at the expense of Congress, and this has proved to be the case. But the difficulties Henry Kissinger faces are not, in my view, simply a product of Watergate; they also stem from a misconception of the limits within which an American secretary of state must operate. One may rail against the system, one may argue that to be denied support or funds in one's policy toward Vietnam, Turkey or Angola, undermines ones credibility in dealing with the Middle East or in relations with China. But the American political system is what it is. Possibly over the third century of the country's existence as an independent state, it may have to undergo profound modification, but such change can take place only very slowly.

Let me turn now from the past to the present and the future. We are in a period of perplexity for many reasons, to some of which I have alluded. We have witnessed the growth of new problems without the disappearance of the old ones. The simplicities of the cold war years have been left behind us. There is an important agenda of business between the United States and the Soviet Union, on which SALT and the control of the strategic balance seem to me the most important, and which not even the most dedicated anti-Communist would wish disrupted. There is also a certain significant agenda of business between the Western powers and China, whether its importance lies in its intrinsic substance or in the opportunity to create greater leverage on Soviet policy. At the same time the alliance between the United States and its major allies remains as important to her as to them, because it expresses an organic relationship that involves not just questions of defense and security, but trade, employment, economic stability and social and cultural interpenetration. Yet neither the alliance nor the adversary relationship overrules the other, and the result is a situation of complexity from which we are often tempted to escape by reverting to the simplicities of the past. Professor Rosecrance recently outlined our dilemma clearly when he wrote, "The choice that is involved is essentially between a mixed international system in which allies and potential adversaries are held together in a network of fundamental cooperation, and a system in which lines of conflict are starkly drawn, with the United States and its allies more or less firmly on one side, and its new enemies more or less firmly on the other. It is a choice between a new form of bipolarity and an ambivalent system in which neither cooperation nor conflict is permitted to dominate patterns of alignment." It is a period that is doubly perplexing, moreover, because not only are Great Power relations changing but many of the assumptions of the quarter century of golden economic growth in the West are now also in doubt, complicating relations not only within the developed world but between the developed and the developing countries.

Speaking as a European whose country has been an ally of the United States for thirty-five years, I think there is little doubt about our particular decision between Rosecrance's alternatives. No one wishes to see the lines of conflict more starkly drawn again, just because it would simplify alliance relations or make it easier to get defense appropriations from parliaments. The development of Soviet-American *détente* has been generally welcomed, even if the Madison Avenue language in which it was described a year or two back occa-

sioned raised eyebrows. Senator Henry Jackson is not a popular figure in Europe. The breakdown of the Soviet-American
Trade Agreement occasions no delight, even if the Nixon administration's strategy of seeking to immobilize the Soviet
Union appeared too optimistic. It is my own fear, which I
think is shared by both Europeans and Americans, that if the
Vladivostok agreements cannot be translated into firm restraints on innovations and, indeed, into reductions of Soviet
and American strategic weapons systems, the process of
mutual deterrence may become so complex that it will
become increasingly accident-prone, difficult to comprehend
or operate, and may perpetuate an antagonism whose political motivation may otherwise be ebbing. It may be, of
course, that the United States by itself now lacks the diplomatic leverage to negotiate such agreements successfully, in
which case diplomatic support of her major allies, Germany
in particular, will become highly relevant again.

One difficulty, it seems to me, is that in a world of increasing complexity we either lack an organizing concept or
tend to be too much influenced by those of the past. *Détente*
is not, I would submit, an organizing concept, but simply a
description of a state of affairs. It is vulnerable to the vagaries
of domestic politics, to the competition of the superpowers
or of East and West in areas beyond those of their original
confrontation and to the misperceptions of each others' intentions, except where it can be translated into specific agreements or into codes of behavior that are explicitly recognized. The concept of a five-power balance advocated by
President Richard M. Nixon some years ago, is either premature or irrelevant by reason of the very different kinds of
power and influence which the United States, the Soviet
Union, China, Japan and the European Community exert,
quite apart from the fact that it leaves no place for the interests of the 120 or so other states in the world who would
appear to be objects rather than subjects of its operation.

The notion of an adversary partnership between the two superpowers has some merit, but it also has limitations. For one thing it takes very skillful diplomacy to defuse the accusation of collusion, not only in the minds of the Chinese and the French but in those of other powers as well. For another, it is not clear how effective it has been or could be in controlling conflict, or the means of conflict, such as nuclear and conventional weapons, nor in stabilizing our economic and other material relationships over the whole spread of world politics. A situation in which the United States and the Soviet Union were seen to be in a sort of semi-alliance might be one in which they had less, not more, influence over the policies of the increasingly influential middle powers. The older notion of Atlantic partnership, which indeed is as old as Victor Hugo's remark of 1847 that he looked forward to the day when the United States of Europe could grasp the hand of the United States of America, has suffered, since John F. Kennedy formulated it, from the ambiguity created by wholly disproportionate levels of American and European strategic power. It has been set in further disarray, partly by the recent statemate in the progress of the European Economic Community, and partly by the raw material crises which have accentuated the disparity in American and European autonomy. Moreover, in recent years there have been increasing ambiguities in alliance relationships. Does a close working relationship between the United States, Europe and Japan strengthen the American position in dealing with the Soviet Union and China, or does it inhibit her? Would the United States prefer to deal with a European entity, a coherent political entity, even if it is not a United States of Europe, or does it prefer to be the dominant member of a multilateral alliance system even with all the additional obligations it imposes upon her. Nor are the ambiguities entirely about American policy. Do the European powers—Britain, France and Germany—prefer a position of diplomatic unity in dealing with the United States, so that Europe as a whole may have a more autonomous relationship with her, or do they prefer to deal individually with her and less intimately with each other? Can the Atlantic Alliance system continue to be manageable when there is a difference of view, though not necessarily a profound rift, about relations with the Third World and with the oil states in particular?

There are two words or concepts that have more or less dropped out of the lexicography of modern diplomatic and political thought and which it may be desirable to bring out into the light for reexamination. One is "concert" and the other is "coalition." I am sure that in some dictionary of political science they are given a precise definition, but to me the word "concert" or a "concert of the powers" has always meant a relationship between major states who feel a high obligation to concert their policies, especially on issues that may relate to peace and war, because each has a range of alternatives to concert which it can pursue and has carefully considered what these alternative options and initiatives may be. It need not imply common action against another state, but may be motivated more by dread of a common problem, as the Holy Alliance was animated by fear of domestic revolution and subversion. In some degree the EEC, despite its elaborate institutional superstructure, is a concert because in the last resort its functioning depends on concerted action by the member governments and their legislatures.

The term "coalition" by contrast can properly apply only to a group of states with a base of common interests and values who have banded together to balance or offset the power of another country or another bloc. Modern history is strewn with them, whether for the purposes of deterrence, like the Franco-Prussian alliance of 1894 or the Atlantic Alliance of 1949, or for fighting wars, like the United Nations of 1941–1945. And so is the contemporary world. The United States alone is allied with over forty countries in multilateral

or bilateral security treaties. But coalition is a more significant term than mere alliance for it implies, to my mind at
least, a relationship of reciprocal advantage rather than one
of guarantor and dependents.

To take the concept of coalition first, I have been struck, in
reading through the documents of the late 1940s, by the extent to which the architects of the Atlantic Alliance—Dean
Acheson, Robert Lovett and Kennan, as well as Lester Pear-
son of Canada, Ernest Bevin of Great Britain and Robert
Schumann of France—saw it in terms of a coalition of reciprocal advantage rather than a relationship of guarantor and
guaranteed. Without a European alliance the reach of American strategic and political influences was confined to the
Western Hemisphere; without the presence of American power in Europe the Europeans felt no assurance that it would be
mobilized if Western Europe were again attacked. Not only
was the Atlantic Alliance a reciprocal bargain; its authors assumed that its leadership would be provided as much by the
major European states, once politically and economically
revitalized, as by the United States. The same sort of considerations underlay the Japanese-American Security Treaty.

We know the reasons why the NATO system became during
the 1950s less like a coalition and more like an American
proconsulate. The whole nuclear equation upset the original
assessment: the introduction of tactical nuclear weapons,
mistaken in my view but ardently desired by European governments at the time, meant that not only strategy but tactics had to be centrally controlled by the United States; the
collapse of British and French prestige fatally damaged the
notion of coalition. But with the gradually increasing political coherence of the European Community, I believe that
some of its characteristics are reemerging, nearly a decade
and a half after Kennedy asserted their desirability in his
formulation of "Atlantic Partnership."

And until recently I thought this was a development the

American administration desired to encourage, with the formulation of the Nixon Doctrine five years or more ago, which seemed to suggest that the United States should devolve greater responsibilities upon her major allies while trying to preserve a broad framework of stability within which they could reach decisions. But some of the political essence of the Nixon Doctrine seems to have got lost. There has been no American encouragement that I am aware of to Japan to assume a larger proportion of American responsibilities to East Asia, and the consequence is that some of them are going to default. An example of the serious failure of coalition diplomacy was the Cyprus crisis of 1974 when the British government hesitated to intervene against Nikos Samson, the creation of the Greek colonels, though it had adequate military force on the island to do so, until it had secured American backing; but Washington was paralyzed by Watergate, and when the German government, which has considerable influence in Ankara, offered to use it, it got support from neither London nor Washington. And the failure of these three capitals to support each other led to the unhappy situation of Turkish intervention. Coalition predicates a situation in which the strongest power, rather than considering itself as the nerve center through which every minor action and reaction must be channeled, preserves its influence for those situations that it alone can handle, allowing leeway to its allies in other matters.

Concert is a conception that is more applicable to the Soviet-American relationship. The reason why the term has dropped out of fashion is that it has traditionally been used in multilateral context: the five or six powers of the old European Concert; Roosevelt's "Four Policemen," and so on. But a concert of two is perfectly conceivable, and its development has not only had the effect of keeping perils such as world war at bay but has had a beneficent effect on coalitions. The Nonproliferation Treaty of 1968, which was the consequence of concerted policy by the two superpowers, had the effect, by allaying Soviet fears of German nuclear weapons, of laying the basis for the *Ostpolitik* in which the initiatives were German but which benefited not only Germany but her coalition partners. And still more forthright action to control proliferation may yet be necessary. Concert between political adversaries implies a degree of continuous diplomatic understanding which creates a climate in which it is possible to explore—sometimes at short notice—whether common action is necessary or attainable, given the fact that the alternative of conflicting action is always present. Concert has its own rules, just as does coalition. I am not, for instance, certain that an Arab-Israel settlement, for whose enforcement the United States is almost solely responsible, obeys them.

We, all the nations of the international system, now face a common enemy, not pollution, or floating exchange rates or exhaustion of raw materials, but complexity. Unless we can emphasize and define the characteristics of coalition and give substance to that of concert, we run the risk that a multipolar world to which some characteristics of balance have been restored, in which medium-sized powers have acquired greater autonomy, partly by intelligent American diplomacy, will become a fragmented, a disorderly and a dangerous one.

3

Détente and the American National Interest

CORAL BELL

Some Washington scoffer once defined *détente* as "building bridges to our enemies and burning those to our friends." Much of the dissentient comment on this strand in Henry Kissinger's assiduous and elaborate diplomatic knitting has been of that sort: the advantages of *détente* are assumed at best barely to outweigh its costs and it is implied that the balance may well be negative. I propose to dissent from this dissent, to be skeptical about this skepticism, to maintain that the doubts of the doubters may themselves be dubious —in short, to argue that the benefits of the policy to the American national interest greatly outweigh its costs, and that it not only has proved, but is likely, if it survives, to continue to prove a useful (and at times essential) stratagem to serve the American national interest, as well as the interests of peace.

I do not think that Kissinger himself could or should necessarily present the policy in this manner. Secretaries of state are of course charged with the defense of the U.S. national interest, and I hope usually take the obligation to heart—by their lights, which in the past (though not at present) have often seemed to us outsiders somewhat clouded. But it is not thought becoming in them, even nowadays, to say too candidly that this is what they are about. There is still a wistful assumption in the American soul that the pursuit of the American national interest is so naturally synonymous with the pursuit of the good, the true and the beautiful in international life that anyone who indicates he is able to distinguish between them must be some kind of un-American, amoral, Machiavellian cynic who should never have gotten to be secretary of state. I do not subscribe to that view: on the contrary, I would maintain that the ability to distinguish the national interest from the general good is the beginning of moral judgment in international politics. To serve the U.S. national interest seems to me an entirely proper motivation for any secretary of state: the quality of his moral judgment will be shown by the generosity of mind which he can bring to his concept of the American national interest and to the problem of reconciling it with other interests.

However, I am of course conscious that there is a group of Americans who might say, "Even if you can show that *détente* has been in the American national interest, we hold that it is morally wrong and ought therefore to be discarded." I will look at the case in due course, and adduce some arguments which I hope may meet it.

But let me first try to define the nature of *détente.* There is an American usage which tends to confine it solely to the American-Soviet relationship, or even just to the arms control and trade negotiations within that relationship. This seems quite misleading, though understandable enough in that arms control has been a sort of symbol of the *détente* relationship. The two, however, should not be equated. If one takes the word in its normal diplomatic meaning, relaxation of tensions, one has to conclude that the transformation of relations with China since 1969 represents a greater measure of *détente*—i.e. a more substantial reduction of tensions—then the change in relations with Russia over the same period, even though the relation with Russia incorporates arms control measures and the relation with China is not likely to do so. The argument

behind this judgment is that the *détente* with China was induced at a time when tensions between China and America
had been continuously high for twenty years. The American and
Chinese soldiers had actually been in combat—in Korea—for
two years, the brink of general war had been approached five
times in the period concerned—1950, 1954, 1955, 1958 and
1965—and there had been no diplomatic representation between the two in the whole period. Taken together these
signs indicate a very high level of continuous tension. By
comparison, the level of tension between America and the
Soviet Union over the same twenty years seems comparatively low, especially after 1963. Thus the American-China *détente* represents a more notable reduction of tension than the
American-Soviet *détente.* I would also argue that it has had,
so to speak, *logical* priority. That is, an opening to China was
necessary, in Kissinger's strategic understanding, to the further improvement of the level of *détente* with Russia which
had already been obtained by the time he came into office
in 1969. More especially it was necessary to the diplomatic
leverage which he hoped (and has in fact managed) to extract from the triangular balance constituted through this
mode of managing American relations with China and Russia.
Russia.

So I would define *détente* as *an artifice of statecraft* by
which a reduction of tensions is induced in a diplomatic relationship. I choose the phrase "artifice of statecraft" quite
deliberately, to emphasize that *détente* is not an accidental,
natural or popularly created phenomenon: it is something
consciously managed into being by policy makers, often
rather against the grain of political ideological expectations in
their constituencies. One can see this most clearly perhaps by
looking at the situation of the Chinese policy makers concerned. When Mao Tse-tung and Chou En-lai began sending
the signals by which they indicated China's interest in a *détente* with America, China was just recovering domestically

from the paroxysms of the Cultural Revolution, which had been marked by a good deal of xenophobia. (Mobs burned the British Embassy and presumably would have burned an American one with even more enthusiasm if one had been available in Peking at the time.) So there was certainly nothing in the domestic or ideological situation of China in 1967 –1968 to foreshadow the zeal with which the Chinese leadership began to play ball—in several senses—with America in 1969, as soon as Kissinger unleashed his barrage of signals via the French and the Rumanians and the Pakistanis, and anyone else who happened to be in contact with a Chinese official. Thus for Peking even more clearly than for Washington or Moscow, one must see *détente* as an artifice of statecraft, brought into use by policy makers in pursuit of their own good and sufficient power calculations, not so very different from Kissinger's.

The technique has proved copyable, so that the press now speaks also of a *détente* between East and West Germany, or even the possibility of *détente* in such unpromising relationships as that between Albania and Yugoslavia, or South Africa and Black Africa. President Nixon used to use the phrase "moving from an era of confrontation to an era of negotiation" for the change. But like many other things the former President said, that was not entirely accurate. Whether the international climate is Cold War or *détente,* there is almost always confrontation (in some sense) and negotiation (in some measure). It is the mix of the two that is different in the two climates. Obviously, in a *détente* phase, the level of negotiation and more especially of communication is kept deliberately high: the characteristic institution of the contemporary *détente* is the summit meeting. Contrariwise, in a cold war phase, the level of negotiation and communication tend both to be kept low: there was no summit meeting with the Russians in the coldest ten years of the Cold War, 1945-1955.

Looking at foreign policy quite dispassionately as a mode
of defending the national interest—or of defending the concept of the national interest held by the existing generation
of policy makers—one might for any given period compare
the advantages of *détente* and Cold War as alternative strata-
gems to this end. For some periods and countries (for instance, Britain in the mid-thirties) one might say that clearly
Cold War would have been the preferable choice, if the concept had been invented then, even given a general moral lean-
ing towards *détente.* So the case I am about to make relates
strictly to the contemporary period.

If I had to put this case into a single sentence, I would say
that *détente* has reduced the costs and burdens of America's
necessary role in the world, in a period in which it was domestically essential that these costs should be reduced, and
has acted as a sort of international safety net in what otherwise would have been a very dangerous period of transition,
diplomatically and politically. Let me put the reduction-of-
costs strand of this argument first. Looking back over the
cold war epoch in American foreign policy as a whole, one is
struck by the inordinate burden of costs which the diplomatic
and military processes involved in Cold War imposed on
American society. I am not here speaking primarily of financial costs, though if one adds up the arms budgets for those
twenty-two years, and the costs of economic and military aid
for allies and potential allies, the total is no doubt staggering.
But these financial costs seem to me less important than the
moral, social and political costs of the Cold War.

Let me illustrate this point by looking at the connection
between *détente* and Vietnam. To my mind, the original
American combat involvement in Vietnam was the most painful and damaging error in the whole two-hundred-year history
of American foreign policy. Even those who disagree with
that view must, I think, concur, on the basis of the published

evidence of the Pentagon Papers, that the process of involvement was intrinsically connected with the notion of "containment" as applied in Asia, and that containment was the
central politico-strategic doctrine of the Cold War. Vietnam
was one of the episodes of the Cold War in Asia. But it was in
my view the psychological costs of Vietnam which were instrumental in producing the mutation in the American national mood which permitted and required *détente*. The *détente,* in turn, (or rather the two *détentes* for the changed
relationship with China was even more important than the
changed relationship with the Soviet Union) provided a vital
part of the mechanism by which Kissinger ended the direct
American combat involvement. It also, to my mind, provided
the essential psychological basis on which America in 1975
could accept the final defeat—for defeat it was, though not
directly for American aims—with a shrug of resignation.

The change in the central balance of power between 1969
and 1975 was what made this feasible. In 1969, the sight of a
Moscow-oriented government being established in Saigon,
and a China-oriented government being established in Cambodia, would have been interpreted as enormous swings of
the world balance against the West. I am not saying that this
interpretation would have been right or reasonable, only that
it would have been *made,* and would have been dangerously
destabilizing for the whole society of states. In 1975, six
years on in the *détente,* the power relationship between
America and Russia on the one hand, and America and China
on the other had been almost completely "insulated" from
the situation in Southeast Asia. Very little of the comment
on the final collapse was preoccupied with notions of a dangerous expansion of the Soviet power base, and still less with
alarms concerning "the southward drive of Chinese power."
This latter absence was especially ironic, when one reflects
that the "containment" of such an assumed Chinese drive

southward was exactly what the American involvement in Vietnam and the protectorate in Southeast Asia were originally intended to ensure.

The *détente* with China was undoubtedly the major factor in the change of mood. If you have found you can construct a very reasonable *modus vivendi* with the Communist great power in Peking, the prospect of a minor Communist power in Saigon or Pnompenh does not appear particularly alarming. The *détente* with Russia was also important, however, in the American ability to accept a reduction of its sphere of power. *Détente* and Cold War are both competitive relationships; but the diplomatic-strategic competition of the cold war phase has a kind of edge of assumed desperation, which induces the illusion that every stretch of allegedly strategic real estate has to be denied to the adversary—even such disadvantageous and costly-to-hold real estate as South Vietnam turned out to be. That is why American policy makers from 1954 to 1968 walked, open-eyed and determined, deeper and deeper into the quagmire. They recognized that it was a quagmire, but the notion of containment, as interpreted in the psychological ambiance of Cold War, required that no inch of territory be conceded to the adversary.

As the politico-strategic doctrine of containment went with Cold War, so the politico-strategic notion of balance goes with *détente.* And the notion of balance enables one to relinquish a disadvantageous battlefield in favor of a preferable one. America has in effect relinquished the disadvantageous battlefield of Southeast Asia, not directly either to China or to Russia (as was once assumed would inevitably be the case) but to a variety of contending forces, mostly local. The "loss" of Southeast Asia was not a result of the *détente:* the true origin of any damage to the American national interest in the whole episode was with the decisions taken at a high point of the Cold War, 1954, to sustain a Western-oriented government in Saigon. What the *détente* did was to enable America to cut its losses, and in a way that insulated the central balance of power from the shock of this local defeat. The weeks of the final collapse were still painful for Americans, but they were not dangerous for the world in the way they would have been without *détente*. There was no "confrontation" with Moscow or Peking, and not much true sense of crisis in America. The "safety-net" aspect of the *détente* operated to ensure against such developments. *Détente* cannot, of course, turn a defeat into a victory, as some of its critics seem to assume it should be expected to do. But it can limit the damage and danger of such episodes, and to my mind it did so in the Vietnam case.

The Cold War was a high-ambition, high-cost policy for America. Exactly how high the costs might be, and how very unfavorable the "cost-benefit" ratio, if any, was not seen until Vietnam. *Détente* is a stratagem for the management of adversary power which aims at securing the essential power interest of America and maintaining its essential diplomatic competitiveness at less exorbitant costs. The transition from a "high-profile" to a "low-profile" policy in Southeast Asia did not really represent a diminution in American power, but a redeployment toward less disastrous objectives. The ability to choose the right battlefields is the most essential talent in diplomacy, and one lost sight of in the undifferentiated globalism of the Cold War.

The use of the *détente* relationship as a sort of fulcrum or base from which to exert American diplomatic leverage in a "Third World" situation is to be seen, in my view, in the Middle East negotiations, especially the crisis management of 1973–1975. One might note in passing that in the Vietnam negotiations, both the Russian *détente* and still more the Chinese *détente* were important in enhancing American diplomatic leverage and maximizing its options—including strategic options like the mining of Haiphong. In the Middle East crisis, and I would argue, the Cyprus crisis, it is of course only the Russian *détente* that is important, since China has no power to act and very little to exert influence. But both in the Middle East and in Cyprus, Russia had or has plenty of opportunities to act, both diplomatically and militarily, to the detriment of Western purposes. My argument is that in both these crises its diplomacy and even (in the Middle East case) its military resupply policies have been subdued to the necessity of maintaining the *détente* with America. I do not see any phase within those two crises in which Russia persisted in a policy after receiving a clear American signal that it would endanger the *détente*. This includes the Russian moves which produced the American strategic alert of October 24; the clearest thing about that loud, unambiguous American signal is that it was successful—if Russia had any dramatic intentions, they were relinquished. Similarly the failure to resupply Egypt for eighteen months with the level of armaments which it would need for a fifth round of the war has in effect held the ring very usefully for American diplomacy, at the considerable sacrifice of Soviet diplomatic influence with Egypt. The relatively ample arms supply to Syria, as against the parsimony toward Egypt, does not contradict this argument. Everyone, and especially the Russians, knows that the Syrians are not about to go to war against a very well armed Israel, if the Egyptians are unable to do so. So in effect by not resupplying the Egyptians adequately, the Russians did their bit toward preventing a fifth round for the time being, and so made their contribution, however grudging, to preservation of the general peace as well as the *détente* with America. After all, why else should they have gone in for this policy of restraint by relative arms denial? It was not out of tenderness for Israel. It certainly did not help their standing in the Arab world or even, one would say, their prestige as an ally in general. They have in effect been persuaded to sacrifice some marginal possible gains in diplomatic influence in the Middle East by the inducements of the *détente* with America.

Again, in the Cyprus crisis, considering the degree to which the Russians might have found diplomatic or even military opportunity (either in the original coup against Archbishop Makarios, or in the Turkish invasion, or in the very shaky internal situation in Greece during the fall of the colonels, when the Left seemed to have a good deal going for it), the very restrained level of Soviet maneuvers seems to indicate a decision that what they might hope for from the *détente* was more important to them than anything they could pick up in Cyprus in the way of extra influence. They really, one is glad to say, did nothing with some rather handsome opportunities.

On the whole, then, the *détente* has been a source of diplomatic leverage to American's foreign policy makers, and a cause of restraint—almost of loss of diplomatic leverage—to Soviet policy makers. But why should this asymmetrical result hold good? Surely, if peace is of equal value to both parties, *détente* should tend to operate equally as a restraint on both? My answer to this is that even assuming that peace is an equal value for both parties, *détente* has differential advantages as between the two. It is precisely because it was assumed to be more valuable to the Russians in the direct Russia-America relation, especially economically, that it has been diplomatically a source of leverage to America. (In a word, the Russians could less readily afford to disrupt it, given its assumed economic benefits to them.)

I find that this asymmetry on the economic plane is what many Americans seem to have against the *détente*,—they argue in effect, "The Russians get wheat and computers and maybe most-favored-nation status out of all this, and what do we get?" The answer in my view is that the United States gets nonmaterial but very important things, like diplomatic leverage, a safer relationship in the central balance and better prospect of long-term stability in the world. Since I am not an economist, I shall judiciously decline to discuss the level of economic advantage in American-Russian trade. But even a noneconomist may venture one observation in this field. Until a couple of years ago, I would have said that an economic comparison between the Western powers and the Communist powers showed an enormous superiority in the West —even the weakest Western economies, like Britain, did infinitely better by their citizenry in material goods than the Communist powers, and no one who had done any relevant traveling could doubt this, on the evidence of his or her own eyes. But now I think one has to admit doubts about the West's ability to cope with its characteristic economic problems of inflation and instability. So that even in the economic field, where *détente* has up to now been assumed to be more useful to the Russians, the trade relationship may come to seem quite useful to the West too.

It is precisely because these hoped-for economic benefits of the *détente* were made to seem doubtful to the Russians (mostly through the ill-considered machinations of Senator Henry Jackson and his allies in the Congress) that the chief apparent danger to its life was conjured into being. That is, Senator Jackson's tactics on the trade bill allowed the economic fruits which *détente* had seemed, in 1972, to promise to the Russians to become excessively belated, wizened, and poisoned by the time they were actually offered in 1975. Belated in that the Russian deficit had changed to a surplus between 1972 and 1975. Wizened in that the export-import credits were cut to a derisory level by Congress. And poisoned, of course, from the Russian point of view, in having the emigration clause attached to the trade bill. Little though one may sympathize with their argument that this amendment was an intrusion into Soviet domestic sovereignty and a slur on Soviet legality, these are obviously arguments that could be and probably were used in Moscow, by the hawks against the doves in the Politburo, and might have genuinely endangered Leonid Brezhnev, as well perhaps as the would-be emigrants and the *détente* in general.

So undoubtedly this episode did represent a setback to *détente*—an occasion for the Russians to ask themselves "Do we need it? Does it pay off? Is the *détente* game worth the candle of 'opportunity cost' we are burning to get it?" If they had cause to answer all these questions negatively, the *détente* might well have sunk without trace. But what was avoided, thanks to Kissinger's efforts, and one would say that the *détente* is continuing, despite Angola, though its path will necessarily be through a minefield until after the 1976 election.

I said earlier that I regarded *détente* primarily as a stratagem for the management of adversary power, and I think that this is the case not only for American decision makers but for Russian and Chinese ones. Moreover, I think that it can be seen as a successful stratagem for all three, because each nation seeks its "payoffs" in a different area: the Chinese in improvement of their strategic position, the Americans in greater flexibility of diplomatic maneuver and a reduction of burdens, and the Russians primarily in economic benefit. This was not always the primary Russian motive: when the Russian drive for *détente* began, in Georgi Malenkov's time, in 1953–1954, it seems to have been motivated largely by domestic difficulties, and in Nikita Khrushchev's time, around 1959, by difficulties with China. But for the present Russian decision makers it seems mostly that seeking Western technology, and import-led growth in the Russian economy is the prime objective. There is also of course a wish to see the "legitimization" of their hegemony in Eastern Europe, but I do not believe that *détente* necessarily provides that. The sphere of hegemony was secured in 1945, and the inability of the West to do much about it was made plain in 1953, 1956 and 1968, all in the cold war period. The best hope now is of obtaining some mitigation of the rigor with which it is enforced, and *détente* seems at least as likely as Cold War to do that.

The episode of the trade bill, and also Angola, make a point I regard as important; that the most dangerous enemies of the *détente*, in America, are those who would load onto it too much of a burden of moral expectation, or extract from it too hard a bargain. Some people seem to expect that it ought to mean that the Russians should bow out of the competition for power and influence in the world: give up the contest. But why should it mean that for the Russians when it clearly does not mean it for the Americans? *Détente* is a set of ground rules to make the contest less dangerous and in some senses less expensive, not an agreement to abandon the contest altogether. I do not think any such agreement to abandon the contest altogether is possible for either the Russians or the Americans. That is really what the Russians mean when they say that the ideological struggle goes on, despite the *détente*.

The other major source of resentment felt about the *détente*, especially on the Right in American politics, is that the arms control negotiations which have been part of it have conduced toward what is officially called "essential equivalency" in nuclear strike forces, which is generally interpreted as meaning parity at best in the general balance of forces. And dark suspicions are felt that the Russians will sneakily find some way of twisting this into strategic ascendancy and of using that situation to the West's disadvantage in some future crisis. A really dedicated pessimist will maintain that the Soviet Union looks to manipulating the economic advantages and the strategic parity conceded through the *détente* in order to develop its general economic and military strength, so that in fifteen years or so it will be strong enough to overwhelm the West, militarily, or in some unspecified political manner. The dread word 'Finlandization' is frequently used to denote the fate likely to overtake Western Europe in this scenario.

While I would not deny that this may be a favorite vision of various hawkish characters in the Politburo, I am doubtful that it will actually happen. The rate of growth of Soviet military strength is not necessarily enhanced by *détente:* possibly the reverse. The main Soviet drives to catch up with and overtake the West have mostly been fueled, as indeed is only logical, by some Western demonstration of advantage. The initial Soviet efforts to build A bombs and H bombs, after 1945 and after 1952, were made in the coldest period of the Cold War. The first drive to build missiles came after the successful recruiting of Germany to NATO in 1955. The first intensive drive to build a navy followed the Western success through naval forces in the 1958 crises. The second-stage effort on both navy and missiles was after the West's demonstration of its superiority in both the strategic balance and local conventional forces during the 1962 crisis. So one might reasonably conclude that the sense of danger, disadvantage or vulnerability is a more effective spur to Soviet arms efforts than *détente,* which is exactly as one would expect. Since 1969, the main source of the Soviet sense of vulnerability has seemed to come from the direction of China and that, along with the various other factors, is certainly enough to make the Russians determined to keep their military capabilities—both nuclear and conventional—at a high level.

If, as I assume, the essential "infrastructure" of the *détente* is a stabilized balance of power, then Russian determination to sustain military capabilities at a high level must clearly evoke a Western willingness to do likewise. Otherwise, of course, the balance of power would no longer be stable, and the superstructure of *détente* would come crashing down on the ruins of its infrastructure, the no-longer-stable balance of power. A preoccupation with this possibility is very clear in a good deal that Kissinger says about the *détente.*

The right-wing opponents of *détente* make use of a rather defeatist extension of this argument, saying in effect that it is impossible in conditions of *détente* for the Western powers to maintain the military alliances—chiefly NATO—and the level of arms budgets required to keep the balance of power stable. They are still echoing John Foster Dulles's arguments of 1955, when he was resisting the first summit conference and making American policy on the basis that a high level of tension was necessary and valuable to the West since only in such conditions could rearmament proceed.

This argument seems to me to rest on unexamined and, as I said, rather defeatist assumptions. Looking in the first place at the two alliance-structures, American and Russian, it is historically quite arguable that *détente* has since 1955 provided more problems for Moscow than for Washington. The various East European ferments of 1956 and later really owed a good deal to the thaw produced by Malenkov's *détente* policies. And above all, the wedge that was to split the Sino-Soviet alliance, from 1958-1959, was introduced into the relationship by Khrushchev's determination to pursue the *détente* with the Americans—Camp David and all that—at a time when the Chinese themselves had no incentive to do likewise. So compared with the troubles of the Russian alliance system, the little local difficulties that have beset NATO during the twenty years now of increasing movement towards *détente* do not seem to amount to much.

On the side of military expenditure—defense budgets—the hawks might seem to have a better case, for *détente* does undoubtedly foster a tendency to cut arms spending, in real terms, though this is disguised as far as money terms go by galloping inflation. Putting it very broadly and oversimply, one might say that in the coldest years of the Cold War,

1952–1953, American defense expenditure rose to about 15 percent of the GNP. With the process of *détente*, it is falling toward 5 percent of the GNP. And other NATO arms budgets have followed a similar pattern. It seems to me that this pattern is, or should be taken as, irreversible: that strategic planners looking to their future tasks over a long period of *détente* should assume that they must evolve a strategic posture and doctrine that can be maintained on 5 percent (average) of Western GNPs. They will not like tailoring their coats from this restricted measure of cloth (or chain-mail?). But politically it is going to be a necessity, and so it should be faced without delay. This is the point at which the arms control measures become relevant. Now it is true that the measures so far established do not actually provide reductions, but considering what ABM systems, for instance, would have cost if they had not been negotiated almost out of prospective existence, one must, I think, concede that without such *détente*-engendered measures the prospect of holding costs must be very thin.

To return to the actual strategic nuclear balance between the Soviet Union and the United States, I think that if anyone had reasons for apprehension, it would be America's allies rather than its citizens. The Western world since 1945 has in effect been living under an American nuclear protectorate. That includes Australia, and Japan as well as the NATO powers, of course. This protectorate, one might maintain, has depended on the margin of American nuclear superiority which was absolute up to 1949, and has been shrinking slowly but steadily ever since then. And this shrinking of the American nuclear umbrella is bound, one might say, to leave America's peripheral allies out in the cold. Extended deterrence is reduced, if the process goes on long enough, to minimal deterrence, which seems likely to inhibit only attack on America itself, or an America's direct interests. The American capacity for nuclear strike is reduced to same diplomatic function which the British, French or Chinese nuclear capacities now have: last-ditch sanctions against nuclear attack.

The process may work out like that, but in my view only over a period of time which will make the original system of extended deterrence no longer necessary or relevant. The system was essentially created by and for the cold war world —that is, to combat a single central threat. As that threat is replaced by a variety of quite different threats, the system of extended deterrence must inevitably be transmuted into something else. It was hardly so agreeable a concept as to cause much regret for its passing, since after all it depended on a morally repellent level of "overkill capacity."

The alarms over the prospective American loss of strategic ascendancy which were evoked in some right-wing quarters by the Vladivostok guidelines therefore seem rather unnecessary. I think most European opinion would regard it as a very useful—even advantageous—bargain for the West. It leaves the British and French nuclear forces out of account, which disposes of one source of difficulty. It leaves the forward-based systems to be argued about in the European context at Vienna, which reduces suspicion of a bargain being struck over European heads on a subject very vital to them. The principle of "freedom to mix" within the total of 2,400 delivery systems should work out very advantageously for the West, the margin of U.S. technological superiority being what it is. The ceiling for MIRVs may be rather high, but the argument that it is so high as to incite either party to aim at a "first-strike capacity" does not seem sustainable. What discourages thoughts of an effective first-strike capacity for either is surely the existence and the invulnerability of the submarine-launched missiles. And the freedom to mix principle, combined with the advantage in invulnerability of these systems, surely provides the maximum incentive for "putting the missiles out to sea," as they said in SALT I. One might even hope to see an agreement to phase out land-based missiles, though the Russians will presumably be very slow to move towards this position. On the present state of their technologies it seems doubtful that the Soviet (or for that matter the U.S.) chiefs of staff could have been persuaded to agree to anything less, but one might hope that the ceilings could be progressively lowered. The Soviet advantage in throw weight is much less important, by all accounts, than the American advantage in accuracy, not to mention its advantages in other technological areas.

Still, to be politically viable, arms control agreements must not only provide strategic stability; they must *look* like good bargains to a relatively inexpert electorate. They must not provide psychological handles of apparent disadvantage to politically ambitious persons who might want to overturn them, in the interests of their respective careers. This might impose a process of "leveling-up" for America in megatonnage or bigger missiles as against the far more desirable process of "leveling down." But there also seems a third option, which should prove more advantageous, that of expediting the process of "putting the missiles out to sea." If America exchanges its present complement of silo-based ICBMs for Tridents of improved accuracy, which are at once practically invulnerable and yet accurate enough to be used against hard targets, it must surely induce the Russians to follow suit as rapidly as they can. And this will produce a long-term balance which in my view should both be stable, and have a built-in element (for technological and geographical reasons) of American advantage. Unfortunately all this will be rather expensive in the short term, but it will have such advantages over the longer term that one might hope it will be chosen.

I have thus far been arguing on what might be called expedential grounds: pointing out the benefits of *détente* to the American national interest in terms of reducing the material and psychic costs of America's role in the world, and permitting it to maintain its overall diplomatic leverage without damage to its long-term strategic situation. But I am of course aware that many Americans who might concede that *détente* is expedient would go on to argue that it is nevertheless wrong: that it disregards the moral component which they feel ought to dominate American foreign policy, or at any rate be enshrined in it. I want therefore to sketch the reasons why I find this argument unpersuasive. The position is essentially that *détente* is immoral or at best amoral, since it involves consorting with two tyrannies of the Left, Russia and China, whose domestic political systems operate in ways intolerably at odds with liberal and humane political values, as defined in the West. There is a suppressed premise in this argument that, being contrary to American ideals, these societies are also dangerous to American interests, and that therefore America should have no part in helping them to flourish, but on the contrary should do what it can by unspecified means to cause them to wither, so that they will in due course be replaced by what is usually called "the open society," by which the speaker tends to mean a society very like the United States.

No doubt it is inevitable that *Realpolitik* and its practitioners should be vulnerable to both the right-wing moralism of the true cold war hangover, which remains suspicious of Russia and China, and the left-wing moralism of the post-Vietnam, post-Watergate period, which is suspicious of power, authority and secrecy and is interestingly reminiscent in some ways of the Woodrow Wilson period. In that sense Kissinger as he goes about his diplomatic errands necessarily does so under the reproachful scowls of the ghosts of both Dulles and Wilson, and their contemporary intellectual heirs.

I am not going to argue against the judgment that the regimes concerned are tyrannies or oligarchies disregardful of human rights, as defined by Western liberals: I fully agree that they are. Nor am I going to argue that moral judgment is not applicable in international politics: I would agree that both means and ends in foreign policy are eligible for moral scrutiny and moral judgment. What I do want to argue is that the moral values that are being applied are not the most relevant ones. I would base my case on the argument made by Eric Voegelin that the basic moral value in political action is prudence, by which he means a reckoning of consequences. And similarly, Max Weber remarks that a political ethic must be an ethic of consequences. So hand in hand with these eminent authorities, I am prepared to take my stand on the proposition that moral judgments on the rightness or wrongness of *détente* should be based on assessment of its consequences. And I maintain that these consequences are predominantly good. I am not arguing that there are *no* debits on the moral plane any more than I would argue that there are no debits on the power-political plane—only that the net balance is favorable, on the moral as on the power basis.

So what are the moral credits that I would claim for the *détente?* First, I think that it will free resources, both material and otherwise, for the more constructive tasks of international cooperation—the fairer sharing-out of food and energy and so on. These projects may not have much of a chance even with the *détente,* but without it they would have still less. In a true cold war situation, commodities have to go into stockpiles, and resources into arms production. Arms budgets are still quite high, but as a proportion of GNP they are undoubtedly likely to be lower in a *détente* phase than in a cold war phase, for both sides. And at the more reduced level of tension, other modes of combat should also be less important. For instance the CIA and the KGB were in many ways the true combat soldiers of the Cold War. With the *détente,* there may be some chance of demobilizing even them. Further, I think the moral results on the human plane in former areas of tension like Berlin are good. There is no doubt that the residents of that city live much more easily since the *détente* was enshrined in the 1972 agreements than they did before that time. Elsewhere in Europe much the same is true: there has been much more prospect of Soviet concessions on reunification of families, for instance, in a *détente* climate than in a cold war climate.

Some of the enemies and skeptics of *détente* speak or write as if these concessions were offset by a more rigorous enforcement of tyranny or party orthodoxy in Russia or the satellites. But this simply is not true. The worst years for such oppression and denial of elementary human rights were certainly the early cold war years. Anyone who remembers the anticosmopolitan compaign just before Stalin's death, or the Zhdanov terror a few years earlier, must be conscious of how pale a shadow of earlier horrors are the present ones. Russia and Eastern Europe are nowhere near being liberal societies, and the *détente* is not going to make them so. To expect that this should be required of it would be, so to speak, to expect the Soviet leaders to sell the roof in order to pay for the lightning rod upon it. The lightning rod is useful and valued: it reduces the chances of the most dramatic danger. But it is less necessary than the roof: they lived without it through the years of the Cold War and could again. The sort of changes in Russian practices that some people speak of as necessary for what they call "true *détente*" would be far more dangerous to the Politburo and the party than a return to Cold War, so if some Soviet policy maker of the future were forced to choose on this basis, he would logically choose the cold war option. And that, to my mind, would represent a very sad worsening indeed for the moral prospects of mankind on both sides of the curtain.

So I would be willing to make my case for the *détente,* if necessary, primarily on a moral basis. But in fact I think moral enthusiasm—even for causes I believe in—is a rather shaky foundation for foreign policy making. So let me retreat to the plane of *Realpolitik* for my final paragraph. The main impact of *détente,* to my mind, is to redistribute diplomatic leverage. This redistribution is rather subtle and unexpected in some of its effects, but on the whole, though not in every case, it works out advantageously for the American national interest. Certainly this seems to me to be so in the main relationships, vis-à-vis Russia and China and the more crucial NATO allies. Now why should I, a citizen of two countries (England and Australia) whose policies are both considerably influenced by *détente,* be in favor of this redistribution of leverage toward America? I must admit that both my countries find their interests well served by *détente,* but the real reason, I hope, is a less self-regarding one. Essentially I think it vital to the stability and creativity of the international system as a whole that America should be able to maintain a long-term role as the anchor man of the Western alliance. That in turn means that the costs to America of sustaining that role over the long term must be kept as low as possible. And it is to my mind possible to keep these costs low only in a long-term climate of *détente,* rather than in the more morally and diplomatically ambitious climate that produced the Cold War. *Détente* is a triumph of civilization — diplomatically civilized artifice—over nature, nature in international politics being notoriously red in tooth and claw. There will no doubt be dangers in living with it, but much greater dangers in trying to live without it.

4

Europe and the Contradictions in American Policy

PIERRE HASSNER

For more than twenty years, Americans, when pressed to pay more attention to Europe's interests and aspirations, have asked in exasperation: who speaks for Europe? This question has lost none of its relevance, nor of its potential for frustration; but, more than ever before, it is reciprocated by Europeans who ask today with more anxiety than anger: who speaks for America? Again, Americans are used to the constant need of the Europeans (especially the Germans) for reassurance and to their constant and contradictory complaints (especially those of the French) about America's domination or about her lack of leadership, about her excessive hostility to communism or her excessive intimacy with the Soviet Union. The trouble is that nowadays all these contradictory complaints have some foundation, precisely because American policy itself is contradictory or, worse, because it has been replaced by the divergent voices of conflicting forces.

For instance, it is true that Henry Kissinger has been guilty of excessive ambition in trying to impose an excessive American control over the management of the energy crisis, over the Middle East negotiations or over the conflict between Greece and Turkey; but it is also true that it is hard to see just what the American line really is on the price of oil, that

the United States lags behind other countries in the definition of a credible energy program, and that, while the administration's past policy hampers its relations with Greece, Congress has dealt a decisive blow to its leverage on Turkey.
Similarly, the administration may be accused of excessive
emphasis on *détente* with the Soviet Union and at the same
time, of a too rigid excommunication of the Italian Communists, while Congress, through the Jackson amendment, takes
the wind out of the former and the Italian elections show the
self-damaging irrelevance of the latter. It would seem, then,
that American policy seen from Europe combines the worse
of both worlds, i.e. assertiveness and impotence. Kissinger
wants to manage everything—*détente,* economic interdependence, the evolution of Mediterranean Europe—but he cannot
make good either on his promises or on his threats.

Of course, the fluidity of both the American and the international environment, and the imaginativeness, secretiveness
and deviousness of Kissinger's strategies combine in making
any impression of this kind a highly provisional one. At the
beginning of 1975, the magician reigned supreme. The early
spring seemed to witness the collapse of all his policies and a
decisive blow to America's position in the world. In the late
spring and early summer, the administration seemed to regain
its composure and to pick up the threads of its foreign policies with certain results in relation to its major adversaries
and allies. Surely by the time these pages are printed, other
impressions will predominate. Yet one cannot escape the feeling that there is more behind the variations than the ordinary
unpredictabilities of international life—that we have entered
a period where America's relation with the world is dominated by a strange and contradictory combination of uncertainty and fatality rather than by a coherent policy based on
relatively solid assumptions about the domestic consensus
and the international system. The European response to this
general impression is a mood of anxiety. While critical, Eu-

rope is afraid that its criticism may be taken too seriously and thus worsen the illness or the "rogue elephant in the forest" syndrome, by making the process of American decline more irreversible and American reactions to it more unpredictable.

Foreign policy, as such, is by definition supposed to counteract both uncertainty and inevitability, mitigating uncertainty with an element of predictability through commitments, alliances and institutions, while on the other hand modifying the determinism of impersonal forces through the freedom of political decisions. Now this role of foreign policy is being challenged, in the American case, by four types of uncertainties, two of a classic political kind, and two of a more basic and troubling kind.

The first two are on the one hand the diplomatic style of Henry Kissinger, based on the search for maximum secrecy and flexibility and on the other hand his domestic base, characterized by a rebellious, self-assertive but divided Congress. There obviously is a tension between flexible diplomacy and institutionalized alliances; between the desire for greater freedom of decision of the policy maker and the desire for greater predictability through commitments and alliances; between unilateralism and multilateralism. Many of the criticisms of Secretary Kissinger coming from Europeans or members of the older, pro-Europeanist, school of foreign policy, like George Ball or Robert Bowie, stem from Kissinger's preference for flexibility and surprise, to the neglect of community building and alliances.

Recently, however, the same have found less reason for worry in the secretary of state's search for freedom of action than in the paralysis of his diplomacy by lack of domestic support; less in his distaste for permanent commitments than in Congress's jeopardizing the credibility of *any* American commitment; less in the intricacy of Kissinger's strategy than in Congress's ability to wreck any of these strategies combined with its inability to come up with any coherent alternative.

   But the really serious question is whether these two political uncertainties are not rooted in two historical and structural changes concerning America's position in the world and the reactions of American society to it—or, in the last analysis, concerning the relation between the evolution of modern society and that of the international system. In a way, our fears about not knowing where Kissinger is going to spring up next or whom he will support or oppose have been superseded by the more basic uncertainty about the framework, the very basis of foreign policy. One has the impression that the activeness and inventiveness of the last few years were really a strategy to gain time and to mitigate the decline of foreign policy in the priorities of the American public and the decline of U.S. economic and military supremacy and general imperial position. Now, as in Vietnam, the borrowed time is coming to a close and the hard questions have come into the open. But the reaction of American society toward isolationism or interventionism, toward moralism or cynicism, toward revulsion from foreign policy, a bitter debate or a new consensus, are more in the dark than ever, if only because the very relationship of national consciousness and international reality, of domestic values and of international constraints is in doubt for Americans, for Europe, and ultimately for all modern societies.

   In a way, we are back to square one. Going back in time, the present moment reminds us, in different ways, of three different situations: 1968–1969, 1960–1961, and 1945–1947. When the Nixon-Kissinger administration entered office, American policy was in disarray: the Tet offensive and President Johnson's decision not to run again had demonstrated the failure of the Vietnam War; the invasion of Czechoslovakia had challenged *détente* and pushed back American hopes for a summit meeting in Moscow and, more important, the opening of the SALT negotiations; the student revolt and the reaction of the American establishment showed that the old cold war consensus on foreign policy had broken down. Not only was it necessary to get out of Vietnam in an orderly fashion, without jeopardizing American credibility, but, in order to achieve this aim and, more generally, to rebuild a foreign policy consensus, a new diplomatic style and a new political rhetoric were needed. A similar situation obtained, in a sense, at the close of the Eisenhower administration: one had the impression of problems arising everywhere (the shock of Sputnik and the supposed missile gap, the Berlin ultimatum of Khrushchev and the failed summit meeting of 1960, the growth rates of Communist economies and stagnation in America) and of the Eisenhower administration running out of ideas and energy to deal with them. The role of the Kennedy administration at that time was to rebuild a consensus through dynamism and a new rhetoric. This time, however, one may wonder whether rejuvenation in style, energy and commitments at the service of an ultimately identical American role are sufficient, or whether the postwar period (with its definition of the domestic consensus and of the international challenge) is not really coming to a close, so that the task of defining a consensus around America's role in the world and, in particular, her relationship to Europe, is as open and momentous as it was after World War II.

This may be the key both to the successes and to the failures of Kissinger's foreign policy. It can be formulated in the words of his 1968 analysis,[1] when he characterized the new international reality in terms of three factors: military bipolarity, a new political multipolarity and a third aspect, the change in the nature of power. While the classical components of power (force, territory, allies) are still present, their relevance is declining as compared to changes within societies;

1. See "Central Issues of American Foreign Policy" in H. Kissinger, *American Foreign Policy* (New York: Norton, 1969), pp. 51–99.

power has become more elusive, more unpredictable, more abstract and unmanageable. Hence, one cannot reproach Kissinger for not having been able to manage the unmanageable; but one can see his failure in his concentration upon the first two aspects and his practical neglect of the deeper changes within societies which he had so eloquently described. We shall deal briefly with his successive and often successful, attempts at manipulating multipolarity, and with the new and unsolved challenges posed to America, particularly in its relations with Europe, by the deeper forms of psychological, social and economic diversity and change.

The goal of the Nixon-Kissinger administration was to keep as much of a central role for the United States in world affairs as possible under new conditions that require skilled diplomacy and bargaining. It meant taking domestic evolution into account by reducing the credibility of the Vietnam War, then by withdrawing without bringing forth a right-wing reaction or a loss in the external credibility of the United States. It meant restoring flexibility to American foreign policy by increasing centralization and secrecy (to an extent which is dearly paid for today) and by making use of the new multipolarity, i.e., of the new strength of America's allies and of the new divisions among her adversaries.

This attempt has essentially taken the shape of four formulas for international order, which have often overlapped but can be seen in rough succession: burden-sharing, multipolar (three- or five-power) balance, cooperative bipolarity, and multidimensional concert. The first represented the initial, and unsuccessful, attempt at maintaining the essentials of the status quo; the second may, to a large extent, have represented a rhetorical and diplomatic instrument aimed at influencing the third; the fourth probably represents the real conception of Henry Kissinger, both in his aims and in his tactics.

The first formula is that of the Nixon Doctrine: the essential bipolarity of the structure remains, and so does the leading role of the United States, but this role becomes less direct, less visible, and less costly, since America's allies assume more responsibility for their own defense. The notion was that a certain reduction in American commitments and a certain lowering of the American profile, made necessary by the breakdown of the domestic consensus, could be absorbed without real loss to America's position because they would be compensated for by the polycentrism of the Communist world on the one hand, and by the growing multipolarity among America's allies on the other.

However, as James Reston pointed out in 1970, the crucial issue was the reaction of America's adversaries and allies: were the former prepared to tone down their pressure because of their divisions and the latter to increase their contributions in money and blood enough to relieve the United States without compromising either its ultimate leadership or the overall balance? Certainly, the results of Vietnamization, after an initial success, have shown that both assumptions were false, at least regarding both the solidity of the South and the moderation of the North. In Europe the formula did not lead to such negative results but because it was not really applied, due both to the Europeans' reluctance to increase their contributions and to the Americans' reluctance to decrease their control. As usual, the Europeans were asking themselves why they should assume more of the costs if they were not going to enjoy more of the decision making, and they reasoned that if the general structure stayed the same the Americans would have to provide their overall defense no matter what they did themselves.

The policy had a somewhat greater success in other regions, where the United States has been able to rely on regional powers as pivots for its policy and as supports of its influence. This is the phenomenon which neo-Marxists call "sub-imperialism" and of which Brazil and Iran are obvious illustrations. In this type of situation, however, the nature of the relations between the regional power, its environment and the United States is usually more complex than that allowed for by the notion of a global alliance and of restructured bipolarity: it is usually more adequate to speak of a regional hegemony, effective or attempted, which implies a certain support of, but also a growing independence from, the United States. On the other hand, in quite a few regions, the United States, rather than relying upon one power, is playing a balancing or conciliatory game between two or more, as with Iran and Saudi Arabia or Israel and Egypt. While the situation still has aspects of indirect hegemony, this role is exercised more through the politics of flexibility and balance than through those of bipolarity and alliance.

On the global plane, too, the second formula, multipolar balance, can be seen as going further in the same direction. Instead of a mere internal restructuring of bipolarity, it means a more flexible relationship, including a more real independence for the different partners, and a mixed-motive relationship between them, varying between coalition and opposition, rather than an unconditional alliance. The question is, however, to what extent such a flexible balance exists today, either in reality or as a goal of American foreign policy. The answer seems very different when one speaks of the notion of a five-power balance (including the United States, the Soviet Union, China, Western Europe and Japan), or a three-power one (including the first three nations) or a multiplicity of balances according to issues and regions.

The popularity of the five-power idea seems to have resulted from the coincidence between an interview with *Time* magazine in which former President Nixon mentioned it (incidentally, in the context of increased economic competition between these five powers) and the fact that Henry Kissinger was a student of Metternich and Bismarck, and hence of the five-power European diplomatic Concert of the nineteenth century. Many critics have trained their guns on the notion, demonstrating the differences between today's situation and that historical precedent. There may have been some overkill, for it is doubtful that the five-power balance idea was ever meant seriously or had any genuine reality. For one thing, in the light of Kissinger's subsequent actions (the new Atlantic Charter, the demand for unity under American leadership in the management of the Middle East and the energy crisis, the pressure for an American solution to the problem of NATO standardization), it is doubtful that the Nixon administration was ever prepared to encourage real independence on the part of Western Europe and Japan. On the other hand, it is just as doubtful whether the latter are prepared to exercise this independence or whether their lack of psychological as well as of mineral energy makes them prefer a second-class status. It is likely that the five-power ideas was meant only to give Western Europe and Japan a certain degree of psychological satisfaction, as well as to justify an increasingly assertive economic competition against them. Anyway, the whole notion, at least as a global formula for the present international system, has been completely discredited by the energy crisis with its show of weakness by Europe and Japan and its show of strength by the oil producers.

But the same fate has befallen other formulas which have been advanced as a counter to the five-power one. For instance, Zbigniew Brzezinski has suggested that, rather than a five-power balance, the international system should be seen as made up of two triangles: the strategic one consisting of the United States, the Soviet Union and China, and an economic one, consisting of the United States, Western Europe and Japan. But this too leaves completely aside the new economic poles of power in the Third World, as well as the economic role of the Soviet Union. In fact, it is extremely doubtful that any geometric or arithmetic formula is able to encompass the diversity of international inequalities and alignments in any meaningful fashion. On the other hand, the idea of a multiplicity of triangles or balances, of associations and conflicts, with the United States directly or indirectly present in all of them, has a real validity, which we include under the label of a multidimensional concert.

There are, however, two specific relationships which have a global reality: the triangular game between the United States, the Soviet Union and China, and the bilateral, partly adversary and partly cooperative bipolarity between the United States and the Soviet Union.

The triangular game, based upon the Sino-Soviet split, was crucial to the early success of the Nixon administration and still plays an important role. Some important questions have begun to be raised about it, however. First, the ability of the triangular relationship to settle the problems arising from other centers of power or of resistance has been questioned. The Nixon-Kissinger administration seems to have thought that the road to Hanoi went through Moscow and the road to Moscow went through Peking. While the latter assumption appears to have paid off, the former did not prevent the defeat in Vietnam. Second, the question has been raised—not least, perhaps, by the Chinese themselves—whether, precisely, the triangular relationship was taken seriously by the United States or whether China was not simply used as an instrument to get to Moscow. After 1972–1973, after the Moscow summit and the Paris agreements on Vietnam, China seems to have lost some of its appeal for the United States, though the visit by President Ford in the autumn of 1975 kept Sino-American relations on an even keel. As for the possibility of reconciliation between the Soviet Union and China, while it is certainly not likely for the foreseeable future, it does raise a serious problem for the very basis of American policy. The Soviet Union and China see the tremendous advantage which their complete hostility is giving the United States, and they seem to inject small elements of uncertainty into their mutual relationship so that the United States cannot take their enmity (and their consequent need for American support) totally for granted.

A degree of reconciliation between them would give a more genuinely triangular character to the relationship, and would require from the United States a more deliberate balancing act, involving a more careful cultivation of the Chinese side than has been the case since the breakthrough of the Peking visit and the Shanghai communiqué. This is more necessary than ever, for Europe as well as for the United States, since, especially at a time when the West is in trouble and the Soviet Union is consolidating her empire, the Chinese connection is one of the few leverages left through which to influence the Kremlin's policies in positive directions. On the other hand, this is easier said than done, since the list of concrete cooperative endeavors in which one can engage with China seems a fairly limited one. By contrast, the Soviet Union has been concerned to make its link with the United States as irreversible as possible, at least for the latter, so as to counter any risk of the Sino-American link gaining an equal priority or substance.

In this, Russia has been helped both by objective factors and by the trend of American diplomacy in the second phase of *détente,* after 1972. This is why it seems that the Soviet-American relationship (with its mixture, as Uwe Nehrlich put it, of "bipolarity based on retaliatory power and bilateralism resulting from cooperative political postures,") deserves to be singled out among the various combinations which characterize American foreign policy and the international system.

In a sense, there is a certain inevitability about this. Every American administration starts by criticizing its predecessors for their overemphasis on the Soviet Union and by promising to put more emphasis on America's allies or on China, or on Eastern Europe, or on the Third World. The Nixon administration, by means of presidential visits to Western Europe and to Rumania and Yugoslavia before Nixon went to the Soviet

Union, and by the opening to China, did indicate such a shift in priorities. Yet, fairly soon, every administration finds that the danger of mutual annihilation, the need to control the arms race, the impatience with troublesome allies, the difficulties of controlling one's sphere of influence, the dilemmas of expansion, arbitration or abstention in distant lands and confusing situations are problems it shares exclusively with the only other nuclear and global superpower, and about which a dialogue with allies or with the Third World can offer no substitute for the bilateral relationship with the Soviet Union. No American administration could afford not to give priority to the latter over Western Europe or Japan when dealing with SALT or the Middle East.

On the other hand, the Nixon-Kissinger administration allowed itself to be identified with a dangerous generalization and overselling of this priority, to the point of giving the impression that it saw in it the basis of world order. This happened through the abuse of summitry, through the building up of the importance of personal relationships between the leaders of the two superpowers, and through the rhetoric of the era of negotiations. Particularly important in this respect were, first, the acceptance of Soviet-inspired declarations (like the Moscow one of May 1972 on the principles if coexistence and the June 1973 treaty for the prevention of nuclear war) which suggest the idea of joint action for the management or prevention of military and even political conflicts, then the creation of standing bilateral commissions (on SALT, or on trade), then the primarily bilateral handling of problems involving European security, like the Conference on European Security and Cooperation (CSCE) and Mutual and Balanced Force Reduction talks (MBFR). In these negotiations themselves, the United States adopted a stance which, on certain points (like the issue of constraints on the use of force) suggests a common interest of the superpowers against control by the small and middle ones, or an unwillingness to challenge Soviet domination in Eastern Europe (through the encouragement of peaceful contacts), coupled with an implicit invitation addressed to the Soviet Union similarly to respect the political status quo in Western Europe.

All this has created European fears, most vocally expressed in 1973 by the then French foreign minister, Michel Jobert, of a Soviet-American condominium or a new Yalta. Naturally enough, the European reaction to the Soviet-American relationship is fear, both when there is too much conflict and when there is too much *détente*. This dual fear of confrontation and condominium, of collision and collusion between the superpowers, common to most third parties, has been best expressed by the prime minister of Singapore, Lee Kuan Yew, who, quoting the Indian proverb: "When two elephants fight, the grass gets trampled," added: "When two elephants make love, it gets trampled too." Europeans feel that there is space for them—both as prizes to be coveted or protected and as independent actors—when the superpowers are close enough neither for war nor for love.

Some of their fears of a Soviet-American agreement, explicit or tacit, on joint global management or on separate but parallel management of their respective spheres of influence are justified and may even become more so in the future. In particular, the nuclear factor requires a certain degree of joint management. If the problem of nuclear proliferation becomes more dramatic, it may well require joint intervention, not to speak of a joint policy on the sale of nuclear reactors and the like. Already, in Europe, SALT and the treaty on the prevention of nuclear war adumbrate an alternative or supplementary security system, based upon the joint surveillance by the two superpowers of a passive Europe. On the other hand, nuclear deterrence, in the bipolar system, requires a degree of clarity in the identification of all allied territories which inevitably creates spheres of protection, hence spheres of responsibility, hence spheres of control and of influence.

Essentially, however, the fears of condominium are as exaggerated as the corresponding hopes. First, the Soviet Union might actively promote superpower bilateralism, but her conception of a "dynamic status quo" and of a "correlation of forces" moving in favor of socialism, thanks, in particular, to the alliance between her mounting global power and emerging social forces within the capitalist and the Third World, do not allow for the forgoing of unilateral advantages required by any static policy of global condominium or partition. This has become increasingly clear since 1973, with the October War, the economic crisis in the West, the Vietnam *débâcle* and the events in Portugal and Angola.

Second, not only is domestic American awareness (and, sometimes, exaggeration) of this Soviet attitude putting Henry Kissinger's conception of *détente* on the defensive, and making it difficult for him to deliver on the American (in particular economic) side of the cooperative relationship; his own policy has sometimes preferred an exclusive and unilateral American role to a joint approach with the Soviets. This applies to his mediating efforts in the Middle East.

Third, whatever the intentions of the superpowers, the domestic and national sources of conflict and change both in their respective spheres and in disputed, ambiguous areas are such as to make strict geographical delimitation, joint abstention or joint management equally illusory. Mutual restraint and caution in a case of potential escalation, when the issue becomes the avoidance of nuclear war, are balanced in earlier stages by the temptation to exploit the other side's difficulties or by the pressures to support one's own friends or allies. In particular, the hope of Soviet help being available or sufficient to maintain a crumbling status quo in Western, particularly Mediterranean Europe, is likely, even if initially encouraged by Moscow's passivity, to be a costly illusion.

Finally, on economic issues, especially the emerging global ones, even a perfectly functioning dialogue with the Soviet

Union could not be the decisive answer. On energy, on food, on the monetary system, on the general issue of a new international economic order, the Soviet Union cannot and should not be excluded, but she is one interlocutor among others, sometimes an important, but just as often, a relatively marginal, passive or undecisive one in a bargaining which combines North-South and West-West issues more than East-West ones. While the Soviet Union *is* a global superpower, she is still not so to the same extent and in the same sense as is the United States. America alone is a decisive actor in every type of balance and issue. This is precisely the perception which would seem to lie at the heart of Kissinger's foreign policy, and which the imperfect expressions of multiple concerts and of issue-linkage are trying to capture.

The other formulas may, in fact, have been little more than a dazzling succession of smoke screens, aimed essentially at preserving a maximum role and freedom of action for American policy. That policy's apparent inconsistency and unpredictability may, of course, be just the result of day-to-day pragmatism disguised under successive and incompatible rationalizations. It might, however, reflect a more subtle and complex attempt to establish a new international system designed to operate according to different rules and with different participants in different regions and on different issues, but with the United States always, directly or indirectly, singly or jointly, in the managing or balancing role. In either case, a host of formulas are used, which academic critics take very seriously, but whose apparent universality is in fact essentially instrumental to the adaptation of American policy to a variety of situations.

Henry Kissinger sometimes uses a rhetoric of cooperative bipolarity, sometimes the rhetoric of a multipolar balance of power, sometimes the rhetoric of the Atlantic Charter and of free world unity reminiscent of the 1940s and 1950s, sometimes the rhetoric of global interdependence and world community. But the aim is to preserve or increase the role of the United States directly or by relying alternately on one pivotal power (as in Latin America), on superpower relations as in the SALT agreements, on arbitration between various powers (as in the Middle East), or on coalition diplomacy, as among the energy-consuming nations or a revitalized NATO.

The central perception is that in a world of multiple centers of power and of unequal vulnerabilities, the United States may have lost its position of dominance and its ability to rule alone but have gained a greater freedom of action and mobility. The new situation could lead the United States either to paralysis because of contradictory impulses towards intervention and withdrawal, or to a new flexibility by the simultaneous manipulation of interdependence and multipolarity, compensating for its relative weaknesses by its relative strengths and playing one opponent or competitor against another. For the administration, the new world role of the United States must be seen in a differentiated, relative and comparative perspective, and its policies must involve the art of selectively separating or linking issues, regions and dimensions.

This is possible to the extent that in the political economy of power, vulnerability and presence, the United States has a more balanced panoply of strength, or more instruments to play than any other nation. Like the Soviet Union, it is a global and nuclear superpower; like Western Europe and Japan, it is a rich and technologically creative society; like the members of the Organization of Petroleum Exporting Countries (OPEC), it is an energy and, more important perhaps, a food producer which may enjoy, in the coming crisis, as favorable a bargaining position for cereals as the Middle East does for oil. Hence it can use its economic power to exploit the Soviet Union's need for technology and grain, to extract concessions on diplomatic and strategic issues. Conversely, it can use its military protection to extract economic concessions from Western Europe, which is rich but militarily weak; it can use a combination of military help (through protection and arms sales) and threat of intervention, of diplomatic leverage (via Israel) and of economic leverage (via technology, food or the search for alternative oil resources) to bargain with the oil producers.

In all these respects, however, it does have to use bargaining, because it has become vulnerable itself: to nuclear attack, to economic crisis, to an oil embargo. But, in an optimistic version, it is less vulnerable, in all these respects, than anyone else; in a more realistic one, it is less so than *some* others in *some* respects and can play on its comparative advantage in terms of vulnerabilities. This, in particular, is at the core of American-European relations at the present stage, both in terms of what might be called the balance of leverage and the balance of dissatisfaction.

The Europeans are used to being vulnerable, and to being protected by the United States at a political price. Now they are even more vulnerable, but the United States has become so too, so the protection has grown less secure but the price is going up, and is becoming economic as well as political. The old transatlantic bargain, like the whole U.S. imperial position of which it was a part, was based on America's being in such a superior situation that it could afford to define its own interests in a broad, generous, indirect or multilateral way, and to defend them without really having to bargain, to maneuver, or to sacrifice some nations at the expense of others. Nor was there any real conflict between U.S. interests and the collective interest of the West both because the United States had the decisive voice in defining the latter and because, objectively, neither security nor prosperity were scarce commodities which could not be maximized for America and Europe at the same time.

Now, however, the United States has discovered successively that it is vulnerable to strategic attack from the Soviet

Union, to economic competition from Japan and Western Europe at a time of unemployment, and to a boycott on oil and possibly other raw materials from the Third World. But it is still much less vulnerable in all these respects than its Western European and Japanese allies. For them, the U.S. position creates the most uncomfortable combination of circumstances. Being vulnerable, the United States cannot put general interests ahead of its own, but being less vulnerable than its allies, it is in a better position to impose its own wishes, especially by using the analogies and links between the military and economic dimensions to suggest that it alone can really defend the common interest, however defined. In both cases, Europe's security is ultimately based on the state of U.S. relations with the Soviet Union and with the Arab world; but if something goes wrong (in terms of the threat of nuclear war or oil boycott), it is the first to suffer, both directly and in its bargaining relations with the United States itself.

There is, then, a combination of European-American solidarity and difference of interest leading, on the European side, to a mixed feeling of identity and impotence, of reluctant alignment and resentful resignation. Europe has to play the common game although (partly because of objective factors, partly because of its own lack of unity and resolve and its tacit preference for the dangers of multiple dependence over those of a costly independence) it cannot have the decisive voice in either economic or military decisions. Militarily, the United States will be less willing to take risks for its allies, giving less protection, whereas economically, it will be less willing to accept immediate sacrifices for the sake of the system, entailing less tolerance. The common factor in the American response may be a new unilateralism or nationalism, which may be manifested either in withdrawal or in intervention. Strategically, the danger Europeans fear is "decoupling" or neo-isolationism. Economically, it is penetration or neo-imperialism. In both cases, as in the danger of condominium, fears have proven exaggerated and may well remain so. But it is already true that the Europeans *are* being asked to pay more for less security, to show a more unconditional solidarity for a less unconditional protection.

This is one of the reasons why the linkage formula has its limitations too. The traditional French position of refusing any linkage, of asserting that the United States must commit suicide to defend them but remain as their main adversary in energy and monetary matters was obviously untenable. But other Europeans, who would not go along with the French in provoking the United States, would also not accept that their need for American protection and their common interests with America as oil-consuming nations should lead to renouncing any distinction between their national or regional interests and the common Western one, and unconditionally deferring to American leadership. Hence the failure of the "Year of Europe" and the tensions over the October war, the Euro-Arab dialogue and such matters as the German sale of nuclear reactors to Brazil.

With the Soviet Union, too, linkage works only to a limited extent. The Soviet Union was ready to accept linkage at the expense of the North Vietnamese and was willing to have the SALT summit at the time of the bombing of Hanoi and the Blockade of Haiphong; but it is not willing to make any spectacular concessions in order to obtain technology or credits, especially when they are not forthcoming and when the need for them has lessened.

There are other difficulties with the concert formula. The whole notion is based on an acceptance of diversity, but in Kissinger there is always a tension between accepting diversity and wanting to orchestrate it. He has a tendency, for instance, to say, "Yes, Germany should have its *Ostpolitik,* but it's not the right moment now. It's not the moment for Brandt to go to Moscow because right now I want to punish the Russians for not behaving in the Middle East,'' and so on. While the United States pays lip service to an independent Europe, every time the Europeans try to do something on their own, they find that it does not exactly fit the role that Kissinger had in mind for them in his global orchestration. In the Middle East as in Cyprus, Kissinger wanted to be the *maestro,* and the situation inevitably emerges that if one instrument plays out of tune, the whole symphony is spoiled.

Hence, another difficulty with the concert notion is that it is extremely fragile since even with the best will on the part of the United States, it depends on others for success. The failures of American policy have been caused to a certain extent by events beyond U.S. control. In a multipolar balance of power, or a directly ruled empire, a power can be responsible only for its own actions. However, in the concert formula, one necessarily relies on his partners to perform their parts, and if one of them, for instance, King Feisal, collapses, there is not much one can do about it. Success depends on events beyond one's control.

But the major threat to the concert notion comes from the character of domestic and international diversity and change. Domestic evolution in the United States, especially during the last two years, has made a flexible policy of linkages next to impossible. Time and again, when watching the apparent contradictions of American policy on energy or the Middle East (switching from opposition to support of high prices for oil, or combining threats of military intervention in the Persian Gulf with the sale of sophisticated arms and the providing of instructors to the very targets of the threat), a foreign observer has been prompted to wonder whether all this confusion was part of a deliberate stick-and-carrot policy of Kissinger's or whether it was a result of the clash among different forces within the American bureaucracy pursuing diverging policies.

The provisional answer is that both are true, but that they

tend to cancel each other out. Kissinger's orchestration of policy is made impossible by the unorchestrated diversity of forces on the domestic front, if, when he is pursuing one energy policy, the Treasury is pursuing another and Congress a third one. Similarly, the task of exercising leverage on the Soviet Union or Turkey and Greece over Cyprus or over NATO is made next to hopeless if American foreign policy is determined by the balance of domestic ethnic minorities and of particular economic interests—especially if these practice a linkage of their own, as happened when pro-Israeli and anti-*détente* forces joined pro-Greek ones in blocking aid to Turkey. When linkage comes to haunt the secretary of state with a vengeance and bargaining with unpredictable foreign states is conditioned by bargaining with unpredictable domestic allies, even Kissingerian acrobatics seem unable to make a concert policy work.

This is made both all the more evident and all the more serious by the character of international diversity and change. In the author's opinion, these are such as to show the dangers and the limits of Kissinger's U.S.-dominated concert policy and of the populist, Americano-centric reactions to them. The issues we have mentioned—energy, the Jackson amendment, relations with Greece and Turkey—are related to wider ones, having to do with the economic, social and ideological turmoil and transformation of the world, and particularly of Europe. In all these cases, the transformations of the international and of the domestic American scene, while having some common sources, may in fact go in conflicting directions leading to paralysis or collision.

The economic issue at hand ultimately concerns the survival or the transformation of the international order, of the Western capitalistic system, and of America's place in it. All three concerns are urgent for any American foreign policy, but they do not necessarily coincide, and the order of priority does not necessarily look the same from the point of view of specific American interests and of the outside world. Clearly, the issues of resource management and of economic redistribution which have been put forcefully on the table by the OPEC countries, followed by the Group of Seventy-seven (the countries of the Third World), fall outside the conceptual framework and the familiar solutions of Secretary Kissinger. But it is also clear that the alternative framework or solutions do not yet exist. It does seem certain that, for reasons both of equity and of power, the new international economic order, even if it does not represent a radical departure from the present one, will not be as Western-centered and that, at the minimum, a new balance with the Third World and the Communist one will have to be struck. But it is far from clear whether the objective to be pursued, or the likely outcome, go in the direction of global management, of an open system, or a new regionalism, or a proliferation of new nationalisms based on neo-mercantilist thinking.

Nor it is obvious what America's and Europe's respective roles will be, in particular, whether Europe's interest is to see an American-centered system or a more multipolar one, an American policy based on penetration through multinational corporations or on domestic rejuvenation. What does seem certain is that the outcome will be in large part outside the reach of American and European foreign policies and will lie at least as much in a combination of unpredictable transnational factors and of struggles of domestic interests. There is no guarantee that the results will be mutually compatible. At any rate it is likely that the United States will be faced more than once with the dilemma of reconciling the interests of the system, whose collapse it is vitally interested in preventing, with its own special interests, as well as the interest of the emerging new economic order with the special interests of the various industrial-capitalist-liberal-democratic countries.

The other issue is that with which we started, the passing or the revival of the Cold War and of the consesus (within the United States and Western Europe and between them) which was built upon it. There is a double paradox here. On the one hand, *détente,* the revulsion against America's role in Vietnam and the primacy of domestic concerns have almost universally spread the notion that the Cold War is dead and the danger of Soviet power a myth, just at the time when the Soviet Union is indeed becoming a global military, particularly naval, power. Its influence is expanding, from India to Europe and Africa, and the political-military balance, particularly in the north and south of the Continent, is for the first time in danger. On the other hand, the reaction against *détente* may revive some of the reflexes of the 1950s and, particularly under the influence of concerned ethnic minorities, make a differentiated response difficult. In particular, an approach opposite to Kissinger's may produce, for partly similar and partly different reasons, a similar result, by equally misjudging the relation between the role of the Soviet Union and developments in Western, particularly Mediterranean Europe. In fact, the Cold War is more relevant than ever as far as relations between the Soviet Union and the West are concerned, but many developments within the West which may or may not be exploited by the Soviet Union or bring her an automatic advantage, are not caused by her and must be addressed on their own terms.

The paradox of Kissinger's diplomacy has been the combination of probably excessive hopes for *détente* and cooperation with the Soviet Union (which implies indifference to the fate of Eastern Europe and to the domestic evolution of the Soviet system) and intransigent opposition to Communist parties or regimes where they are both more popular and less dangerous to the United States: in Vietnam, in Chile, in Italy and Spain. This could be justified in terms of *Realpolitik* by the notion of accepting realities, but only when one has to —hence of building a "stable structure of peace" with the

Communists when they are strong, of "destabilizing" or at least isolating them when they are weak, or preventing them from coming to power when this can still be done. But it implies, at bottom, a decision to wage *détente* only with the Soviet Union, to ignore the evolution of societies within the two camps, or to repress it, directly or by appealing to the Soviet Union.

This also implies, however, that each superpower is willing and able to control its own sphere of influence and its direct or indirect allies on the other side, which runs directly counter to the nature both of modern society and of Western political regimes.

Other American reactions are possible, to judge from ambiguous domestic trends. Public opinion and Congress may, soundly in our view, judge that there is something wrong with considering the Soviet Union fit to participate in a stable structure of peace but the Italian Communist party unfit to participate in a government coalition. Congressional opinion, however, would associate this notion (as well as, for instance, indignation towards Turkish misbehavior) with the feeling that, the Cold War being over, Europe should be left to its own devices because the Soviet and security factors are obsolete. Conversely, the anti-Communist impulse or the solidarities and memories of minorities like the Italian or the Greek one, may lead Congress to see in the evolution of Italy or Greece a replay of the struggles of 1945 or 1948 and oppose it in the same way, with the same means or the same rhetoric.

All these reactions miss the central paradox of European politics, i.e., the growing discrepancy between the structure and the requirements of the diplomatic-military balance on the one hand, and the nature and evolution of individual countries and domestic societies on the other. For roughly twenty years, between 1948 and 1968, the two appeared to coincide, a country's military, diplomatic, geographic and

ideological alignment and her domestic regime being determined in relation to cold war lines. Since 1968 it has become
clear that various domestic and transnational evolutions were
taking place in different countries which were at odds with
their external alignment. They were repressed in the East but
have developed in the West, sometimes in an explosive, sometimes in a diffuse and barely perceptible way. *Détente* has
legitimized Western Communist parties, some of which appear as the main challengers to obsolete or corrupt regimes
and/or have become, like the Italian PCI much more part of
their own societies than instruments of Moscow. The transitional societies of Mediterranean Europe, Greece, Turkey,
Spain, Portugal, have little in common with each other, except that they all have undergone an identity crisis, that they
all are torn between the appeal of Europe and of affluence on
the one hand, and a greater identification with a regional or
non-European environment or tradition (the Balkans, Islam,
the Mediterranean, the Third World) on the other. They have
bilateral relationships with the United States which their
public opinion has come to resent (partly because of past
American support of oppressive dictatorships for reasons of
security and stability), and their security concerns have more
to do with civil war or with conflict with each other than
with the Soviet threat. Any attempt to constrain them into a
rigid Atlantic framework in the name of the latter, or to support anti-Communist and antineutralist forces indiscrimi-
nately and exclusively, is likely to fly in the face both of the
diversity of these countries (in terms of traditions, social
situations, the character of their Communist parties and their
armed forces) and their common aspiration to change and
unwillingness to be manipulated from outside. On the other
hand, it is no less true that a certain imitation effect exists,
that domestic evolutions which are harmless or desirable by
themselves can have disastrous effects if they lead to the loss
of militarily vital bases or to Soviet advances. Neither NATO

nor the Common Market can be the same if each southern country goes its own way or if France is ruled by a Communist-dominated Popular Front.

The problem, then, is to reconcile these two contradictory considerations, the need of the international system for stability and the need of domestic societies for change. The only possible direction is a policy of flexible containment, adapting the response from case to case, and trying to distinguish between military and political considerations, between NATO's hard core center and its south, between attitudes toward the Soviet Union and toward indigenous regimes, between the role of the United States, that of the European Community and that of individual countries. It means trying to maintain the balance without identifying it with antidemocratic and ineffective repression and, conversely, making NATO and the European Community safe for diversity without making them ripe for Soviet domination. Probably the United States should apply a policy of "Bay of Pigs, no, Missile Crisis, yes"; it should concentrate on preventing the Soviet Union from shifting the European balance in her favor and warn her that any attempt at gaining a foothold in present NATO or American territory bases would jeopardize SALT, *détente* or whatever she expects from her relationship with the United States. The European Community could exert a more direct leverage on the countries concerned, to the extent that they are interested in entering a multilateral cooperative relationship, and encourage friendly domestic forces. Institutionally, an inner differentiation of NATO or the emergence of a partial regional European or Southern European alternative to it, or a network of bilateral American relationships with various countries might have to be envisaged or combined.

The challenge is to find new forms for the American-European relationship which would enable it to fulfill its functions in terms of military balance and cooperation without being identified, in each country, with an oppressive or crumbling status quo. The problem is made all the more difficult by the fact that not only is a division of labor between America and Europe required, but it must rely on distinctions, differences and contradictions between countries and between issues, which run counter both to the traditional legitimation of the Atlantic relationship and to the rigidities induced by the very lack of an American and of a European consensus. America and Europe can find the proper combination of unity and diversity between them only if each of them finds it within itself.

5

The United States and European Community

FRANÇOIS DUCHÊNE

At first sight, it may seem a waste of time to write of American foreign policy and the European Community. America has moved in dramatic new directions since Western Europe all but monopolized its field of vision during the Cold War. It has turned to the superpower triangle (if China can really qualify), to global bargaining, to domestic concerns and, not least, to the delights, however delusive, of diplomatic freedom of maneuver as the strongest nation among many and no longer the muscle-bound Atlas, the paralyzed prop and stay, of one of two competing world systems. The European Community's own vision of its future has itself changed radically. Ten years ago George Ball was saying to the Europeans: "You complain of America's lack of interest. What are you doing that is interesting?" Worse than that, Charles de Gaulle was standing on its head the original argument of Jean Monnet in 1950 that a dose of federalism was essential to overcome national vetoes in an intergovernmental system. De Gaulle showed that provisionally at least it was possible in a semifederal set-up to generalize the veto of a single power to the whole group.[1] He taught governments of

1. This was less true than it sometimes seemed. De Gaulle was careful not to test Germany too far, as he might have done by preventing the Kennedy Round of tariff negotiations (for instance). But it was sufficiently true to impress observers.

member states that the Community was not a school for the new European virtue but an arena like any other for the rough and tumble of political competition.

The nations have relearned this highly traditional lesson without any difficulty at all. The federalists' idea of a united Europe has gone from disappointment to disappointment in the past ten years. With the single exception of agriculture, the European Community has failed, despite repeated efforts, to follow up the initial success of the creation of the Customs Union by effective entry into the field of common policies. It has failed to Europeanize the policies of economic, social and other government intervention which are the stuff of modern domestic politics. The initial assumption that the creation of a Customs Union would promote giant European companies able to compete with the American multinationals has not been borne out. The difficulties of the few exceptions, such as Agfa-Gevaert and Dunlop-Pirelli, and the demise of Fiat-Citroen, have virtually proved the rule. Georges Pompidou's misbegotten attempt to relaunch the European enterprise on European monetary union by 1980 wasted a number of years and hopes.

Financial engineering could not bridge the differences between societies, especially in the wages sector. Far from producing a set of European currencies floating together against the dollar, the years of would-be progress to monetary union saw first the Italian lira and the British pound and then the French franc peel off from a DM zone left as the core of the hoped-for European currency system. Changes in monetary relationships also cut up the common agricultural market based on the idea of fixed prices valid throughout the Community. Little better luck attended the second relaunching of the European enterprise around the extension of the Community to Britain, Denmark and Ireland in January 1973. Within eighteen months the new British Labour government was locked in conflict with its own left wing on whether to stay in the Community at all, on the grounds that membership clashed with progress toward socialism at home. The conflict between the assumptions of domestic radicalism and commitments to the Community also diluted the hitherto unquestioning federalism of the Dutch and (to a lesser extent) the Italians. Disappointment reached a peak in late 1973 with the spectacular failure of the Europeans to stick together in response to the Arab oil embargo. No wonder the chairman of the European Commission himself spoke of the following year as a catastrophe for European integration.

It is no wonder too, that the third attempt to relaunch the European vessel late in 1974 seemed quite different in its aims and methods from any previous ones and from the original federal concepts of the European Community. There was no grand design like monetary union by 1980, no vaulting institutional ambition. Instead, the new dispensation underlined the control of the national governments by regularizing summit conferences as the *fons et origo* of Community decision making. The new German chancellor, Helmut Schmidt, seemed to take a special delight in denouncing the costliness and ineffectiveness of the Community bureaucracy (ignoring the role of the nations in seeing it was so); and Germany, as the struggle against domestic inflation hardened, rapidly became a byword for its refusal to finance Community projects on the old easy terms. These assults, widely believed to be ultimately aimed at the cost of the common agricultural policy, led the French in 1975 to study whether a change would harm French agriculture. The answer seemed to be that on balance it might not, but that it was hard to see how any alternative system could be *communautaire.* In a world of food shortages, the French (like other Community food exporters) might have no difficulty in selling their surpluses on the world market. This suggested the possibility of retreat from the single major area where a common European economic policy had been established. The Customs Union itself still had to stand the test of prolonged recession. Though it stood up well between 1973 and 1975, the cooperation that took place between member states, for instance on money or reflation, was essentially conducted bilaterally between the most appropriate major powers and not in the Community system. It was not very different from whatever leadership was provided in the world setting, where directorates of select groups of the Six (or the Five or the Twenty or whatever the number might be), were becoming the norm of international decision making. The specific role of the Community was not too evident.

The contrast with the dynamic presumptions of the federalists in the Community's early days is so striking that there can be little surprise at talk of its demise as a political force. This possibility underlies both the *Realpolitik* of some Americans who proclaim the greater use of dealing directly with Japan and West Germany as bellwethers of the industrial world and the lamentations of European Old Believers without whom there would have been no Community at all. Even in the formulation of Steven Warnecke, that Community policy has been reduced essentially to the preservation of the Customs Union, there remains little of the federal vision of the Schumann Plan a quarter of a century ago. Others speak of the essential irrelevance of regional integration, such as the Community represents, in an era of "global bargaining." Nothing is as dead as yesterday's tomorrow. Why, then, bother to consider the European Community as a sufficiently important feature of American foreign policy to warrant specific treatment?

The reason is that, paradoxically, in the midst of so much failure and dilapidation, the European Community in some ways seems astonishingly alive. Both in the economic field and in foreign policy cooperation, the signs of vitality would appear considerable were they seen as themselves and not in the light of diappointed hopes of another kind. Economically, one of the more impressive features of the reaction of Western Europe to the abrupt increase in the price of oil in 1973 and 1974 has been the ability of most of the countries to switch resources into exports and to damp down the inflation aggravated by the energy crisis. Britain aside, there seems to be a growing convergence in the economic behavior of the Community countries when faced by the cyclical variations of the market. Few practitioners would doubt that this phenomenon is linked to the fact that even the larger member countries (except the latecomer Britain) have over 8 percent of their GNP involved in Community trade while, at the extreme, the proportion for Belgium rises to the extraordinary figure of almost 40 percent. In modern conditions, in contrast to the pre-1914 era when similar interdependencies seem to have been attained,[2] such commitments cannot be trifled with because of their enormous social and political implications. On the same grounds, in a period of recession, when the strains upon the economic harmony of the member nations grow, they feel the need to influence the world situation more than when conditions are buoyant. Collectively, the European Community, representing one-quarter of world output and trade, can influence levels of world activity where even the Germans may feel they carry too little weight alone.

In these circumstances, the underlying interdependence of the European Community countries seems to be growing. This process may even constitute the kind of preintegration necessary for the emergence of any real economic union later on. It is particularly noticeable with Germany and France, whose monetary policies have been gradually converging. Of recent years, the French economy has tended to follow the trend of the German with a lag of a few months. The French, as the trade figures for 1974 show, have also tended to compensate for deficits with the outside world by a surplus with

2. See R. Rosecrance et al., "The Reversibility of Interdependence," mimeograph paper, Cornell University, 1975, pp. 9–11.

the Common Market. The inference is that, contrary to the fears expressed when the Common Market was established twenty years ago, it has helped the French economy to compete. This has been the unseen foundation of the reentry of France into the monetary "snake" with the countries of the Deutschmark zone in August 1975, and the simultaneous German and French announcements of reflation programs. Whether France can remain in the "snake" is doubtful.[3] The fact remains that the very presumption is tied to a growing compatibility of the French and German economies and that this could be the key to the future world role of the European economy. If the French economy proves weak, on top of the Italian and British ones, this will confine Europe's effective role to the DM zone, comprising the Germany economy and its satellites, Benelux, Scandinavia, Austria and Switzerland. But if all the other major European economies are in trouble, the capacity of Germany to maintain its own health and give a lead to the world economy will be greatly weakened, if not nullified. This was clearly one of the factors behind the German loan to Italy in 1974 and the cooperation with the French from 1974 to 1975. For, if the French economy proves strong as well as the DM zone and is added to, not subtracted from it, there will be a massive basis for Western European responses to international economic problems and a core to which the British and Italians can ultimately return. The distinction is between a European region able to play a role in the world and one fragmented to the point where the strength of Germany itself is placed in question. The very fact that the distinction can be made is rooted in the interdependence encouraged by, and now associated with, the Common Market. In these circumstances, the ability to have effective European cooperation even at the bilateral or intergovernmental level is bound up with the existence of the Common Market as a going concern on which

3. France left the "snake" again in March 1976—Ed.

economic actors at all levels in the member countries continue to count.

The common agricultural policy tends to reinforce this general solidarity by giving the powerful farm lobbies a common stake in the system. This cohesion will certainly be affected by current changes in the international market for food. The common agricultural policy, attacked by the consumer countries of the Community (and outsiders) as protectionist for its tendency to produce surpluses in a period of relatively abundant and cheap food, suddenly became a factor of price stability during the recent world shortage of grain and boom in prices. This factor could again become politically important if renewed Soviet purchases in the United States were to become the antechamber to more lasting future world food shortages. The common agricultural policy could yet become popular in Europe with consumers as a factor of more stable prices and above all safer supplies. By the same token, the interest of the Community food producers might wane, as French reactions have already suggested. On the other hand, in such conditions producers could still get higher prices and consumers safer supplies, so that a bargain between the differing producer-consumer interests in the Community seems quite feasible, while the difficulties and unknowns of unscrambling the omelette could be very great. On balance, the common agricultural policy is likely to become more and not less of a stabilizing factor in Europe in a period when the supply of food is shorter than it was in the years of abundance for the rich.

Politically, too, there have been unexpected signs of progress. Much the most remarkable has been the growing diplomatic cooperation of the Nine. Given the relative lack of interest of the United States in the European Security Conference, the main bargaining tended to be between the Soviet Union and the Community's nine member states, usually maneuvering as one. The Nine have also coordinated their approach to the mutual force reduction talks at which most of them, including France, are not even represented. In both negotiations, they have particularly resisted East-West commitments, notably on defense, which might undercut their chances of future political union. Similarly, the Nine have become increasingly involved in the political, and by implication security, problems of southern Europe. Though they have not been very effective as a group over Cyprus, there has been a complex interplay between French influence in Athens, German in Ankara, and the magnetism of the European Community, prospective membership in which has served the new Greek regime as an alternative to close relations with either superpower. On Portugal, the Nine, surprisingly in view of the Community's usual timidity, have interfered with the progress of the revolution a great deal more blatantly than either the Soviet Union or the United States and made their loans conditional on the recipients' "democratic" behavior. The so-called Lomé Agreement of association with forty-six African, Caribbean and Pacific states led by Nigeria has in some ways set the trend for new worldwide arrangements and certainly influenced the American negotiating stance toward the developing countries. This has even been the case where the failures of the Community have been most glaring, in energy. The underlying European determination to work out a cooperative relationship with the oil producers has contrasted steadily with the American tendency at once to woo and to threaten them. Whether these attitudes have been in conflict, as they sometimes seemed, or at bottom complementary, the general trend has been in the European rather than American direction.

All these developments have taken place in eighteen months. On any normal historical reckoning this would seem to constitute pretty rapid progress. They are certainly not at all easy to reconcile with the picture of a Community in the last stages of decrepitude. They also seem to relate to a number of basic features in the Community's situation which are unlikely to disappear. One is the sheer weight in the world economy of a Customs Union which is far and away the largest import market in the world, 60 percent larger than the American. This is bound to have foreign policy repercussions, as it did in the Kennedy Round of talks to cut obstacles to trade in the mid-1960s, that is before Britain further enlarged the Common Market. The same was clear again in the Lomé Agreement, is clear in Franco-German joint policies on reflation, and could be clear once more in the Tokyo Round of trade talks which have now begun. Politically, too, the European Community has an indigenous power of attraction which is not dependent on its relation with the United States and indeed depends on the fact that it is *not* a superpower and bears the label "Made in Europe." Something of this, though probably not much, suffuses the Arab-European relationship. A great deal affects that with the societies of southern Europe.

The most striking recent security development has been the shift of emphasis from the NATO central front, where the superpower presence in effect nullifies any potential European role, to southern Europe and the Mediterranean, where political and economic factors are more influential than military ones. The United States holds the military balance there, but its bilateral relations with each of the riparian states has recently been turning sour. As the Soviet Union has not become more popular with the years, the European Community thus becomes a natural alternative focus of political aspirations. Without major military power, and to some extent for that very reason, it is able to exert a quasi-ideological pull with which the United States cannot compete. There is indeed no reason why it should wish to do so. The interests of the United States and European Community are essentially complementary in southern Europe, except perhaps where

Israel might indirectly affect them. A division of labor between them is natural and makes them both more effective
than either could be alone.

The underlying feature of all this is that *détente* is bringing
to the fore a number of issues which seemed secondary during the Cold War and which now, as the Cold War recedes, are
becoming of primary importance. The European Community
is a great deal freer to act in many of these cases than would
be suggested by an analysis based on cold war categories,
dominated by money and East-West issues, where the link
with America was paramount. This is not to assume that the
European Community will seize these opportunities. It does
not even mean that because foreign policy cooperation has
now been inserted into the procedures of the Council of
Ministers, one can regard this cooperation as a genuine Community rather than multilateral or bilateral affair. But it does
mean that the Nine have options, and a framework within
which to act. Like Japan, like the Organization of Petroleum
Exporting Countries (OPEC), the European Community,
with all its limitations is still potentially a major regional
political force and a world economic actor. Its scope and
limits are of that order, not to be compared with that of the
superpowers, but significant still. Thus, at least potentially,
the failure of the traditional federal *plats de résistance* of
money and defense may be compensated in the case of the
European Community by what could prove to be their functional equivalent today, foreign policy cooperation by the
member states of the largest Customs Union in the world.
In a modest way, an embryo European confederation, now
buoyed by agreement on direct election of a European Parlia-
ment, may already be operating in the ruins of the original
federal dream, concealed from the mourners mainly by their
tears.

How far, then, is the European Community likely to seize

its opportunities? There are a number of reasons for inferring that it may lack the political will to do so. Whenever the international situation requires a major change in domestic policies, especially a sudden one, the member states' differences prove too great for the Community to act. Energy has been the most glaring example, but there are others, such as trade policy to Eastern Europe or money. More generally, it can be argued that the European Community suffers from another form of the Japanese "low posture." Like Japan, operating under the American security umbrella, it tends to play the cautious shopkeeper, offending no potential customer, placating roughs and so avoiding all responsibility that might take business away or bring danger near. But its condition is still more extreme than Japan's. No low posture can diminish the inner unity of Japan, with all that this implies in ultimate capacity to exploit opportunities. Low posture in the case of the European states tends to maintain the divisions between them, since investment in the European Community as a decision making body implies an activist approach, a definite decision to break out of tradition and obscurity and make oneself conspicuous. The British and Germans stand pat on the NATO status quo, the French on their refusal to reenter the military organization. Despite the fashion for the technology gap eight or ten years ago, European nations have done little to meet the American industrial challenge. Domestic factors have come first. So long as the political situation divests the Europeans of prime responsibility for their security, the incentive to the kind of institutionalized vigor that is implicit in using the European Community as an instrument of policy is likely to be low. The problem of political will is posed not only by the institutional difficulty of gathering nine nations into common action, but by the total position of the group in the world balance. Low posture, low political will, low institutional efficiency and low propensity to use the potential of the Community for foreign policy are, on such a reading, all interconnected.

Certainly, the Community is too slow and too hesitant to be of major relevance to the "high politics" of global crisis management. Whatever may sometimes be suggested to the contrary, the behavior of Americans and Europeans alike in actual crises shows that neither are keen to share the joys and sorrows of superpower status. The United States keeps firm control of military escalation in Europe; Kissinger has at no time displayed enthusiasm for European initiatives in Arab-Israeli diplomacy. The Europeans have evinced no desire to compete with the United States in either of these fields. The nuclear King's Peace, the element of fragmentary confederation in the world system, essentially reflects the military stalemate between the superpowers. The ability to manage crises is the very mark of their status. The role of Europe in crisis management, like that of Japan and virtually all other states including China, is very modest indeed.

However, if these limitations of the European Community were the whole story, it would be virtually impossible to account for the zest and speed with which the Nine have taken to foreign policy cooperation in some important areas. The reason for this seems to be essentially that change at least in East-West relations and in southern Europe could threaten the status quo in Western Europe. On such occasions, Community action, far from challenging the domestic arrangements of the member countries, becomes a means of enhancing their joint bargaining power vis-à-vis states or problems which might pose a threat. This in itself can produce change. The Nine may wish merely to maintain their existing interests in the European Security Conference, but by the simple fact of acting together they seem to have become the dominant Western negotiator. If Greece, in order to remain aligned with the West, requests to join the Community, and the Turks, however skeptical, propose to follow suit should that transpire, the security, political and economic situations are all transformed. Again, the very fact that the European Community countries have interfered successfully in Portuguese internal politics, even with secretly bated breath or by agreement with the United States, affects both the member nations' image of the Community, and others' image of them.

In many of the fields of what might be called the civilian fashioning of the international system and which are increasingly attracting attention, the superpowers that monopolize crisis management have neither the common will nor capacity to shape processes which, on the contrary, call for collective action. When it comes to "milieu shaping" in the economic, political and even sometimes security fields, outcomes depend on a large number of countries, or groups of countries, of which Japan, China, OPEC and the European Community are the most obvious but not the only ones. Here the European Community has no monopoly of hesitancy, poor coordination, or cussedness. The difficulties of obtaining decisions from the United States whenever Congress and administration fall out are notorious. So are the extreme external pressures apt to be needed to obtain a reaction from Japan. More generally, one of the dominant characteristics of international negotiation today, involving large numbers of countries, is its snail's pace, the effort needed to achieve change. This is proportionate to the number and weight of the countries whose assent is required. There is compensation precisely in the weight of what is moved once agreement is reached. In fact, where the Community has managed to act as one, there has on the whole been progress beyond the limits of what would have been likely without it. The Kennedy Round of tariff cuts in the mid-1960s began as a reaction on the part of the United States to what it saw as the discriminatory potential of a European Customs Union which would automatically give a preference to member states over third parties in one of the world's greatest markets. That negotiation produced by far the greatest international reduction in trade barriers ever achieved by the industrial powers. Similarly, the insistence of the French that the European Community should have a "Eurafrican" association smacked at first of neo-colonialism, the beginning of a new European preserve which might drive the poor who had been excluded into the arms respectively of Japan and the United States, and so divide the world again into competing spheres of influence. Because of such fears, rather than in spite of them, the agreements between the European Community and what are now the forty-six associates have gone towards a system more open to third parties and more creative of mechanisms applicable to the world than would initially have seemed possible. The main reason is that the width and variety of interests of the nine member states themselves cannot be contained in a straitjacket designed by any one of them. Because of this, the European Community has not slowed up international reforms. Rather, it has made possible outcomes that were impractical before.

In sum, while the European Community can hardly play a direct role in crisis management and will find it difficult to act where foreign policy calls for abrupt changes in the domestic policies of member states, it nonetheless shows potential capacity to play a part, even a considerable one, in two areas. The first is in influencing regions around its own borders, where its power of attraction is greatest. Here, in an era of *détente,* its policies, though not military ones, can have a considerable effect on the security balance. The other is in economic global bargaining, where Europe's resources as a manufacturer, trader and banker inevitably make it, whether united or not, a party to major decisions. In both areas, as I have tried to suggest, there are factors of process, as well as of what is theoretically possible, or to some desirable, which argue that the international context is thrusting upon the

Nine, and will continue to thrust upon them, problems which give a premium to a collective response. In this sense, one would expect the Community countries to take up at least some of their opportunities of common diplomatic or economic action in the current and foreseeable world situations.

On that basis, what should the U.S. policy to Western Europe, and more particularly to the European Community, be? What, for that matter, has it already become? Until the Nixon-Kissinger era, the United States adhered, though with growing reservations, to what might be called the interdependence school of policy. The United States must underpin the West economically and militarily, in return for which a reviving Europe and Japan would gradually help it shape the world in a reformist Western image. General de Gaulle made nonsense of the European end of this from 1963; Nixon and Kissinger duly followed suit at the other end from 1971. But because the United States had the resources of a superpower, it did more than become just another nation seeking individual purposes in a multipolar world. Kissinger's "Atlantic Charter" speech of Easter Monday 1973 enunciated America's right to freedom of maneuver on the grounds of its "global responsibilities" while denying the same privilege to merely "regional" Europeans. Leadership gave the shepherd rights withheld from the sheep. The European Community would have American support only if it strengthened Western solidarity; the member states must consult the United States *before* reaching Community decisions. At the Washington energy conference in February 1974, Kissinger seemed to egg on the opposition of the French Gaullist foreign minister, Michel Jobert, the better to corral the rest. Yet while the oil consumers were supposed to unite behind America to face OPEC, Kissinger continued to threaten the oil producers irrespective of his allies' wishes. The sense of a slide to empire and a growing conflict of attitudes between protector and protected was rife in the wake of what had originally been publicized as the Year of Europe. Yet barely eighteen months later, there was already a sense of a marked return to the civilities of interdependence. The replacement of Pompidou by Valéry Giscard d'Estaing has helped to reduce unnecessary Gaullist controversy. The October War and recession have shown there is a basic Western community of interest in the face of the Soviet Union and the problems of the world economy despite the modulation of 1971–1974. Nevertheless, the tensions of those years have left their mark: is the return to apparent harmony durable? what are its limits? what should American aims be and how might the Community fit into them?

"Most crises take place in the imagination," as a novel by Pamela Frankau put it. Not quite, perhaps, but the imagination does amplify them. One reason for the alarms of 1971–1974 was that the end of the Cold War led to a crisis of allegiance between allies. The Europeans feared the United States would sacrifice them for superpower special relations, the Americans that the Europeans would be a burden on American world diplomacy. In the event, neither fear has proved very substantial, since relations with the Soviet Union remain universally edgy and America cannot manage the world economy alone. Last but not least, the central thrust of the Nixon-Kissinger diplomacy has succeeded: it has shifted American policy away from system building to the conscious and concurrent pursuit of specifically American national priorities within that system. These developments have both restored a certain amount of interdependence diplomacy and profoundly changed attitudes towards it. The old assumption was that interdependence was overwhelmingly positive, and that particular interests should be regarded as secondary to the total good. Now the idea of conflict within interdependence, as was perhaps appropriate after the oil embargo, has received official consecration.

Seen from this point of view, there are fairly obvious arguments for American policy not to encourage the European Community as a partner. If one assumes that obtaining German assent is equivalent, in most economic cases, to getting the assent of the majority of the European Community countries, leaving only France as the odd man out, this becomes an obvious way of breaking European Community logjams or situations in which a European Community view might emerge in conflict with, or merely as temporarily uncomfortable for, American diplomacy. By the same token, it is quicker and more efficient to deal with Bonn than with a group of nine whose difficult compromises, once reached, become blocked. Further, American deals with Germany and Japan as the bellwethers of the industrial world favor the formulation of unilateral policies in the United States. This is more than the Kissinger style. The increased self-assertion of Congress in foreign policy, directly as in arms sales to Turkey or indirectly on questions like energy conservation, suggest that the problem is rooted in the priorities of the domestic American political system. Congress's attitude to energy conservation seems to be that the burden of proof that unregulated American consumption may harm allies rests with those allies. The trouble, of course, is that harm is apt to be "proved" only when it is too late to make the structural alterations to avoid catastrophe. Given this bias of American domestic politics, to downgrade the European Community is clearly a convenience. It speeds up decision making; if necessary it circumvents awkward customers; it makes it more likely that through Germany and Japan, American ideas of how allies should act will prevail. In fact, Tacitus had the word for it: "divide and rule."

Europe's impotence in crisis management situations can also affect the picture, as the history of the establishment of the International Energy Authority (IEA) shows. Kissinger explicitly set it up to ensure that the industrial consuming countries should adopt a collective attitude, led by the

United States, to the oil producers; and the conflict with the French, ineptly though the latter aimed their campaign, lay precisely on the issue of allied influence. In NATO and on money, the long-established institutions based on a world-wide model centering around the United States have undoubtedly inhibited the emergence of a European component within them. The same might happen through other organizations set up in the heat of crisis. In this way the potential for collective European decision making might be crushed between member states attracted to directorates and the United States institutionalizing the leadership system in the alliance.

All this is possible, but whether it is most likely is another matter. NATO is in a class by itself. Both on money and energy, the prime cause of the Europeans' failure to cohere has lain with themselves, not with the United States. The Germans once promoted the idea of a joint European float against the dollar. It failed because of the inability of the nine societies to move in economic concert and so sustain a single currency system. Similarly, in energy, the Europeans could have formed a group in the IEA; that they have not is due to their policy differences, dramatized as usual by the British and French. While the residuary beneficiary of European divisions could well be the United States, even on energy the Europeans have been perfectly able to make their point when they buried their own differences. Their proposals to raise money in the International Monetary Fund because it was a framework for cooperation with the oil producers ran directly counter to the American preference for the Organization for Economic Cooperation and Development (OECD) precisely because this would exclude OPEC members; the final compromise split the difference. French persistence in pursuing a tripartite conference with the oil producers and developing countries has dragged the Americans very reluctantly in its wake. America should not be made the scapegoat of European failures by having ascribed to it a power to dominate events which it does not possess.

It is questionable in any case whether the United States can really have the systematic will to inhibit the European Community. Indirectly, and even directly, there are now so many ways in which the Community is useful to it. It is easy, for instance, to overrate Germany's capacity to play lieutenant to the United States. This may work for NATO, where the halfheartedness of everyone else has reduced the alliance to a largely German-American affair with multilateral embellishments which sometimes seem mainly complications. But important as NATO is, it does not govern everything. The Germans are acutely aware of needing the United States more than the United States needs them. Normally, of course, this makes them toe the line, but it also drives them to keep open alternative insurance policies, of which *détente* is one and European integration, and especially the French link, much more actively the other. This has economic analogues. The Germans may expect, and be expected, to give an economic lead in Europe, but if all their major neighbors are in no condition to act compatibly, this casts doubt not only on the lead Germany may give but even on the viability of its own economy. This, again, leads the Germans to seek European associates in action, especially the French. Thus, to the extent that the Common Market makes France and Germany more compatible, it provides an invisible underpinning even to the bilateral American-German relationship.

The argument becomes still more pointed on trade. It is not only that the United States and European Community together dominate world trade negotiations. One of the reasons why protection has not already moved further in the world today is that both in Britain and the United States, the fear of retaliation by the Common Market inhibits import restrictions. Even in security, the European Community as an alternative pole of attraction to the Soviet Union gives the superpower military balance an invaluable political foundation. The Cyprus crisis has shown that the mere existence of a passive European Community, to which the Greeks and Turks can look as a future focus, has given crisis diplomacy new resources. In all these and many other ways, American and European Community interests are now complementary to the point of being structurally interdependent.

Two conclusions seem to follow. One is that it is no longer possible to draw a clear dividing line between the European nations and the Community. There is too close a relationship between the Nine and the foundations the Community now provides for them. This would limit the power of the United States to pressure the Community even if it wanted to. The other is that the interests of the United States and the Community are too intertwined in too many areas to allow American policy to be at all systematic in circumscribing Community growth. In such circumstances, it is plain that a conflictual view of relations is not practical or desirable. The latter point can be given negative confirmation by the case of the IEA and the domestic American debate on energy conservation. The increase in American energy imports from the Middle East, if resumed, will do more than add to the vulnerability of Europe and Japan; it will weaken America's own bargaining power in the world. A coherent European view on this issue, actively pressed, could hardly do less than the European nations in the American debate now. It could arguably, and on the record of trade or the financial talks in the IMF and OECD, make a far greater impact. Both the United States and Europe are more likely to see issues in their total international setting when they have to take account of each other's priorities than when they contemplate their navels. A dialogue between them, because of the diversity of their connections and outlooks is a giant step toward taking a world view of the problems they face. Western and world views are not alternatives, they are more often mutually reinforcing.

Today this is probably the heart of the matter. The world seems to be entering a new phase, post-cold war and in a less familiar sense post-*détente* too, because of the relatively low relevance of the Soviet Union to many of the problems that matter most to the rest of the world. Also because of the slow (though not necessarly irreversible) confirmation of the nuclear stalemate between the superpowers, the problem of the relations between them that seemed dominant in the last ten years now seems considerably less acute than the issues of how to organize a rapidly shrinking world. Here the centerpiece is still relations between the Western industrial powers and the other non-Communist countries. Computations of who is up and who is down in the scales of power are really rather secondary to the ability to adapt to the new challenges posed by food and population, the revolution in communications, changes in social aspirations, the problems of the environment or the dangers (in an age of unsurpassedly accurate weapons) of civil explosions between rich societies and increasingly militant and self-conscious poor. Whatever the problems of the nineteenth century, national societies struggling with the industrial revolution had one asset: institutions whose legitimacy to order conflict and political and social change were recognized. The only international substitute for them today is negotiation between clusters of powers which can mobilize major resources and between which the deals and the construction of new relationships and institutions are beginning in effect to take place. These groupings include the United States, the European Community, Japan, OPEC and, some way behind, the Soviet Union, China, and the various trade unions of the poor.

The United States, like all other powers, has to make the most of this untidy system which we will no doubt have with us for generations to come. The significance of the apparent shift in Kissinger's diplomacy from the delights of summitry between superpowers to the less congenial routine of constructing economic foundations for an evolving international system, seems to be essentially that constraints are imposed by the situation on even the most powerful states. These constraints not only limit the field of maneuver, they also dictate to a considerable degree the partners to deal with. From this point of view, the role of the European Community, not as sole partner of the United States in a dumbbell concept à la Kennedy, nor as one of Nixon's Pentagon of great powers in a traditional directorate, but as one of the inevitable groups of any international structure, should be among the necessary consequences of America's own priorities.

There is no point in Americans being more European than the Europeans, à la Dulles, nor are they likely to be. There must also be no return to the overweening rhetoric of the Year of Europe, which is also unlikely. Today's ambiguities are more covert than that. Neglect, from the benign to the hostile, is more plausible, the tacit understanding of the happy few that they concoct the decisions and the rest is window dressing. This is both true and not true—true in the obvious sense that directorates take many of the decisions, and not true in so far as the happy few are themselves dependent on networks which buttress and condition their power. The European Community is one of these networks. Even though it cannot compete with the happy few, it is embedded in many of the systems they are trying to administer and is also a building block for new ones. It is not from mere politeness that the Community was an invisible member of the European Security Conference and now of the Tripartite Conference while it is a highly visible one in the Tokyo Round of trade talks. Far from being the astral body of a federal corpse, the European Community seems, in a disorderly, pragmatic way, a necessary and useful element of the international functional agreements American (and Western) policies are condemned to seek. More modestly than in its cold war heyday, the whole interdependence school of policy with which the Community's origins are bound up, seems to be reviving, not for ideological reasons but from necessity. This suggests that the European Community is slowly taking root as an important part of the international system and that American policy should cooperate with it for that reason, notwithstanding the demise of yesterday's grand designs.

6

West Germany's Place in American Foreign Policy: Pivot, Anchor, or Broker?

PETER KATZENSTEIN

In the first half of the 1970s the main business of American foreign policy has been to bring about a change in the structure of the international system. Its main business in the second half of the 1970s will be to cope with the consequences of that change. One consequence of central importance is the growing prominence of cooperative elements in the relations between adversaries and of conflictual ones in the relations among allies. In recent years, the gradual improvement of America's political relations with the Soviet Union and China illustrates this change as does the simultaneous deterioration of relations with her Asian, Latin American and European allies. The ambiguity which this "mixed international system" imposes and the "elusiveness of power" to which it contributes create new problems for the conduct of American foreign policy.[1] There is a growing probability that the magnitude of these problems may prompt American foreign policy makers to search for a partner who might lighten their load. In a field of diminishing size the German Federal Republic appears today to be the only serious contender for that position.

1. Richard Rosecrance, "Détente or Entente?" *Foreign Affairs*, 53 (April 1975), 464–481. Stanley Hoffmann, "Notes on the Elusiveness of Modern Power," *International Journal*, 30 (Spring 1975), 183–206.

The American-West German relationship is the only alliance of central importance to American foreign policy which has not been undermined either by the process of *détente* or by the frictions in the international economy. Political relations between the two governments are better than at any point since the celebrated *entente* between John Foster Dulles and Konrad Adenauer in the mid-1950s. Forgotten are the divisiveness which the "Western European option" had created in Bonn in the early 1960s and the unease which the "Eastern European option" had caused in Washington in the early 1970s. Today there exists, instead, a similarity in political perspectives and objectives which offers the prospects of fruitful cooperation between Washington and Bonn on some of the central problems in international politics. In the summer of 1975 the meeting of foreign ministers in Paris, the NATO summit in Brussels, and the mutual visits of the West German and the American presidents illustrated how great a value the two governments set on close and cordial bilateral relations.

On this point American preferences are easy to understand. The military and economic affairs of the Atlantic Alliance are in desperate state. The unresolved conflict between Turkey and Greece over Cyprus, Turkish reaction to the arms embargo imposed by the United States Congress, and the seizure of power by a left-oriented military government in Portugal have exposed a grave weakness in NATO's southern flank. Domestic economic and political pressures, furthermore, have forced some NATO members to put a smaller emphasis on their defense policy at the very time at which the United States prefers to conduct the force reduction talks with the Soviet Union from a position of strength. Protectionism in trade relations, volatility in international finance markets, and concern over raw material supplies have added economic troubles unprecedented in the history of the Atlantic Alliance, and these troubles are accentuated by the inflated cost of oil imports and a worldwide recession. The reform of the Atlantic Alliance and of the international economy are two critically important tasks of American diplomacy. Both tasks are easier if Washington succeeds in enlisting the active support of the Federal Republic rather than eliciting its indifference or outright opposition.

Intimate political relations between Bonn and Washington also suit the interests of the Federal Republic. Until recently West German foreign policy revolved around the inconsistencies of its answer to Germany's national question: national reunification through supranational integration. But Chancellor Willy Brandt's Eastern policy and the renunciation of the goal of reunification for the foreseeable future have set free political capacities which, for the first time in postwar history, make West Germany's political and economic power commensurate. Adenauer's "policy of strength" was an unsuccessful attempt to act the role of a political giant while the Federal Republic was still an economic dwarf. In the 1960s the relation between political aspirations and economic achievements was reversed. Successive West German governments hesitated to participate in *détente* policies while the stature of the Federal Republic in the international economy grew. Under the government of Helmut Schmidt, West Germany has finally ceased to play the role of economic giant and political dwarf and attempts instead to contribute to the economic and political stabilization of international affairs. That task of stabilization, the West Germans know, can be achieved only if West German and American policy makers follow jointly a coordinated political strategy and avoid working at cross-purposes.

Both governments are, then, becoming increasingly aware of the advantages they derive from close cooperation; that awareness, furthermore, is shared by their domestic opponents whom they will face in electoral contests in the course of 1976. But the structure of the current international system, its high rate of change, and differences in the position of the two governments in world politics impose limits on the degree of cooperation feasible. American observers, at times, are inclined to overlook these limits and tend to choose an inappropriate image of American-West German relations. Three images are discussed in this essay. First, there is the image of West Germany as the *pivot* in the global economy. Calling for joint leadership by Washington and Bonn in the international economy, Fred Bergsten, among others, has recently favored this image in his plea for concentrating American foreign policy initiatives on Bonn rather than Brussels.[2] Alternatively, West Germany could become the *anchor* for a recalibration of the military, economic and political problems of the Atlantic Alliance. This second image has precedents in the bilateral relations between Washington and Bonn in both the 1950s and 1960s.[3] The first image envisages bilateral relations centered around economic questions of global significance; the second image points to bilateral relations focused on military, economic and political concerns of regional importance. The third image incorporates elements of the first two in assigning the West German government the role of a *broker*.[4] While the first two images of American-West German relations are dominant in American thinking, the West Germans apparently favor the third. This paper

2. See, for example, C. Fred Bergsten's testimony, Joint Hearings before the Subcommittee on Foreign Economic Policy of the Committee on Foreign Affairs, House of Representatives, 93rd Congress, *American Interest in the European Community*, November 8, 1973, pp. 89 ff. See also Wilhelm Hankel, "West-Deutschlands Aussenwirtschaftspolitik nach dem Zweiten Weltkrieg," unpublished paper, 1975.

3. Roger Morgan, *The United States and West Germany 1945-1973: A Study in Alliance Politics* (London: Oxford University Press, 1974).

4. Although it is not explicitly mentioned, that image apparently underlies Karl Kaiser's arguments in his article "Die Auswirkungen der Energiekrise auf die westliche Allianz," *Europa Archiv*, 24 (1974), 820–821. See also the English translation of this paper under the title "The Energy Problem and Alliance Systems: Europe," *Adelphi Paper*, no. 115 (London, International Institute for Strategic Studies, 1975), pp. 17–24.

argues that the third image provides a better map for policy makers than the first two, for only brokerage offers a satisfactory way for coping with the unavoidable, conflictual elements which the mixed international system creates for all alliance relationships in current world politics.

West Germany as a Pivot

A brief glance at the economic statistics of the Federal Republic should convince even the most critical skeptic of the contribution which West Germany, together with the United States, could make toward a reconstruction of the international economy. In 1974 the West German share in total world exports was 12 percent, that is, as much as French and British exports combined and only slightly less than the share of the United States. For the years 1973–1975 the West German trade surplus will amount to roughly $40 billion. West German reserves stand at roughly $35 billion, more than twice as much as the reserves of the United States as the second strongest power. Between March 1972 and March 1975 the value of the German mark increased by about 40 percent against the U.S. dollar, and if one goes back to 1969 the revaluation amounts to as much as 60 percent. The German mark is rapidly becoming a second international reserve currency and is the backbone of the European "snake in the tunnel," the joint float of several European currencies. West Germany's inflation rate continues to be the lowest of all industrial states, and although unemployment in the current recession has been sizable by West German standards, both in terms of its magnitude and duration, it is little more than half of the unemployment rate of the United States. In short, an economic connection linking Washington with Bonn might return to the United States an economic base comparable to the one it held at the pinnacle of its power in the early 1950s.

The October War of 1973, furthermore, has strengthened the relative standing of both the United States and the Federal Republic in the international economy. The oil embargo and the ensuing controversy over raw material supplies have helped to halt the slide of the United States in international affairs, for they revealed that the United States is less vulnerable than any other advanced industrial state to the cutoff of raw material supplies. Although it is not clear whether this relative gain in strength is temporary or permanent, Secretary of State Kissinger has been quick to recognize the political advantages which this condition confers upon the United States. The Federal Republic has been the only other industrial state whose relative standing has improved because of the oil crisis. In 1974 the West German trade surplus exploded to record heights, and the financial strength of the German mark has encouraged the Arab states to funnel a portion of their new wealth back to the industrial states through the West German currency.

Since both governments take a very similar approach to questions of international economic reform, joint economic leadership could rely on more than raw capacity. Both governments favor a liberal, open, international economy, and both prefer multilateral political solutions to the current economic problems. These political inclinations, furthermore, can now serve as guidelines for policy making as both governments, for the first time in the last decade, have shed traditional political shackles. After Vietnam and Watergate the United States is again in a position to follow a policy designed to serve what it regards as its national *interest.* Brandt's Eastern policy, on the other hand, was an indispensible requirement to liberate the Federal Republic from the burden of its past foreign policy failure, to reduce the political leverage of adversaries and allies on Bonn, and to create a *national* interest centering on the Federal Republic.[5] Chancellor Schmidt is primarily interested in the stabilization of

5. Gebhard L. Schweigler, "German Foreign Policy," *World Survey,* 74 (February 1975), 1.

the shaky economic underpinnings of the current international order, and on this critical point West German and American political objectives are identical.

These, then, are formidable reasons which speak for an
American policy which treats the Federal Republic as a pivot
of the international economy. Yet such an analysis is partial,
and the prescriptions for policy making on which it is based
are fundamentally flawed. In current world politics questions
of economic interdependence have been superimposed but
have not supplanted questions of military security. Although
anticommunism in West Germany is waning as a political
force, the security needs of the Federal Republic are, in the
eyes of its government, as large as ever. The West German
security deficit is, in fact, much larger than the raw figures
of American troops stationed in the Federal Republic indicate. Chancellor Schmidt and his cabinet are convinced that
the American nuclear umbrella is the critical component in
West Germany's defense posture. This assessment is shared by
other members of the right wing of the Social Democratic
Party (SPD) not represented in the cabinet, by the centrist
segment of the SPD around former Chancellor Brandt, by the
small coalition partner, the Free Democratic Party (FDP) and
by the opposing Christian Democratic Union and Christian
Social Union. Only the younger generation, representing the
left wing of the SPD, disagrees in part. But if at some future
time, in the 1980s, that faction should succeed in controlling
the SPD leadership and through it, possibly, West German
politics, the political relations between the Federal Republic
and the United States most certainly would undergo drastic
changes. For the foreseeable future, however, the relations
between the United States and the Federal Republic in the
area of military security resemble not those among equals but
among patron and client. The renegotiations of the agreement under which Germany offsets American balance of pay-

ments expenditures on U.S. troops in the Federal Republic are a periodic reminder of that fact.

There exists a corresponding asymmetry in the posture of the United States and the Federal Republic in the international economy. In contrast to the United States, the West German economy is highly vulnerable to any cutoff of its sources of supply of raw materials. The scarcity in raw materials, which both governments must now anticipate as a probable future development, inevitably leads to the adoption of different political strategies. This difference was evident during the October War. The clandestine resupplying of the Israeli army from American army depots in West Germany was tacitly tolerated by the West German government. But when these shipments continued after the cease-fire and were discovered by the press, the West German government, fearing Arab reprisals, reacted strongly and asked that all shipments of war materials from West German territory be halted immediately. That demand caused a serious diplomatic quarrel between Washington and Bonn. Dependent on Arab oil imports, the government of the Federal Republic, like the governments of most other West European states, was primarily interested in receiving adequate oil supplies in the short run. The United States government, on the other hand, was more interested in longer-term political solutions and proposed to take a harder stand against the Arab states. That difference in perspective was inevitable given the different degree of economic vulnerability. This episode illustrates that the Federal Republic is a Croesus with feet of clay.

These differences in policy are not trivial. It is quite possible that in the years ahead questions of raw material supplies rather than the management of aggregate demand through the international trade and finance system will become critical in world politics. If this happens, American-

West German economic conflicts are likely to recur. One such conflict, the recent West German-Brazilian reactor deal, gives a foretaste of how far the two standpoints might diverge. Although the sheer size of that contract was a very strong financial incentive, the prospect of securing a long-term source of uranium supply may have convinced the West German government that in this particular instance it would have to stand fast against American opposition. West Germany opposed the United States on the critical question of financing the International Energy Agency. Like all other Western European states, with the exception of France, the West Germans are of course interested in sharing in the relatively plentiful United States oil reserves in time of need; but the financial provisions on which they insisted in the interest of protecting their financial reserves are sufficiently complex to make it unlikely that the oil sharing plan would ever become fully operative.

The asymmetry in the military and economic vulnerability of the two countries is complemented by the greater sensitivity of the West German economy to changes in international markets. West German exports amount to 23 percent of GNP as compared to 4 percent for the United States. For reasons of sheer size alone the United States economy is, thus, more insulated from demand changes in the world economy. The recession into which the world economy has moved during 1974–1975 has affected West German exports so strongly that the economy of the Federal Republic has failed to respond to government-initiated investment programs. With vital industries such as iron and steel, engineering, chemicals, and automobiles selling more than 50 percent of their products abroad in 1974, the sharp decline in export orders in the first half of 1975 has led to the worst recession since 1949. The United States economy, on the other hand, is less sensitive to conditions in world markets. Because of its enormous absolute size, the American economy gives signals for the world economy which are especially important in their phychological impact. Since late 1974 Chancellor Schmidt has, therefore, repeatedly urged President Ford to steer a more expansive course in his domestic economic policy because a change in U.S. domestic policy may be crucial for a revival of world exports.

The greater sensitivity of the West German economy to changes in international demand suggests a different basis for the preference for a multilateral, liberal strategy to world economic problems to which both governments subscribe. In many ways their strategies reflect the structure of their domestic institutions, which embody different types of economic liberalism. But there are other reasons. As was true of Britain in the nineteenth century, the United States has also followed an "imperialism of free trade" as the most appropriate way to exercise the hegemonic position which it acquired in the world economy after 1945. But with a weakening of that position the influence of domestic political interests favoring protectionism and a unilateral approach to foreign affairs is again growing in the conduct of American foreign policy. As the industrial rump of the defunct German Empire, the Federal Republic, on the other hand, came to a liberal approach to world economic problems not as a tool convenient for ordering international relations but as a device indispensable for the reconstruction of its shattered economy. More than for the United States, a liberal international trading system and a resilient international financial system are essential to the economic prosperity and stability of existing political institutions of the Federal Republic. The shared liberal preference in international economic affairs thus conceals differences in the intensity of interests in problems of reform of the international trading and financial system.

At first glance the image of West Germany as a pivot and the prospect of a joint leadership by the United States and the Federal Republic in international economic affairs is appealing, especially for American policy makers. What is more natural than a combination of the economic strength of two states which have already been close allies for a quarter of a century? But even though West Germany's economic strength looks imposing from Washington, the West German government is inclined to take a different perspective on these matters. Chancellor Schmidt, in his own words, "sees a certain danger in the fact that some Americans are currently inclined to overestimate the importance and capacity of the Federal Republic."[6] The security needs of the Federal Republic as well as the vulnerability and sensitivity of its economy to international changes expose a weakness in the West German position of which its government is acutely aware. To be sure, in certain areas (international trade and finance, and domestic stabilization policy) the West German government is eager to exert its influence in international affairs. On the whole, though, there exists a recognizable unwillingness to exert political leadership in other, critically important, policy areas (energy, raw materials, and food) because the hand of the West German government is weak, its expertise is limited and its financial resources, though vast, could easily be overcommitted.

West Germany as an Anchor

The second image, of Bonn as an anchor, suggests an alternative political strategy for American foreign policy. A special partnership between Washington and Bonn would not serve global but regional objectives. Its primary aim would lie not in the reform of the international economic system but in the recalibration of the complex military, economic and political problems which are troubling American-Western European relations in the mid-1970s. For American policy makers this second image has great attraction. For ideological,

6. See Schmidt's interview in *Der Spiegel,* 29, 1–2 (January 6, 1975), 33.

military and economic reasons the Atlantic Alliance continues to be an area of vital concern to American foreign
policy. The weaknesses in the West German economic and
military position which make the first image unattractive
to Bonn, but in particular the security needs of the Federal
Republic, ensure that the United States would retain its position as the senior partner in the alliance. In the 1950s and
1960s, furthermore when strategic issues were still of overriding importance, the relations between Washington and
Bonn, at different times, approximated a special partnership. This image is, then, a diplomatic blueprint which has
already been tested in reality.

A special partnership has, thus, much to recommend itself
to Washington; but it does not fit political realities in Bonn.
Current West German foreign policy making is decentralized
and rests in the hands of three men. Although Chancellor
Schmidt, Foreign Minister Hans-Dietrich Genscher, and SPD
Party Chairman Brandt all favor good relations with the
United States, none of them subscribes to the image of a
"special partnership" between Washington and Bonn. All
three are acutely aware of the great economic and political
weight of the Western European states in the Federal Republic's external relations. For example, roughly one half of West
German exports are sold within the EEC as compared to less
than 10 percent shipped to the United States. The Federal
Republic's entanglement with Western Europe is, in fact, so
strong that the West German government feels compelled, as
it did recently in the case of Italy, to subsidize massively the
economies of its most important trading partners.

The political weight of Western Europe presents an equally
important obstacle to the development of a special partnership between Washington and Bonn. Although West German
foreign policy has traditionally been oriented toward a
strengthening of the Atlantic Community, that policy was
always based on the assumption that a united Europe might,

possibly, play a more active role in world politics at some unspecified future date. The major thrust of American foreign policy since 1971, on the other hand, has been to eliminate that possibility. For Bonn a special partnership would, at best, relegate West Germany to the role of a transmission belt for an Atlanticist conception. It might, at worst, seek to use West Germany as a means of avoiding U.S. domestic opposition in the implementation of American foreign policy.[7] While Bonn takes a regional perspective on the possibility of Europe's global future, Washington takes a global perspective one the probability of Europe's regional future. This basic difference in political perspectives explains why the Federal Republic has strictly avoided any semblance of privileged treatment by Washington as the objective economic gap separating West Germany from its Western European neighbors has widened.

East-West relations are a second area which reveals a basic difference between Washington's global and West Germany's regional perspective. America's policy of *détente* has, from the mid-1950s on, caused numerous frictions between the American and West German governments. Most of these frictions developed because West Germany's foreign policy, after its initial Western orientation under Adenauer's leadership, remained immobilized in its insistence on German reunification as a precondition for the initiation of a process of *détente* in Europe. American interests, however, pointed in the opposite direction: toward a rapprochement with the Soviet Union, especially from the early 1960s onward. In 1970, at the outset of Brandt's Eastern policy, these frictions recurred albeit this time apprehension was voiced in Washington. Brandt's foreign policy had two components, one na-

7. Gebhard L. Schweigler, "A New Political Giant? West German Policy in the 1970s," *The World Today*, 30 (April 1975), 138–139. Stanley Hoffmann, "No Trumps, No Luck, No Will: Gloomy Thoughts on Europe's Plight," in James Chace and Earl Ravenal, eds., *Atlantis Lost* (New York: New York University Press, 1976).

tional and the other regional. The national German component was to maintain a united German people linked through
numerous cultural and economic contacts but living under
two different forms of government. The regional, European
component was Brandt's interest in the strengthening the
process of *détente* between the two superpowers then under
way and in the preparation of the ground, both politically
and psychologically, for relations between East and West Europe should the process of *détente* lead to a sizable reduction
of America's military presence in Western Europe. American
apprehensions in the early stages of the Eastern policy arose
from the fact that the timing and speed dictated by these
national and regional considerations threatened to interfere
with the global policy of *détente* (involving China as well as
the Soviet Union) on which President Nixon was then em-
barking.

Although this episode has been largely forgotten, the difference between a global, American and a national or regional
West German orientation toward East-West relations has remained, and is a likely barrier to the development of a special
partnership between Washington and Bonn. The difference in
perspective on the European Security Conference and the
Mutual Force Reduction talks illustrates that point. The
American government has shown a notable lack of interest in
the progress of the European-wide negotiations which were
concluded successfully in Helsinki in July 1975. At best,
American reasoning ran, the prospect of a European Peace
Charter would offer political leverage for pushing the Soviet
Union on the force reduction talks. These talks, after all,
promise to lighten the military burden the United States
carries in Western Europe while blunting powerful critics of
the American defense posture in the United States Congress.

The Federal Republic, on the other hand, has taken an
active interest in the European Security Conference, which
it regards as touching upon its national objectives. Like West

Germany's Eastern policy, the conference is a further brick in the edifice of a stabilized status quo in Europe. The "human rights basket" of the Helsinki Accords, furthermore, sets standards for the liberalization of the flow of information and personal contacts between European states which introduce international elements into the relations between the two German states first defined in the Basic Treaty of 1972. Unlike Brandt, Chancellor Schmidt favors the liberalization of contacts between the two Germanies not for reasons of national unity but because it offers some diplomatic leverage in East Berlin after West Germany's de facto recognition of the German Democratic Republic. Although noted for his stinginess in Brussels, Schmidt is willing to pay a tidy sum for increasing that leverage. Complementing the asymmetry between Washington's global and Bonn's regional perspective is the fact that the West German government views the force reduction talks with some apprehension because the size of West Germany's armed forces is one possible subject of negotiation, and because these talks could be a preliminary step to a sizable reduction of America's military presence in West Germany.

The difference between America's global and West Germany's regional perspective is also evident in the relations of the two governments with the Communists in Western Europe. In the currently most crucial area in Western Europe, the Mediterranean, American and West German foreign policy objectives diverge. The United States is inclined to treat the Latin countries in Europe like Latin American ones. Its strong support of the Greek colonels between 1967 and 1974 betrayed a preference for military dictatorship over leftist regimes which has also marked American foreign policy in Chile and elsewhere in Latin America. Motivated, at least in part, by an interest in maintaining secure military bases, important especially for influencing military developments in the Middle East, the critical stance which the United States initially took toward Portugal after Marcelo Caetano as well as its demonstrative show of support for the present Bourbon government in Spain illustrate one consequence of the global perspective of American foreign policy for political developments inside Western Europe.

The West German government, on the other hand, is forced to develop alternatives to a rigid anticommunism in Western Europe. For it faces the prospect of dealing, in the near future, with an Italian government in which the Communist party might be a major political force. This is not to deny the interest which the Schmidt government shares with the United States in the stabilization of southern European affairs. But it prefers economic over diplomatic means, and shows a greater interest in economic than political ends. There is, in addition, a second, ideological element in West German foreign policy more closely associated with the name of Brandt than Schmidt. Influenced by the German experience after 1945, the SPD party chief believes that, beyond all considerations of national or regional interest, the Federal Republic has a special obligation in Portugal, as elsewhere in southern Europe, to aid the successors to the fascist governments in their attempts at developing viable political institutions and practices.

With regard to critical problems facing the Atlantic Alliance —the future shape of Western Europe, East-West relations and political developments in southern Europe—there exist considerable differences between the political objectives of a global and those of a regional power. The increase in the political and economic standing of the Federal Republic during the last decade has widened the scope for effective action in its foreign policy. Besides traditional national concerns (symbolized by West Germany's continued interest in securing the status of West Berlin), questions of stabilization at both the regional and global level have now come into the purview of German foreign policy. Even if it were willing, the government of the Federal Republic can no longer play the role of junior partner in an alliance dominated by the United States. Karl Kaiser is right when he writes that "the Federal Republic would no doubt choose a close relationship with the United States if the choice were to emerge as a last alternative, with all other avenues of cooperation between an integrating Europe and the United States closed. But the choice would be deeply regretted, if not resented.[8] Short of last alternatives the relations between Washington and Bonn are not served by attempts to establish a special partnership.

West Germany as a Broker

The Federal Republic should thus become neither a pivot nor an anchor in American foreign policy. Weaknesses in the position of the Federal Republic prevent it from accepting an invitation to exercise, jointly with the United States, leadership in global economic affairs. An increasingly tight web of economic and political relations spun between West Germany and its European neighbors make unlikely the formation of a special partnership linking Washington with Bonn. The first two images of American-West German relations are thus based on incorrect assumptions. Neither the management of global economic affairs nor the reconstitution of the Atlantic Alliance permit the Federal Republic to act consistently against vital interests of its European neighbors. At the same time, though, the first two images highlight elements which facilitate close cooperation between the United States and the Federal Republic on some aspects of the reform of the international economy and on a partial reordering of the affairs of the Atlantic Alliance. The image of Bonn as a broker offers a third way for organizing American-West German relations which has the advantage of accu-

8. Karl Kaiser, "Europe and America: A Critical Phase," *Foreign Affairs* 52 (July 1974), 739.

rately depicting reality. Since there are limits to Bonn's capacity to act the role of broker, American foreign policy should make use of West German brokerage primarily in its relations with Western Europe rather than Third World countries or the Soviet Union.

The great economic strength and enlarged political freedom which the Federal Republic has gained during the last five years predestines it for the role of broker in international affairs. With increasing determination, it appears, the West German government has seized on that role. Like any of its potential successors, the Schmidt government prefers to maintain a low political profile and a maximum distance from all international conflict spots. Awareness of international sensibilities over West German capabilities, as well as fear of financial expense and political trouble, make that preference comprehensible. The West German government prefers instead a multilateral, consensual approach to international politics in which it can fulfill the role of a broker.

This is the role in which West German foreign policy makers travel most comfortably throughout the world. Even after his fall from power, former Chancellor Brandt still attempts to fill the role of intermediary in the evolving relations between East and West. In the Middle East, West German foreign policy has managed to change its traditional pro-Israeli course toward a more even-handed one without seriously offending either side in the conflict. In the conflict between Turkey and Greece, Bonn, more than any other government, can count on receiving a sympathetic hearing on both sides. In its relations with the OPEC countries the West German government speaks for Western Europe at large when it advocates that producer and consumer states alike need a new institutional order governing raw material supplies which takes account of their many mutual interests as well as the needs of the very poor states which constitute the Fourth

World.[9] On all these questions West Germany's overriding objective has been directed toward the stabilization of international affairs. This conservative trait has made its brokerage largely compatible with what remains a central objective of American foreign policy.

The West German government plays the role of a broker also inside the Atlantic Community. As was true of the strategic debate in the 1960s and the discussions over the reform of the international financial system, the sharpest clash on the question of energy and raw material supplies for the industrialized states exists between France and the United States. Bonn's penchant for multilateralism and a consensual approach to international conflict leads it to reject both the American and the French position. The preference of the United States for the organization of a cartel of consumers, proposed first in the context of the oil crisis, smacks too much of confrontation which Bonn, with its high degree of dependence on imports of raw materials, rejects as politically too risky. The first response of the French government to the energy crisis, on the other hand, was a search for bilateral arrangements. This alternative, too, is not to the liking of the West German government for it threatens to move the international economy dangerously close to the barter system which in the 1930s led to drastic shrinkages in world trade. A cooperative approach to supply countries in a multilateral framework is the policy most favored in Bonn; it falls neatly between the diverging positions of the American and the French government. It was, therefore, relatively easy for Chancellor Schmidt to propose an energy compromise for the United States and France which was ratified by the two presidents in the agreement at Martinique. This episode is merely the latest illustration, albeit on an issue of critical importance, of the mediating influence which the Federal

9. Helmut Schmidt, "The Struggle for the World Product: Politics between Power and Morals," *Foreign Affairs*, 52 (April 1974), 437–451.

Republic attempts to exercise within the Atlantic Alliance. Overviewing a longer time span, Roger Morgan has rightly remarked that "the pattern in Atlantic economic affairs, where Germany consistently tried to guide Europe's emerging structure and the outcome of substantive problems in a direction favourable to good European-American relations, was similar to the pattern in the military affairs of the region."[10]

Treating the West German government as a broker in international affairs, one sees reasonable prospects for bilateral relations between Washington and Bonn which are both cooperative in spirit and effective in their impact on international developments. To be sure there is a distinct possibility that not all short-term American interests will be achieved, since the Federal Republic will not back all American proposals unequivocally. But the very factors which bar Bonn from being a pivot ensure that West Germany's brokerage should normally lead to compromises which are fairly close to the American point of view. This is true, for example, on questions of military strategy in NATO and questions of reform of the international trade and financial system. Where differences in political preferences are more notable, for example on the question of raw material supplies, the West German broker would act as a gentle brake on American foreign policy initiatives. But this would not be entirely disadvantageous to the Americans for, without the support of Europe, American initiatives on any major issue of the international economy are likely to fail. Finally, taking an approach to American-West German relations which is guided by the image of West Germany as broker is a low-risk strategy, for it merely encourages (or tolerates) the Federal Republic's playing of a role of its own choosing.

Viewed in a larger perspective on German history, the role of broker is attractive and reveals more common sense and moderation than have distinguished the governments of prev-

10. Morgan, *The United States and West Germany,* p. 208.

ious German regimes. It is, however, not entirely clear whether a West German broker can be honest and whether the government of the Federal Republic will be able to play that role effectively over at least a moderate time span. For example, the current economic strength of the Federal Republic which has contributed greatly to its political ascendancy is as decisively affected by its financial policy as its industrial prowess. As the West German government and many of its admirers point out, since the late 1960s the Deutschmark has floated upward against most major currencies. This makes the explosion of West Germany's export surpluses in the same period doubly astonishing. Yet the government and the Federal Reserve Bank of West Germany have seen to it that the revaluation effect has remained smaller than the effect of worldwide inflation from 1973 on. Thus under floating exchange rates during the 1970s as under fixed exchange rates in the 1960s West German exports have remained highly competitive in world markets.

The "liberal" and "international" approach which the West German government has taken in international economic affairs is entirely compatible with a "mercantilist" and "national" perspective, mercantilist in that it leads to the accumulation of vast foreign exchange reserves, national in that it reflects the preference of the West German government for strict antiinflationary policies.[11] But the strictness, it bears repeating, is not only a result of West Germany's past experience with hyperinflation. It is also an indispensable element to the international standing of the Federal Republic. Since the concern of the West German electorate over inflation appears to have weakened somewhat, it is conceivable that the international aspect of West Germany's stabilization policy

11. Hankel, "West-Deutschlands Aussenwirtschaftspolitik," pp. 3, 8, 16. Henrik Schmiegelow and Michèle Schmiegelow, "The New Mercantilism in International Relations: The Case of France's External Monetary Policy," *International Organization,* 29 (Spring 1975), 384.

will, in the not too distant future, become more important in determining West German policy than the fear of electoral sanction. After three wars, Bismarck's preference for maintaining the status quo in Europe made it convenient for him to assume the role of broker because that role was entirely compatible with the national objectives of the new German Empire. The current West German government has a similar stake in maintaining the status quo of the current international economic order. The strength of Bonn's commitment to the status quo affords other governments, including that of the United States, diplomatic leverage which is uncommon in the relation among clients and brokers.

A second potential weakness in treating the Federal Republic as a broker lies in the gap which separates foreign and West German observers of the foreign policy performance of the Federal Republic. That gap is due to the growing importance of domestic politics of advanced industrial states in the current era of world politics.[12] After its adjustment to the division of the country, ratified de facto through Brandt's Eastern policy, the West Germans have turned inward, toward the tasks of social reform and preservation. But even without this specifically German legacy, domestic constraints on foreign policy have increased everywhere, which interferes with playing the role of international broker. The orchestration and coordination of foreign economic policies is problematic precisely because the range of domestic interests tangibly affected by international developments has expanded greatly. Expectations and experiences of gains and losses lead to pressures which may make the conduct of a diplomacy, exercised in the spirit of fair brokerage, increasingly difficult. For example, with drastically growing budget deficits a likely issue in future electoral campaigns, the West

12. This argument is developed at greater length in my paper "International Effects and Domestic Structures: Foreign Economic Policies of Advanced Industrial States," *International Organization,* 30 (Winter 1976).

German government may feel pressured to find a new policy
for dealing with its enormous foreign exchange reserves. The
losses due to revaluation have amounted to roughly $12 bil-
lion since 1969, and they no longer go unnoticed by taxpay-
ers or local and state governments crushed by the growing
burden of the welfare state. If they were to become sufficiently strong, such pressures might not be compatible with
West Germany's role as honest broker in international affairs.

A third area of potential weakness lies in the future course
of world inflation. Should that inflation level off only briefly
before rising further throughout the industrial world, it is
probable that West Germany would soon find itself not as the
broker of international conflicts but as the target of diplomatic maneuvers by other governments unable for domestic
reasons to join the Deutschmark bloc and eager to push the
West German government to adopt more expansive domestic
economic policies. Under different guise, the recurrent political conflicts over the revaluation of the mark in the 1960s
might repeat itself over the question of West Germany's domestic economic policy in the latter part of the 1970s. If,
on the other hand, inflationary pressures weaken, so would
the effective rate of "subsidization" of West German exports.
The current export slump of the West Germany economy is
partial evidence for the great sensitivity of West German exports to changes in world demand due to the de facto under-
valuation of the mark during the last fifteen years. Such
sensitivity affects West Germany's domestic economic performance and thus the political staying power of its government.

There is, finally, some legitimate doubt that the quality
of West Germany's diplomacy permits effective exercise of
the power conferred upon it as an international broker. In
the arena of most complex bargaining, Brussels, the West Germans have traditionally been "policymasters" only to the
extent that they were also "paymasters." But even the great

financial strength of the Federal Republic is insufficient to maintain such a posture in an expanded EEC, not to speak of wider regional or global economic arrangements. As the financial constraints imposed on West German policy makers grow, the demands placed on the skill of its diplomats will increase. If a sensible division of labor can be agreed upon in Bonn, the existence of three spokesmen for West Germany's foreign policy has undeniable advantages for a broker dealing with different issues and diverse clienteles. Chancellor Schmidt, it appears, is concentrating on economic questions, Foreign Minister Genscher on security questions, and SPD party chief Brandt on East-West relations. But these different issues are not easily separable. There exists, furthermore, a contradiction between making fine distinctions in diplomatic parlance with political clients abroad and scoring debating points in political contests with political opponents at home. German foreign policy in the 1870s had one juggler and many different balls. West German foreign policy in the 1970s has only one ball but many jugglers. *Both* games, one might add, require a great amount of political finesse. It is by no means clear whether the present West German government, or its successor, can command the diplomatic skills necessary for successful international brokerage.

Today, the Federal Republic has its feet in many political camps, and it conceives of its role as a broker in international conflicts. American foreign policy can gain most by calling on West Germany's services where the credibility of its brokerage is least in question, in the Atlantic Alliance. For military, economic and political reasons any West German government will prefer to mediate between the Western European states and Washington rather than to choose sides in any possible conflict between them. But in other problem areas, such as East-West or North-South relations, military weakness or economic vulnerability undermine the credibility of West German brokerage. To some extent this may be offset by

West Germany's self-consciousness in acting the role of broker. At times it thus may be to the advantage of the United
States to call on West Germany's services in these problem
areas. By and large, though, psychology is a shaky foundation for a foreign policy. The voice of the Federal Republic
should carry its greatest weight in the management of the
affairs of the Atlantic Alliance.

The contemporary international system is distinguished by
the complexity of its structure and the rapidity of its change.
Compared to the last quarter century, elements of cooperation and conflict are now more mixed and power has become
more elusive. As the burdens imposed on American diplomacy grow, it is possible that a current mood might become
future policy. If firm political support were to be sought
abroad, that support, it seems, could be found more easily
in Bonn than anywhere else. Past diplomatic practice suggests that the United States would treat West Germany either
as a fellow leader (through whose manipulation the behavior
of several other actors in the global economy could be influenced) or as a special partner (in an attempt to secure the
shaky foundations of the Atlantic Alliance). Organized
around the image of West Germany as a pivot, the first
strategy would risk failure since it disregards the security
deficit of the Federal Republic as well as fundamental differences in the vulnerability and sensitivity of the American
and West German economies to international economic developments. Following the image of the Federal Republic as
an anchor, the second strategy is flawed for its neglect of differences which exist between Washington's global and Bonn's
regional perspectives on critical problems of the Atlantic
Alliance.
      The specific requirements of bilateral relations between
Washington and Bonn as well as America's general objectives
in world politics are served equally well by treating West Ger-

many as a broker whose voice should carry special weight in the management of the political problems of the Atlantic Alliance. This third strategy avoids possible weaknesses in the first two. On the one hand, it circumscribes the place of West Germany in international affairs without being unduly restrictive; the most caustic critics of the Federal Republic would have to agree that it will inhibit the *nouveaux riches* in Bonn from becoming the *nouveaux boches*. On the other hand, this strategy accords the Federal Republic a prominent place in international politics without asking the impossible; the greatest admirers of the Federal Republic would have to concur that Bonn cannot become the Atlas of the Atlantic Alliance. Treating Bonn as a broker in international affairs is a modest proposal with low risks and moderate payoffs. It prescribes an attitude for American foreign policy, not a course of action.

7

America in the Far East: Political & Military Dimensions

KENNETH HUNT

The United States plays a key role in the security structure of much of Asia. This was not always so; it is an outgrowth of the dramatic changes brought by World War II and its immediate aftermath. But changes in the three decades since that time have been no less dramatic, and there are tensions and problems in the region still. Does American policy help to solve these problems? How desirable and how durable is the American position in the Far East?

This position has, of course, itself changed considerably over the years, responding to international events and domestic pressures. In the 1950s the policy had a marked anti-Communist, anti-Chinese coloration. The Korean war was fought; SEATO was formed as an alliance of anti-Communist countries; and the train of events was set in motion which eventually led to Vietnam. The strain of the drawn-out Vietnam War produced in 1969 the Guam, later Nixon, doctrine, which severely modified American willingness to provide military manpower to help Asian allies. The watershed year of 1971 brought the *volte-face* of a rapprochement with China, foreshadowing the redundancy of SEATO (essentially an anti-Chinese alliance) and the withdrawal of U.S. forces from South Vietnam two years later. The fall of Saigon in 1975 finally brought to a virtual end the U.S. commitment to the mainland of Asia, only the forces in South Korea and those in Thailand remaining.

What has been left at the end of this period of change is a political and military strategy based mainly on a maritime presence in the Pacific, and certain commitments, notably to Taiwan, South Korea, Japan and the Philippines, plus a treaty with Australia and New Zealand not much affected by all this. SEATO is still in being, but its military side is now a dead letter.

This is, of course, to state the policy very briefly and barely. In full awareness of the doubts about American constancy caused by the Vietnam *débâcle*, the United States has been at pains to reaffirm its remaining commitments throughout the world, to reassure its allies (and potential enemies) that these will be upheld. There has been no rush to build a brand new Asian policy from the remnants of the old but rather a period of consolidation and reflection.

With the ending of the mainland commitment in Southeast Asia, however unwelcome this may have been, the United States now has freedom of maneuver there. And maritime strategy is very flexible. The forces in the region are largely air and naval, and there are few entanglements. Though there will be political frictions about the occupation of foreign bases, only Korea presents a serious risk of American troops being caught up in conflict. The forces are perfectly capable of meeting the commitments to the defense of Taiwan, Japan and the Philippines and to Australia and New Zealand. They are also appropriate to the important task of maintaining the freedom of the seas, including some ability to operate in the Indian Ocean, and additionally of playing a part in the defense of the continental United States. But a maritime strategy offers only a limited ability to affect events on land. In Asia change is apt to be brought about by men crossing frontiers or overthrowing governments, and only soldiers on land can combat this. Air power has some deterrent value but not much direct military utility when unsupported. And its use can have high political visibility and often disadvantage. So a maritime strategy does involve being willing to tolerate events that one is no longer able to alter.

The present policy and position, as truncated by the events in Southeast Asia, may then, for the time being at least, be a not unsatisfactory one, but whether it is likely to be adequate over the longer term is another matter. Exactly what American foreign and security policy in Asia and the Pacific basin should set out to achieve is not easy to decide. There are many detailed issues in different parts of the region for which policy needs fairly precise definition, but perhaps broad aims can be established. Clearly it should avoid the risk of the United States being drawn into conflict and allow it the maximum political and economic access to all countries in Asia. The United States has an interest in international order and stability and for this needs to cultivate good relations with China and the Soviet Union in particular. She is, however, concerned that neither of these powers nor any combination of powers should be able to dominate the region, and so it is in her interest to cultivate allies—notably Japan, a key country on many counts. The policy must ensure as far as possible the freedom of the seas and the protection of allies where necessary. All this must be at a cost that the public will stand; events in Asia have left a legacy of disenchantment and congressional jaundice, and no policy that is not proof against this, and is seen by others to be so, will stand up in adversity.

At a quick glance it is evident that not all elements in the present policy satisfy these criteria. The military and political commitment to Taiwan, for example, does not help improve relations with China. The military presence in South Korea is a hostage to fortune, which presents some risk of entanglement in a mainland war. It is necessary, therefore, to look more closely at the various commitments that do exist, to gauge their worth, but it will be as well to look first at the international context in which policy has to be set. The main framework for this is the relationships among China, the Soviet Union, the United States and Japan.

China and the Soviet Union

Satisfactory relations with China are a desirable prop to any American policy in Asia, but this is far from just a bilateral problem. For each one the Soviet Union also looms large, and relations are therefore a matter of priorities. For the United States there is no doubt where the priority lies; she must and does give first place to relations with the other global superpower, the Soviet Union, not least because each has the power to destroy the other. For the United States the links with the Soviet Union are overriding. China has nothing to give that can match their importance, and so relations with her cannot be at the cost of worsening those with the Soviet Union. China naturally dislikes this. Her whole policy is anti-Soviet in orientation; she prefers her friends to be the enemies of the Soviet Union. It is true, of course, that improved relations between China and the United States put pressure on the USSR and may actually improve the climate of negotiations between the superpowers.

The quarrel between China and the Soviet Union is, central to the security setting in Asia not just for its impact on American policy, but because of the military dangers that it presents and because it permeates every other political situation in the region. The two powers clash on ideological and on national grounds. They dispute the leadership of the Communist and Third Worlds and their common border. Their Asian policies are each dominated by the other.

Militarily they confront each other with very large forces indeed. Those of the Soviet Union are well-equipped, with modern armor and aircraft and tactical nuclear weapons with a variety of delivery means. Strategic nuclear weapons are

certainly targeted on China as well. These Soviet forces in
the Chinese border regions are no doubt designed to dissuade
China from any attempt to redress her border grievances by
force and to win any local clashes that might break out by
miscalculation. The Chinese People's Liberation Army is far
less well equipped though the formations near the border
have fairly modern weapons. China relies for her defense
on sheer mass rather than quality of armament, allied to the
rugged nature of much of the terrain. She has in fact devoted
her resources to the two ends of the military spectrum:
nuclear weapons to deter Soviet nuclear attack and people's
war to defend her territory. Though her nuclear program is a
slow one, she has operational a nuclear force which may indeed deter by its ability to extract a price in the event of a
nuclear clash. There is no doubt about the deterrent effect
of her massive armies.

War between them seems improbable. China is unlikely to
provoke it when so much military advantage, particularly
nuclear, lies with the Soviet Union. The Soviet Union, which
has no need to make border changes, will hardly welcome
war with such an enemy, and the time for nuclear preemp-
tion—if ever there was one—is probably past. Local clashes
are, of course, possible but are unlikely to be allowed by
either side to get out of hand.

The conflict is thus likely to remain political. As a competitor for Communist leadership, each faces the dilemma of
choosing between supporting revolutionary movements in
Asia or cultivating good state-to-state relations. Where North
Vietnam was concerned this particular problem did not exist,
and each gave support in a bid for influence in Hanoi. Elsewhere in Asia the Soviet Union has been wooing a variety of
states, offering the blandishment of an Asian Collective
Security system, only a lightly disguised form of containment
of China. The states she has approached, conscious of the
nearness and sheer mass of China, have been reluctant to

espouse anything so calculated to affront that country, even if they saw any utility in the idea, which is doubtful. China has some cultural affinities with many countries, in some of which there are overseas Chinese in large numbers. This tends to give China the inside track over the Soviet Union, except perhaps where Hanoi is concerned. When the United States changed its China policy in 1971, many Asian countries followed suit, notably Japan and even the fervently anti-Communist Philippines, opening diplomatic links or at least improving relations with China. And China reopened its embassies around the world, closed during the Cultural Revolution, no doubt partly in an attempt to win friends in her quarrel with the Soviet Union. Her attitude toward regional revolutionary movements is ambiguous but certainly muted for the moment, while state-to-state relations are to the fore.

The Sino-Soviet dispute is obviously not entirely to the discomfort of the United States; indeed there are certain dividends from it, though given the importance of U.S.-Soviet relations, playing one side against the other is not easy. Their conflict limits the ability of either to profit much from the American discomfiture over Vietnam. China not only tolerates but welcomes an American presence in the Western Pacific. The Soviet Union faces active political opposition from China all over Asia and indeed throughout the Third World. Each is mesmerized by the other. Probably neither would welcome for the moment, for example, any upheaval in the Korean peninsula or any marked change in the political alignment of Japan, for fear that the other might capitalize on it. So, in a way, the dispute makes for a certain stability.

Is the quarrel likely to go on? Can relations be friendly again, as they were in the 1950s? The odds seem against it. The rift runs deep and the issues that divide them are fundamental. But new leaders are likely to emerge in both countries before many years are out, and this may lead to some degree of adjustment of day-to-day relations, less marked hostility. The United States must allow for this possibility, in order to avoid, if possible, becoming the odd man out. Achieving this will not be easy, of course, but it does argue for improving relations with China as much and as soon as possible so as to undercut the Soviet position. One cannot completely rule out a China that reverts to being hostile to the Western world and to the United States. To guard against this the American alliance and base structure must be sufficiently insulated from events on the mainland to be proof against Chinese antagonisms.

East Asia

With this preliminary analysis in mind, we may look individually at the ingredients of present policy, to see if they serve American interests. It might seem appropriate to start with Japan, since that country is the keystone in the American position. It is, however, easier to begin with Taiwan because the policy there is in a sense a separate one, a relic of the past in a context which has now changed.

Taiwan

For nearly a quarter of a century the United States effectively treated Taiwan as China and ignored, boycotted, the mainland. For many of these years most of her allies did the same, but by the late 1960s the effective refusal of the United States to acknowledge the existence of 700 million people had become an aberration, a strange way to conduct international relations. In 1971 President Nixon changed the policy abruptly and diplomatic relations with China were restored. The American embassy remained in Taipeh however, and only a liaison office was established in Peking. Japan, tied until then to American China policy, quickly went further, despite a substantial pro-Taiwan lobby in the Diet and objections from Taiwan. She opened an embassy in

Peking because good relations with her massive mainland neighbor were vastly more important to her than those with Taiwan. The United States perhaps felt that the initial heave of reopening links with Peking was enough to be getting on with, and the problem of Taiwan could safely be left until later. No doubt she felt moral qualms about abandoning that country, a loyal ally throughout the anti-Communist years.

Looked at dispassionately, this half measure of a policy now seems almost as much an aberration as the earlier one. On any count China has more value for the United States than Taiwan can possibly have and her value should be turned into political capital. There is no legal dispute over the status of the country. China regards Taiwan as part of her territory, but so does the United States. In the words of the Sino-American Communiqué of February 1972, the United States "acknowledges that all Chinese on either side of the Taiwan Strait maintain there is but one China and that Taiwan is a part of China."[1] The United States wishes to see a peaceful settlement of the Taiwan question and would not want any attempt made to resolve it by force. In earlier years U.S. naval forces were from time to time deployed between Taiwan and the mainland as a deterrent, and combat forces were stationed on the island, but the latter have now been removed. There is, however, unlikely to be an attempt at force: China shows no signs of intending this and appears ready to leave a solution to politics and time. In any case, the defense forces of Taiwan are strong, and a major amphibious offensive capability—which China does not have as yet—would have to be mounted in order to challenge them.

But if force were to be used, would the United States intervene any longer? That it would is surely extremely doubtful, and the thinning out of U.S. forces in Taiwan is an indication of this. It may be argued that the situation is an illustration

1. *Survival*, May/June 1972, p. 140.

of the Nixon Doctrine at work: the manpower will be found by the local country while other military aid and a nuclear guarantee is provided by the United States. But the somewhat rubbery Nixon Doctrine has also been defined as a compromise between what the administration would like and what the American public will stand. Would the administration now contemplate committing U.S. forces to what would be a war with China, however limited? Not on any count. And public support certainly would not be forthcoming; Congress would be completely hostile.

Of course this states the problem in an extreme form since the need for force is unlikely to arise. It suggests, however, that American policy is not only and obviously invested in the wrong country but that a military guarantee is valueless in any case. The time has surely come then for the policy to be changed, following the pattern set by Japan. There is clearly a moral case for maintaining links with Taiwan, and there is no doubt some domestic political support for doing so, particularly on the Right, to which the President must listen in an election year. But there is no reason why the Japanese example should not be followed and full trade and other links retained. Taiwan surely realized that the change of policy in 1971 would sooner or later mean a changed status for her and will have been making her adjustments. The present American position is only the rump of a failed China policy and should be abandoned. An ambassador should be sent to Peking, and an impediment to better relations with China thus removed. This may not be an immediate issue nor may any immediate advantage be derived from it. The problem is not so urgent that action need be taken tomorrow, but the sooner the United States makes this gesture the better balanced will be her policy in Asia.

South Korea

The marked exception to the overall American strategy in Asia is in South Korea, where substantial U.S. ground forces are committed. With their associated fighter support there are some 42,000 men there in all, no longer in the front line but in the country as a visible token of American support. The bilateral defense agreement is, of course, a commitment of long standing. It dates from the division of Korea under the Armistice Agreement of 1953, but as has already been stressed, it was strongly reaffirmed in the wake of the fall of South Vietnam. The forces are supported from bases in Korea and Japan. Should fighting break out again in the peninsula, the Japanese bases would be necessary for the effective prosecution of any war by U.S. forces, land, sea or air.

The situation in the peninsula has long been potentially explosive. The division of Korea is resented by both regimes, and each maintains substantial armed forces either as a guard against any attempt to impose reunion by force or perhaps as a means to impose it one day. There is no doubt that the presence of American troops is and has always been a restraining factor, a deterrent against attack by the North and a cautionary hand on the South. Since the senior American officer there is also the United Nations force commander, he controls the South Korean forces as well as his own.

Reunification by peaceful means has been much bruited about, particularly during a brief period of apparent reconciliation between North and South in the summer of 1972. Nothing came of this, however, and the prospect now seems remote. Reunification continues to be a slogan used by both sides but it is difficult to see how Korea could be united; the North would not accept a unified country under a capitalist system nor the South one under Communist leadership. A form of federation, which has been talked of, is theoretically possible but bristles with practical difficulties. It is hard to escape the view that each regime has a vested interest in its own continuance and a division on the lines of the two Germanies will be the eventual outcome—if there is no war. But such a division, made permanent either by agreement or by solidifying over time, is still likely to need external props for a while, rather as it has now. The South is too exposed by its nearness to its three Communist neighbors.

American forces are therefore helping to provide stability in the peninsula, in default of or while waiting for a political solution, as they have done for the last quarter of a century. This is certainly in the interests of international order in the region, which is one reason for keeping them there. Another more specific reason is that unrest or hostilities in the peninsula could produce severe political and psychological stresses in Japan, in whose stability and protection the U.S. has an important stake. The reaffirmation of the commitment to South Korea had partly to do with disabusing the North of any notion that the United States would be willing, if pressed sufficiently hard, to see Seoul fall as Saigon had, but it was no doubt also made to reassure Japan.

It is worth digressing for a moment about the Korean problem and Japan. It is often said by Japanese that Korea is a dagger pointed at their heart, and there is little doubt that when President Truman decided to fight the Korean War in June 1950 it was with the awareness that the fall of the South to the Communists would have threatened a then barely stable Japan. But Japan has changed. She has learned to live alongside large Communist neighbors and to work and trade with them despite ideological differences. Living with North Korea would be manageable to her if the North were willing to establish working relations. Japan has much to offer and requires relatively little in return. The same could conceivably be true if the peninsula as a whole turned Communist. This would not be Japan's preferred solution but might be a tolerable one nonetheless. Depending on how benign Korean policies were, it might mean stepping up her military protection, either by herself or through a reinforcement of the link with the United States. As far as the present position is concerned, it is clear that Japan wants no military part in defending South Korea, nor, for good historical reasons, would that country welcome any Japanese military intervention. Japan's support for South Korea's defense is limited to affording the use of her bases to U.S. forces. Japan does have a strong interest in stability in the peninsula, and to her the status quo is greatly preferable to the alternatives of unrest or a Communist South. She looks, however, to the United States to maintain that status quo and will not do so herself. This is in fact a reasonable policy which suits all the other states affected by the dispute, none of whom wants to see a Japan with a wider military role. But it leaves the United States as the guardian of the peace, the one taking the real risks.

If American policy in Korea provides stability, it has some uncomfortable features, apart from being somewhat static. The government of President Park Chung Hee in Seoul is not the most liberal or enlightened one, and its comparative unconcern for some human rights has alienated an important and probably growing section of the South Korean electorate. In the United States it awakens disturbing echoes of regimes in Saigon, with their failure to command widespread popular support. This could be a serious issue in Congress. If U.S. troops are thought to be shoring up a needlessly repressive regime while running the risks of being entangled in war, the present policy could sooner or later be called seriously into question.

The deterrent role of U.S. forces does make war unlikely but what if it did break out against the odds? The existing garrison would no doubt have to be reinforced and the South Korean army fully supported. This means a war on some scale and at least a proxy confrontation with China and the Soviet Union. The intervention of Chinese forces could not be ruled out. This posture is, to say the least of it, a very uncomfortable one for the United States even if all the risks involved are understood and accepted. Would there be social

consent in the United States for involvement in another war
over Korea? The answer is unclear, which means the administration might have difficulty in prosecuting a war beyond its
initial phases. If this is the case, U.S. policy in Korea rests on
a shaky foundation: if deterrence fails it may not be backed
by adequate U.S. defense. There would be the risk of having
to abandon Seoul under strain, just like Saigon.

There does seem a case for looking for a more balanced
posture, for some safer policy. Are there any practical alternatives short of simply leaving? There is the obvious one of
working for a phased reduction of U.S. forces over a period,
by ensuring that South Korean forces are fully capable of
self-defense, and backing them by political guarantees. It
should be accompanied by initiatives for a political solution
in the peninsula, if any are possible. The policy must be a
genuine one and not merely a device to ensure American
withdrawal. If it were the latter a dangerous situation would
be created and one which would probably not work in the
U.S. interest. To have a continuing chance of success the
government in Seoul would have to command and be seen to
command a sufficiently strong popular following. Here it is
important to make the point that whatever it may look like
from North America, Seoul is not Saigon: though there is
political disquiet in South Korea, a far greater degree of
support exists for the government there than was ever the
case in South Vietnam, and little counterattraction is offered
by the policies and attitudes of the North. Yet there is still a
dilemma: the durability of the Park regime owes much to
American support for South Korea, and if this were seen to
be wavering the government might face difficulties. But
South Korean forces are tough and self-reliant, and if given
the proper equipment and political backing they have every
chance of providing an adequate defense. Their planning is
clearly taking the possibility of American withdrawal into
account, indeed may be assuming it. With U.S. troops re-

duced and then eventually withdrawn, South Korea would have to be given by the United States the same sort of support that Israel now receives—the ability to match the equipment of the opposite side and political support for survival of the state. And South Korea faces nothing like the odds from the North that Israel faces with its Arab neighbors. It is also a robust country, with enough economic strength and potential to hold its own. The policy of a graduated U.S. withdrawal should not be a hasty one but neither need it be long drawn out. Japan should be asked to play a part in its implementation, probably through economic assistance.

Just how such a policy was implemented would depend to some extent on the outcome of the search for a political solution and on the regional political context. The impediments in the way of a political solution are sadly numerous: nothing can be imposed; there is little common ground between the two Koreas; and China and the Soviet Union have to agree as well since it is they who give political and military support to the North. Japan should also be a party to any solution.

An obvious difficulty at the start is that of getting China and the Soviet Union even to talk together. If they will not, which is the present position, then the stalemate continues. If they do talk, then to get them to agree is a major hurdle. China ostensibly wants American forces to leave and so might back the idea—but might quietly prefer them to stay where they are for the moment, reckoning that the Soviet Union might profit from instability and that Japan might guard against it by a measure of rearmament. Nevertheless, for China any solution openly negotiable is likely to have to include the withdrawal of U.S. forces before too long and to be based on reunification finally. The strength of her ideology is such that it is difficult to see her subscribing formally to anything else. Yet she has demonstrated on many occasions that she is willing to live with what she might regard as interim solutions, such as the British occupation of Hong Kong or indeed the division of Korea, if these are tactically useful or tolerable. No doubt she feels that events will move her way one day and the peninsula fall within her orbit. So she might agree, if only tacitly, to an international arrangement that gave the Soviet Union, the United States and Japan no permanent advantage but which was desired by the last two at least for the political movement, however slight, that this might encourage. Of course, neither China nor the Soviet Union can actually prevent North Korea from taking military action but they can exercise a degree of discouragement, and in many ways, that is a powerful restraint.

The Soviet Union might bring a slightly different historical approach to the question, since she has behind her the experience the division of the two Germanies. She agreed to this because for her it represented some political gain and because the ideal of reunification under Communist leadership was effectively blocked by the unwillingness of the West Germans and the strength of the Western Alliance. The parallel in Korea is close, but there is the extra ingredient of China. It is possible that the Soviet Union could accept the division of the country, or federation if this were a possibility, but only if China did as well, since otherwise Soviet influence over North Korea might be forfeited. To obtain such agreement would require very tough negotiating by the United States and no doubt a great deal of time. It must be admitted that the prospects are distinctly unpromising—forbidding, indeed. Which leaves the more practical alternative of reaching some understanding that the status quo will not be disturbed militarily and that more time must elapse before a political solution can appear. This is not, perhaps, as hopeless a task or outcome as it may sound. If accompanied by practical support for South Korea, it would enable the United States to withdraw from her present exposed position within a very few years.

Japan

American security policy toward Japan has evolved from that of the occupation of a defeated enemy to the provision of military protection and a nuclear guarantee under the United States-Japan Security Treaty. This treaty, originally negotiated for ten years in 1960, was renewed in 1970 on an annual basis; either party may now give one year's notice to terminate the agreement. The American occupation of bases in Japan itself has steadily been reduced, and Okinawa reverted to Japan in 1971, though there are still major American facilities both there and on the home islands.

The Security Treaty offers mutual advantage. To the United States it provides a most important political ally in the Pacific basin, one with which economic ties are close and extensive. The provision of naval protection and a nuclear guarantee at least partly removes the incentive or need for Japan to rearm beyond present levels or to contemplate the acquisition of nuclear weapons. The bases are useful, operationally and administratively, to the U.S. naval and air forces and are needed for the support of Korea.

For Japan, a trading nation whose economic survival depends on importing raw materials and exporting finished goods by sea, the security of the sea lanes is vital, and the U.S. Navy helps to provide for it. Keeping her own armaments at a low level has benefited her economy and avoids the political strains, internal and external, that would be involved in major rearmament. The nuclear guarantee has helped to prevent the nuclear issue from being an operational one in Japanese or regional politics. As a near neighbor of two large Communist powers, China and the Soviet Union, the first unpredictable, the second difficult, Japan has generally found the link with the United States to be a comfortable basis for her foreign policy. It has enabled her to concentrate on an economic role and pursue a discreet, low-key course in foreign affairs, calculated to give offense, whenever possible, to no one. Though in practice this has usually meant following American policy fairly closely, it has also enabled Japan to shelter behind it on occasion.

The Security Treaty does, however, pose certain problems for the Japanese government. The fact that there is no obvious military threat to Japan has made it possible for the opposition parties to discount the need for the treaty and advocate its termination. The U.S. link is regularly used as a stick with which to beat the government, and the visits of nuclear-armed U.S. vessels made a target for political demonstrations. There have been local frictions over the bases, which occupy coveted urban land, and their use to support the war in Vietnam produced political difficulties for the government and led the issue of consultation and prior permission to loom large. Though Vietnam sparked this off, Korea is also a sensitive case, since the United States will feel impelled to reserve the right to take emergency action that would make prior consultation at least difficult.

It is clear, though, that the Japanese government, as distinct from most of the opposition, sees no sensible alternative to the Security Treaty and in the aftermath of Vietnam is more conscious than before of the role of the United States in Korea. There is now more understanding of the part that the bases play in this role. But there are many in Japan who would like to reduce the dependence on the United States and have the country occupy a position politically equidistant from China, the Soviet Union and the United States, or at least move further away from the American corner of that triangle. This is hardly a matter of practical policy, however. The link with the United States is by far preferable to the uncertainties of future Chinese attitudes, and any real improvement of relations with the Soviet Union depends on that country agreeing to return the northern islands and signing a peace treaty, the prospects for either of which are far from favorable. And what would equidistance mean? It would be extremely difficult for Japan to occupy a detached position politically in Asia. Her economic weight in the region is so great that such a form of neutrality is hardly possible in any meaningful terms. For her, therefore, the United States remains a firm island in a relatively uncharted sea, and the political link with her, reinforced as it is by close economic ties, is the only practicable course to follow, at least for the foreseeable future. And maintaining the Security Treaty is perferable by far to providing her own protection. Japanese rearmament on such a scale would not only involve heavy costs, but provoke marked hostility in Asia and later adversely the political environment in which she must operate.

Present American policy toward Japan seems therefore to be right for both parties. It is of great political advantage for the United States to have Japan as an ally in the Pacific, given her importance and position; to contemplate the alternative of a Japan linked with one or more of the Communist powers is to emphasize this point. But U.S. policy must be a sensitive one, not abrasive as it was in 1971, for example. The United States should not press Japan into any measure of rearmament to lighten her own military burden, and should certainly not do anything that might encourage her to acquire nuclear weapons. And sensitivity is obviously needed over the Security Treaty itself, allowing for full consultation on all issues, emergency and otherwise. The use of the bases will have to be kept to the minimum. Japan in her turn must understand that if the United States is to maintain a forward military presence in the Pacific then the bases are needed. Any pressure by Japan for American withdrawal from the bases runs the risk of encouraging a too hurried change of U.S. policy on Korea, hardly in the Japanese interest in the absence of a political settlement there.

Southeast Asia

After the complexities of policy in East Asia that in the Southeast seems simple. The mainland commitment is at an end. The U.S. maritime presence coincides with American interests, which are in the islands and the Pacific. There is no discernible external threat to these interests, but if there were, the forces available would be well able to compete with it. The ability to influence events on land is now much diminished, but the political freedom of maneuver is infinitely greater than it was a few short years ago. Is is no bad policy to be left with.

Of course it has some limitations. There is a need for forward bases, to give the ability to operate economically and speedily, and the occupation of these in the Philippines, where they are a local political issue, poses problems. It is probable that the argument will be over price rather than tenure, but it will involve giving support to a government with some unattractive aspects and one involved in an insurgency campaign.

The insurgency is symptomatic of the difficulty that the United States would have in formulating a coherent policy for Southeast Asia that went much beyond that of an offshore presence. The region has a number of governments whose policies may be somewhat illiberal, at the least, and whose future is far from assured. There is no common security structure, and indeed there hardly could be since there is no common threat; countries are more often warily eying their next door neighbors or concerned with communal or insurgency problems. Acceptable borders or forms of government have often yet to emerge. The policies of North Vietnam are not entirely predictable; they could be hostile not only to the United States but to local countries too. And Indonesia may not be a wholly certain quantity; she dwarfs her near neighbors and claims some jurisdiction over huge sea areas and important straits. It is said that to be optimistic about the future of Southeast Asia one must be optimistic about the future of Indonesia too.

The United States, faced with this mosaic of largely ex-colonial states in varying degrees of immaturity, shares with many of them economic and political interests. With countries such as Australia, New Zealand, the Philippines, Malaysia, Singapore, Indonesia and Thailand there will be a need to coordinate such interests and others too, a common ocean policy, for example. But though these economic interests have importance, in no case and not even in total are they vital. The American stake in the region is relatively low. The United States is concerned to have economic access to as many countries as possible and to promote stability, in the interests of international trade and order. Given recent history, the means to be used will be political and economic, rarely military. The United States has technological strength and economic vitality, tools that will be sorely in demand. There will be obvious difficulty on both sides in working out any relationship with countries in Indochina for some time to come. Whether Hanoi follows a pro-Soviet or pro-China line is perhaps likely to be less of a consideration than her behavior to nearby states. U.S. policy here will largely have to be reactive. The military role, beyond that of the maritime protection of island allies, is likely to be minimal; it would not be welcomed at home nor is it likely to be much asked for abroad, other than in terms of the supply of arms. Insurgency and local violence may present a borderline case; there may be calls for help which go beyond a request for hardware and which may carry political implications with them. On the whole the rule here is the simple one: local governments must provide their own manpower. It is rarely profitable for an outsider to intervene in a local dispute; if the government cannot maintain its own position, given material aid, then the social system is unlikely to be the right one.

Conclusions

The United States has come through an agonizing period in Southeast Asia. The security structure there largely collapsed around her, leaving one away from the mainland to take its place. In East Asia, on the other hand, the structure was not tested and is still intact. Commitments have been reaffirmed and there is no immediate pressure on them, but they have not gone unquestioned.

No new Asian policy has yet been decided upon, and it is right that this should be so. The events have been a blow to the confidence of the United States and her allies and to American prestige; time is needed for the disasters of Vietnam to recede.

But if the United States faces difficulties in working out a satisfactory posture, China and the Soviet Union face rather more. China has the powerful and difficult Soviet Union on the one hand and an uncertain Vietnam on the other. Her Asian economic environment is dominated by Japan; her own economy is as yet weak. The Soviet Union faces Europe in the west and China in the east, both major military adversaries. Her allies in Asia are marginal: an ambiguous North Korea and a North Vietnam likely only to pursue its own interest. She has been unable or unwilling to offer any attraction to Japan to counter the greater pull that China exerts, or loosen the firm ties with the United States.

So the United States does start with certain advantages and few liabilities. She has two primary concerns: to prevent outside superpower hegemony in the Pacific basin, and to keep Japan in her camp. Neither should pose difficulties, the first because of her great military, economic and technological strength and her island base structure, the second because the advantages are mutual and Japan has no preferable alternative. The United States must, around this centerpiece, erect or help to erect a security structure, notably in East Asia, to maintain international order. She will need to work with allies or like-minded states with interests in the region, as for example, Japan, Australia, New Zealand and the United Kingdom. She must also have a working relationship with the Soviet Union, necessary to both of them in any event, and cultivate relations with China that are as harmonious as possible. Potential points of friction, such as Taiwan, or of danger, such as Korea, need special attention.

It is the contention of this essay that if adjustments are made to the existing policy on Taiwan and Korea the result will be a political and military posture which will leave the United States well balanced in Asia but strong. There are limits to it; there is not a great deal that can be done to affect the mainland, other than by political or economic mechanisms, or by arms aid on commercial terms. In return there is freedom from entanglements and room to maneuver. The United States is what she should in her own interest be and what she is uniquely fitted to be, a Pacific power. The Nixon Doctrine was concerned to effect an American withdrawal from overcommitment in Asia. Policy should now be designed to stabilize the presence and make it durable.

8

America in the World Economy

LEONARD SILK

In retrospect—and by comparison with the present situation—the problem of formulating a foreign economic policy for the United States during the earlier part of the postwar period seems simple. The United States emerged from World War II as the strongest economy in the world and the natural leader of the non-Communist nations; its fundamental mission was to lead its wartime allies and its former enemies, Germany and Japan, toward reconstruction and economic growth. This mission was considered by American internationalists crucial to the future expansion of the United States and world economies and to the defense of the weakened nations of Europe and Asia against the feared expansion of Communist power. Generous foreign aid by the United States would be linked to liberal policies for trade and investment, aimed at integrating the economy of the so-called "free world." The Communist world was essentially cordoned off, and limited economic war was waged against it. In a nutshell, such was the foreign economic policy of the United States in a bipolar world, a mixture of American self-interest, generosity toward friends and hostility toward foes.

The (non-Communist) world monetary system that emerged from World War II was also based on the same blend of principles. The United States, with its huge and undamaged economy needful of work to replace the war production that had lifted it out of the Great Depression, its hard and convertible dollar and its huge supply of gold reserves, constituting almost three-fourths those of the non-Communist world, was more than willing to play banker and manager of the international monetary system.

This American-led system worked like a dream in reconstructing the world economy and setting all the developed nations on a path toward economic growth and prosperity that was to transform them socially and industrially. But such a world monetary system could not last; its expansion depended on the strength of the U.S. dollar and continuous dollar deficits, which, with fixed exchange rates, were the source of growing monetary reserves, essential to expanding world trade. And therein lay a dialectical contradiction you cannot find in Marx: a strong dollar and chronic U.S. payments deficits could not indefinitely co-exist. Either the dollar would weaken and the system would fail, or the American deficits would end, the supply of monetary reserves would dry up and economic expansion of the system would cease.

At first this coming doom of the system was only dimly perceived. In the late 1950s, when the United States decided that the reconstruction period was over and the time had come to close the gap in its balance of payments, the task proved difficult—partly because other nations (though complaining of the American deficits) resisted revaluations of their currencies, burden sharing or trade adjustments that would have made it possible, and partly because the United States was loathe to give up its hegemonic role. Both the Korean and Vietnam wars signified American determination to carry the "free world's burdens." America's persistent payments deficits were not due solely to its military actions and economic aid programs; of growing importance, as the deficits went on year after year, was the overvaluation of the U.S. dollar in relation to gold and other currencies. This hurt American exports and made imports, as well as travel and foreign investment, cheaper for Americans. So the migration of American business overseas went on apace, with the corporations using abundant and overvalued dollars to buy up foreign assets, start branches and subsidiaries abroad, hire foreign labor and use other foreign resources to increase their worldwide profits. The vast pool of dollars that accumulated in Europe—the so-called Eurodollar market—helped provide the capital that nourished the growth and spread of multinational corporations, most of which were American.

Foreigners, in the midst of the dollar prosperity, were schizoid about the trend. Many, especially those in close partnership with the Americans, welcomed the growth that U.S. capital, technology and managerial skills helped bring. But there was increasing concern about the inflation that the dollar inflow was also helping to breed, and growing opposition to the "American challenge" of economic and political dominance—and particularly about the recklessness of American military policy. Vietnam strained the political bonds between the United States and its European allies. It also sealed the doom of the postwar world monetary system that had been built on a strong dollar and fixed exchange rates between the dollar, gold and other currencies. For Vietnam accelerated the outflow of dollars from the United States and, even more damaging, increased domestic inflation. President Johnson unleashed inflation at home by his long delay in going to Congress to ask for higher taxes to pay for the Vietnam War and his unwillingness to cut Great Society programs to make room for the war in the Federal budget.

President Nixon inherited the inflation and eventually made it worse. After a year of trying to stop it by tight money alone, Nixon found rising unemployment politically intolerable and switched to a highly expansive fiscal and monetary policy aimed at restoring full employment, imposed a freeze on wages and prices and ended the convertibility of the dollar into gold—the famous "New Economic Policy" launched on August 15, 1971. If the postwar U.S. economic policy can be said to have ended on a given date, that was the date.

The full change in the international monetary system, however, was still to come. Overvalued dollars continued to gush out of the United States as expectations of what once would have been unthinkable—a dollar devaluation—grew. The first devaluation, aimed at preserving the fixed-exchange-rate system, came on December 18, 1971, but it did not end the massive dollar outflow. In early 1973 there was a second dollar devaluation, and a continued hemorrhaging of dollars; the Germans were no longer willing to take in the flood, for fear of the inflation it was causing. The fixed rate Bretton Woods system was dead, and the whole world monetary system was afloat. But inflation was anything but dead. The world was awash with liquidity, stemming chiefly from the massive dollar outflow that ended Bretton Woods, and all nations were in a simultaneous boom; the perception of rising prices was transmogrified—as inevitably happens when an inflation lasts long enough—into a public perception that paper money was losing its value and was not worth holding. Speculators rushed from currencies into gold and into commodities; by October 1973, world commodity prices had more than doubled from the start of the year.

And then, with the outbreak of the Yom Kippur War in the Middle East, the Arabs launched their oil weapon against the West. World commodity inflation had given the oil producers both the motivation and the opportunity to increase their prices fourfold above the pre-October War level, acting through their cartel, the Organization of Petroleum Exporting Countries (OPEC). The huge transfer of income to oil producers (both foreign nations and the oil companies) created an unprecedented shock for the world economy, including both the developed industrial countries and the oil-poor developing ones. The enormous increase in oil prices and payments put powerful pressure, both direct and indi-rect, upon the industrial countries to increase their export prices in order to cover their current-account deficits. For them the backflow of oil dollars did help to balance their accounts. The greatest ultimate danger of the massive shift of income and wealth to the oil-producing states was to the poor developing countries. For their part those poor states—the so-called "Fourth World"—hoped to follow the example of OPEC and build commodity-exporting cartels of their own to force more income from the rich nations of the North; a new North-South confrontation emerged to take the place of, or complicate, the East-West confrontation that had marked the earlier postwar period.

A dramatically new world situation, and one of baffling complexity, confronts U.S. foreign economic policy in the middle 1970s. The twin threats of inflation and depression hang over the United States and the world economy. The discordant state of the world economy stems not from a de-ficiency of demand (such as racked the world economy in the 1930s) but from the disruption and cartelization of supply. Most disruptive have been shortages of oil and soaring energy prices and shortages of food and soaring food prices. There are also rumors and speculations of many other raw material shortages to come—bauxite, copper, lead, zinc, manganese, magnesium, even iron ore. Yet claims that such commodities can be readily cartelized, like oil, seem exaggerated, as does the more general and even more alarmist warning that we are fast approaching the "limits to growth." The immediate crisis does not resemble the Doomsday that would result from an actual exhaustion of the world's resources. Rather, the scar-cities that have struck the industrial world and many of the developing countries are chiefly the result of the fierce pur-suit of self-interest by governments and businesses, and if these problems are exacerbated in the future, it will be primarily because the international political and economic system has failed to cope with such threats. The upsurge of nationalism and resentment against the rich capitalist powers is a root cause of the new crisis of scarcity; colonialism is suffering its death throes in Asia, Africa and the Middle East. The oil-producing countries have taken the lead not only in acquiring wealth but in avenging old grievances, and the other developing countries are seeking to join with them in demands for a "New Economic Order," a concept that its critics have dubbed "World Populism."

In this new era that is emerging, one of the most difficult problems facing foreign economic policy is conceptual: how can the United States construct a policy that will meet so many different problems of conflict and cooperation with other advanced capitalist countries, with the Soviet Union, China and other Communist countries, with the rich oil-producing states and with the still poor developing countries?

Should the United States hold to its long effort, which began in 1934 with the Reciprocal Trade Act, to build an open international system of trade and investment, and at the same time meet the demands of the poor nations for preferential treatment and greater market stability? Would the interests of the poor really be better served by a more tightly managed system? The classic case for free trade, after all, rested not on its advantages to the rich nations (or multinational business organizations) but on its support for the efficient use of resources on a global scale and hence for national economic development and world economic integration. What sort of monetary system is appropriate to a world in which the U.S. economy is no longer dominant but is still important enough so that no new system can be built without its concurrence and active leadership?

Beneath all the difficult technical questions lies a fundamental issue: how can the United States, in these new circumstances, combine the pursuit of its own political and

economic interests (and those of its multinational corporations) with the traditional American commitment to principles of equality and justice, principles that were never intended
to be for home consumption only?

The relative simplicity of the cold war era is behind us. We
are hoping to build a "new structure of peace"; but if such an
era of peace is to come and to endure, it is unlikely to result
from a willingness of sovereign nations to subordinate their
interests to those of others. Rather, it will depend on the de-
ployment of power in some form to assure world stability.

The old bipolar, cold war era, and its concept of power,
foundered on the inability of the United States, a superpower, to prevail over North Vietnam, a seemingly insignificant
military and economic power. The traditional concept of
national power had two basic elements: the resources a nation could pour into military goods and manpower, as mea-
sured by its total defense expenditures, and the economic
capability of a nation to produce goods and services, as mea-
sured by its gross national product. In the prenuclear age, a
nation's economic capability was considered an even better
measure of its power than its current defense outlays or
forces—since in a wartime situation it could shift resources
from civilian to military use and thereby mount and sustain a
bigger military effort than its rivals. This was the secret of the
successful American military effort in World War II; indeed,
this formula for power was first demonstrated by the way the
North crushed the South in the American Civil War.

The nuclear age seemingly downgraded the significance of
a nation's underlying economic capabilities (at least in a contest between superpowers); what would count in such wars
that were expected to last only a few days, or perhaps min-
utes, were forces in being—nuclear weapons immune from
attack and ready for instantaneous response to any threat.
But in other "conventional" conflicts between nations, great

and small, the old concept of power, based on economic capabilities and the resources diverted to military uses, remained valid.

Vietnam altered that concept of national power by its incredible length and by America's failure to prevail. It demonstrated the constraints upon the use by a superpower of its full military and economic capabilities. Obviously those constraints were not physical but political and social, both at home and abroad. The constraints are linked to four interacting trends in the world: (1) the cold war coalitions have been greatly weakened, with the members of alliances doubtful of the fidelity of their allies; (2) nonsecurity issues—primarily economic—have risen to the top of the diplomatic agenda; (3) friendships and adversary relations have grown more complex and ambiguous; and (4) there has been an increase in the power of "transnational" institutions—not only the multinational corporations but also various types of labor, environmental, scientific, technological, religious and cultural communities, which are creating their own global networks and which may either support or conflict with national policies.

In this world of multiple coalitions and conflicts, the essence of power itself is changing from the direct use or threat of military force to gain national ends to various other kinds of promises—especially offers of economic exchange, investment or technical cooperation, or access.[1] To be sure, the old threat system remains and is of decisive importance, if issues over aggression or national survival develop. But it is the diminished fear of such threats that is forcing us to rethink the concept of national power and economic policy in the post-cold war, post-Vietnam, multipolar era. It would seem to imply that economic strength, balance and flexibility in dealing with different partners and coalitions must become the dominant elements in the conduct of U.S. foreign policy.

1. See Seyom Brown, "The Changing Essence of Power," *Foreign Affairs,* 51 (January 1973), 286–299.

At the end of World War II, it was recognized that, for the United States to fulfill its chosen mission of world reconstruction, full employment and economic expansion had to be maintained at home—to keep up the necessary political climate for a world role, to provide the resources needed by others and to enable the United States to maintain a growing and open market for the exports of others. At the end of the war memories of the Great Depression were still vivid, and there were anxieties lest the U.S. economy, once the stimulus of war production was removed, would lapse back into chronic unemployment. The Employment Act of 1946—and the vigorous policies for stabilization and expansion that American administrations subsequently pursued—eliminated that fear. U.S. economic growth provided a powerful impetus to world expansion in the decades that followed the war.

The situation of the middle 1970s requires a comparable effort on the part of this country to keep its economy operating at a high level of employment. At the same time, it must do a better job of curbing the inflation that has exacerbated the problems of others. International inflation originates basically from domestic sources, and the United States has been as great a culprit as any nation in breeding world inflation.

No monetary formula or technical solution will provide the United States or any other government with the political courage to curb the pressures and demands that propel domestic inflation. Government must, in the broad public interest, curb those special-interest pressures that distort and waste resources, particularly in multibillion-dollar military programs that not only create inflation but increase the danger of arms races and war itself. The military-industrial-congressional complex is only the most celebrated example of the special interests which capture a huge share of national resources. Other interest groups that have won special benefits and protection from government—whether in the form of subsidies, huge appropriations, tax breaks, tariffs, import quotas or other rules limiting foreign or domestic competition—include the oil industry, the maritime industry, civil aviation, the highway-building industry and its supporters, dairy producers, wheat farmers, cattlemen, steel producers and textile producers. Labor unions fight for a growing share of the national pie partly by backing the demands for special favors and protection of the industries that employ them and partly by waging side contests with managements for a bigger slice of the take. A government, sympathetic to business, seeks to curb the power of labor by running the economy at a low level of employment—a solution acceptable to business ideologically, since it avoids the need for price as well as wage controls, but one that is costly and even dangerous to business itself, if it does not achieve its desired results of economic stability in a reasonable period of time.

A program against inflation cannot succeed unless it removes the corrupting influence on government of the special interests and, on the other side of the coin, curbs the efforts of government officials to invite bribes in exchange for favors as a means of consolidating political power in a corporate state. This problem is particularly difficult to handle in the international sphere, where it adds an additional threat to the reputation and possibly to the very life of multinational corporations.

Laissez-faire capitalism, in which private enterprise was supposed to countervail the power of the State, may be dead, but the mixed economy—that mixture of government and private interests that has replaced it—needs better ways of harmonizing competing group pressures in a noninflationary way and of guiding the economy to serve broad social needs, such as protection of the environment, development of crucially needed energy, scientific research and provision of education, medical care and other vital services. In addition, the mixed economy needs an incomes policy, a means of regulating the growing income claims of contending groups, together with their access to money and credit through the banking system.

Similarly, this nation and other democratic states need more effective ways of planning their long-run social and economic development. Increasing the supply of resources, human and material, is essential to preventing inflation in a way that will not require periodic or chronic spells of recession, depression and high unemployment. In an increasingly integrated international economy—especially among the major nations of North America, Western Europe and Japan —such programs need to be international in scope. A single nation that pressed for expansion alone might force its interest rates too low, induce an outflow of funds and a widening gap in its balance of payments, cause its currency to depreciate and thereby worsen its domestic inflation. But a common policy, implemented on a continuous basis, would provide greater assurance that no single country would be endangered and that all could advance together.

To cope with the international monetary problems of a multipolar world, in which the dollar is no longer the fixed center of the system, the world needs to stay with the sort of flexible monetary system that has succeeded the Bretton Woods system. Floating exchange rates have proved to be an effective shock absorber for the double blows of rapid inflation (at widely different rates among different countries) and serious slumps in production and employment; those shock absorbers have made it possible for the world to avoid a disaster as serious as that of the 1930s.

In the late 1920s and early 1930s, the effort to defend fixed exchange rates led to the wild speculation, massive capital flows, the chain of financial disasters, the blocking of trade and investment, and finally the collapse of the world economy into the Great Depression. This time, despite rapid inflation, a huge transfer of resources to the members of the oil-exporting cartel and a serious slump throughout the Western world, there has been no breakdown in the world monetary system or in foreign trade and investment.

Floating exchange rates, however, are no panacea. In one respect they may make the world economy more inflation-prone—for with floating rates, governments may find it harder to muster political support for deflationary policies with the arguments that these are vital to defend the currency's par value, that they prevent a run on money or protect the national honor. Such appeals have rarely worked when a fixed currency was seriously overvalued and when heavy unemployment and depression were essential to deflate domestic prices enough to validate the national currency's par value.

In any event, the fixed-rate system was not really fixed. Those nations that chose to inflate and then devalue their currencies could and did so. Worst of all, the fixed-rate system, as it evolved after World War II, was itself a powerful engine of worldwide inflation. The dollar was the key to the system, and the United States could not or would not devalue. Instead, this country, with its overvalued dollar and its chronic payments deficits which, as we have seen, were the price of political and economic hegemony, fed massive amounts of money to the world economy until the fixed-rate system broke down. That massive outflow of dollars was a basic cause of the communication of world inflation. After the initial period of adjustment to floating rates—and especially because of the inflationary effect of dollar outflows—rates of inflation in the Western world stopped rising and have since been coming down. To be sure, there was so dramatic an exception to this trend as the United Kingdom—but its inflation was clearly internal in causation, not external. Whether individual nations choose to check their domestic inflations or not, national governments are at least in a better position under floating rates to control their money supply than they were under the old fixed-rate system, with the massive capital flows it propagated from nation to nation— and especially from the United States to European creditor nations.

Nevertheless, the United States has been in conflict with many countries—led by France—over the issue of fixed rates versus floating rates as the basis of the international system. France, in addition to wanting fixed exchange rates, originally favored gold as the international monetary standard; elimination of the international monetary role of national currencies—especially the dollar—except in particular regions (such as Francophone Africa with metropolitan France, parts of the sterling area with Britain, parts of Latin America with the United States); controls on capital movements, to prevent their disruptive effect on fixed rates; the organization of world commodity markets to reduce price fluctuations and establish "fair" prices for primary products; and trade preferences as instruments of foreign policy and cultural policy.

The Americans have come to see floating exchange rates as a desirable component of a policy aimed at furthering liberal world trade and investment. Although recognizing that the floating dollar cannot play the unique and dominant role that it commanded under Bretton Woods, the Americans believe that the dollar can and should continue to play the role of a key currency, while gold gradually diminishes in importance. In my view, the American position (as expressed most clearly in the U.S. Treasury but sometimes opposed or at least blurred in the State Department, for reasons of diplomacy and international accommodation) is better suited than the French to further the objective of world economic integration and development. At the Kingston meetings of the International Monetary Fund, the world agreed to a modified floating rate system.

The ideal of a free and open global economic system, of course, is likely to remain far distant from what is achievable in the decades ahead, but it still seems to constitute the right objective for a United States foreign economic policy, aiming at efficient use of the world's resources and closer economic and political relations among all nations and regions, and hence toward peaceful world development.

Doubtless, this general objective will have to be qualified and adapted to deal with immediate and transitional problems, some of which may seem so massive and urgent as to outweigh the longer range objective of a liberal and open world economy.

The "energy crisis"—and the complex confrontation between OPEC and the oil-consuming countries, both developed and developing—is one such problem. Following their success in quadrupling oil prices and in effecting a transfer of income and wealth likely to amount to at least two hundred billion dollars (in constant 1974 dollars) by the end of the current decade, OPEC members have moved to consolidate their gains by calling, pacifically, for "a new economic order founded on justice and fraternity." While it is difficult to know precisely what this concept means to them, it seems clear that what they are trying to do is nail down the gains they have made since the Yom Kippur War in the Middle East in October 1973; to stave off retaliation by the West, whether this should involve countermoves on prices, trade barriers, withholding of access to food, technology or capital, or even military action; to secure the allegiance of the poor, developing countries to their cause; and to avoid a world depression that would wreck the market for their oil and tear their cartel apart.

Some international bodies—such as the World Bank—appear bent on facilitating that process of accommodation between oil producers and consumers, and on refuting pessimistic views about the impact of higher oil prices on the growth potential of both the developed countries and the oil-poor developing countries. Without denying that such damaging impacts exist—which would be rather difficult to do, in light of the widespread slump and unemployment among the advanced industrial countries (in good measure a consequence of the impact on real incomes of the soaring oil bills) and the extreme hardship imposed on many developing countries (some would attribute India's economic crisis and the crisis of its democratic political system as primarily due to the soaring cost of fuel)—officials at the World Bank and elsewhere insist that such problems caused by the oil cartel can be overcome by "international economic cooperation." Cooperation is one of those good things of life that it is almost impossible to be against, but is it not even more important to prevent OPEC from setting prices unilaterally, both as a means of restoring world economic equilibrium and "to encourage the others"—that is, other commodity-producing countries—not to follow the example of OPEC and help convert the world into one of warring blocs and monopolies? Hence I favor a policy for the United States and its Western European and Japanese allies that would put pressure on the oil cartel by conservation and reduced energy consumption and by expanding domestic production of energy. For both the intermediate period and the long run, the United States should put greatest possible effort into research and development to open up new energy sources and technology, especially from the sun and from nuclear fusion, which the world needs to replace rapidly disappearing fossil fuels.

A host of other global economic problems—including our relations with the Communist world; improving our relations with the poor nations and providing for their needs for our food, capital, knowledge, and help in many forms; the role of the multinational corporations and the need to develop agreements among national governments for the multinationals' rights and obligations—will continue to challenge our efforts to help build a more closely integrated world economic system. General statements of policy aims inevitably seem pretentious and vacuous, but I would conclude by expressing my hope that the United States will continue to pursue a foreign economic policy consistent with the high moral aims on which this country was founded. We must aim at equity and justice as well as efficiency. The recent failures of U.S. policy—not only in Vietnam but in the monetary area— should help to restore our sanity and balance and sense of interdependence with other nations. The world is indeed shrinking (and not in just space-time relations but its natural resource base is shrinking) and we shall be feeling, even more than now, the political, economic and environmental impacts of continued growth, the spread of industrialization, the threats of pollution and radioactive wastes, the need to protect and develop our oceans and land and other critical resources. In the emerging, cramped and conflictual world environment, a narrow nationalism is unthinkable. But, as we cannot retreat into isolationism, we cannot pretend to a spirit of self-abnegation that does not meet the threats to our interests abroad nor the political and economic pressures upon government policy at home. We can do most to further world development and stability by maintaining a healthy and prosperous economy at home and by striving to be as flexible, inventive and innovative as we have been in the past —that is the true American economic tradition and contribution to the world's economic and social advancement. We can best play that role in an open and liberal global environment.

9

The Multinational Corporation and American Foreign Policy[1]

ROBERT GILPIN

Over the past several years much attention has been given by scholars, public officials and the media to the looming importance of so-called "multinational corporations" (MNC). These giant corporate entitites with subsidiaries throughout the world have been variously described, praised and condemned. For some they are the salvation of a world which has been plagued for centuries by petty nationalistic conflicts and poverty.[2] Only these truly international (or as some would say, transnational) organizations can transcend the anachronistic nation state and diffuse throughout the globe the capital, technology and managerial skills required for economic development. For others, however, these powerful private corporations are mini-empires producing wealth for the few and poverty for the many.[3]

In sheer assets the multinational corporations are very powerful institutions indeed, many having resources far greater than a large majority of the member states of the United

1. Many of the themes and ideas contained in this article are further elaborated in the author's *U.S. Power and the Multinational Corporation: The Political Economy of Foreign Direct Investment* (New York: Basic Books, 1975).

2. For a highly favorable view see Raymond Vernon, *Sovereignty at Bay* (New York: Basic Books, 1971).

3. See Richard Barnet and Ronald Müller, *Global Reach: The Power of the Multinational Corporations* (New York: Simon and Schuster, 1974).

Nations. The scope of their operations and the extent of the territory over which they range are far greater geographically than any empire that has ever existed. They have integrated the world economy to a far greater degree than ever in the past. They have taken global economic interdependence beyond the realms of trade and money into the area of industrial production, thus impinging profoundly on individual national economies.

I have asserted the importance of multinational corporations before defining what a multinational corporation is. In nontechnical terms it is any corporation in which ownership, management, production and sales activities extend over several jurisdictions. It comprises a head company with a cluster of subsidiaries throughout the world economy. The goal of the corporation is to have managerial control of foreign production units. The two most prominent types of investments are manufacturing investments in developed economies and investment in extractive industries in the underdeveloped world, especially petroleum. These corporations have a common pool of managerial talent, and of financial and technical resources. Most importantly, the whole operation is run in terms of a coordinated global strategy. The multinational seeks to perpetuate its dominant position with respect to technology and access to capital through vertical integration and centralization of decision making. These investments create economic relations of a highly significant and lasting character, and for this reason investment of this kind is highly controversial.

Although the corporations of other industrial powers are among the oldest multinationals (Royal Dutch Shell, Unilever, Nestlé), the multinational corporation today is most frequently American. Eleven of the fifteen largest multinational are American. While European and Japanese corporations are increasingly going multinational, that is, establishing foreign production facilities through foreign direct investment, these nations still lag far behind the United States. In general, these other nations prefer trade and portfolio investment to foreign direct investment. Therefore, the term "multinational corporation" is still largely a euphemism for the overseas expansion of America's giant oligopolistic corporations.

From an initial accumulated investment of only $7 billion in 1946, by 1972 the book value of American direct investment abroad totaled nearly $100 billion with an annual output of approximately $200 billion. Additionally, whereas prior to World War II, Latin America accounted for most of this investment, after the war, Canada, Western Europe and other industrial areas absorbed the great bulk of this investment (see Chart 1). Investment in the production of raw materials and in traditional manufacturing industries has remained strong. However, a large fraction of postwar investment has gone into advanced manufacturing industries (40 percent) where it is heavily concentrated in the so-called commanding heights of the modern industrial economy (automobile, chemicals and electronics). The other large segment of U.S. foreign direct investment is in petroleum (30 percent). This $20 billion investment accounts for about 40 percent of American direct investment in the lesser developed countries (see Table 1).

By the early 1970s, the United States had become more of a foreign investor than an exporter or domestically manufactured goods. International production by MNCs had surpassed trade as the main component of international economic exchange. Foreign production by the affiliates of American corporations was nearly four times American exports abroad. Moreover, a substantial proportion of American exports of manufactured goods were really transfers from an American branch of an MNC to an overseas branch. In 1969, the American multinationals alone produced approximately $140 billion worth of goods, more than any national economy except those of the United States and the Soviet Union, and in 1971

Chart 1. Book value of U.S. foreign direct investment abroad, at yearend 1960, 1965 and 1972 (by area, in billions of dollars and percent of total)

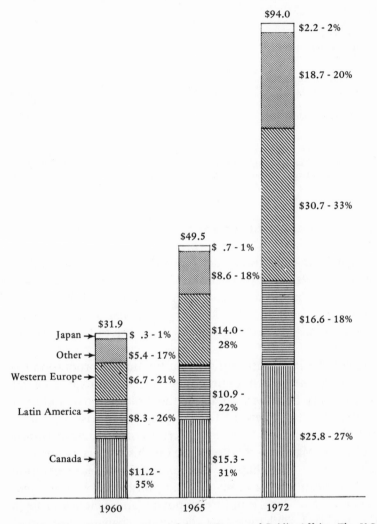

Source: From U.S. Department of State, Bureau of Public Affairs, *The U.S. Role in International Investment,* February 1, 1974, p. 7, with data from U.S. Department of Commerce, Bureau of Economic Analysis, *Survey of Current Business,* 52 (November 1972), 21–34, and 53 (September 1973), 21–34.

Table 1. Sectoral distribution of U.S. foreign direct investment in developed and developing countries, yearend 1972

Developed countries	
Manufacturing	51.2%
Petroleum	22.1
Mining and smelting	6.9
Other	19.8
Developing countries	
Manufacturing	26.4%
Petroleum	39.2
Mining and smelting	10.8
Other	23.6

Source: From U.S. Department of State, Bureau of Public Affairs, *The U.S. Role in International Investment,* February 1, 1974, p. 6, with data from U.S. Department of Commerce, Bureau of Economic Analysis, *Survey of Current Business,* 53 (September 1973), 26–27.

the MNCs accounted for 15 percent of total world output. Many of America's largest corporations have placed more than half of their total assets abroad and more than half of their earnings come from abroad. These earnings in turn have become an important factor in America's overall balance of payments position. The loss of these assets and earnings would be a severe, though not a fatal, loss to the American economy.

Given the importance of the multinational corporation for American foreign economic policy, one would expect a great deal to have been written about the multinationals and their relationship to American foreign policy. Surprisingly this is not the case. Except for ardent critics of the multinationals and a few Marxists, the literature on this subject is not very extensive. In this chapter, therefore, the overseas expansion of American corporations will be considered in the larger perspective of American foreign policy (and America's role in the world). I shall argue that the rapidly changing position of the United States in the world economy is bringing about a reassessment of the role of the multinational corporation in the American economy and in the world economy.

Explanations of Corporate Expansionism

What explains the sudden emergence of the multinational corporation, that is, the overseas expansion of American corporations? Three explanations are to be found in the literature. One line of argument explains the multinational in terms of the contemporary revolution in technology and communications. According to this argument, the compression of time and space by modern technology has made this type of global enterprise feasible. The second line of argument explains the rise of the multinational in terms of economic factors. Here, several economic theories compete as valid explanations: capital market theory,[4] oligopoly theory,[5] product cycle theory,[6] organic growth theory[7] and others. A third explanation, less common than the others, is that American corporations have been able to expand abroad because of favorable government policy, especially tax policy.[8] These tax incentives include tax deferral (that is, the corporation does not have to pay taxes on foreign earnings until those earnings are repatriated to the United States), depletion allowances for oil multinationals and a credit on American taxes for those paid to foreign governments. In short, U.S. tax policy is said to have created an incentive for American corporations to invest abroad rather than in the American economy.

All these positions have varying degrees of validity. However, in this article, I shall emphasize a fourth explanation for the rise and success of American multinational corporations,

4. Robert Aliber, *The International Money Game* (New York: Basic Books, 1973), pp. 187–188.

5. Stephen Hymer, "The International Operations of National Firms: A Study of Direct Foreign Investment" (mimeographed 1960); and Charles Kindleberger, *American Business Abroad: Six Lectures on Direct Investment* (New Haven: Yale University Press, 1969).

6. Vernon, *Sovereignty at Bay.*

7. Judd Polk et al., *U.S. Production Abroad and the Balance of Payments* (New York: National Industrial Conference Board, 1966).

8. Peggy Musgrave, *United States Taxation of Foreign Investment Income* (Cambridge: The Law School of Harvard University, 1969).

one which is seldom mentioned. This explanation centers on the emergence of the United States at the end of World War II as the world's dominant economic and military power. From this perspective, the technological revolution in transportation, economic factors and favorable government policy constitute the *sufficient* condition for the foreign expansion of American corporations. But the international economic and political order created by the United States after World War II is the *necessary* condition. This international economic order over the past several decades has rested on a *Pax Americana* much as the international economy of the nineteenth century rested on the *Pax Britannica.* If free trade was the economic policy of the *Pax Britannica,* then free investment has been the economic policy of the *Pax Americana.*

The foundation of this *Pax Americana* has been, in brief, U.S. monopoly of nuclear weapons at the end of World War II, the role of the dollar as the basis of the international monetary system, the superior industrial position of the United States and U.S. control of the non-Communist world's supply of petroleum. Since the end of World War II, these critical elements of economic and military power have been largely in American hands, though the U.S. role in each area is rapidly diminishing—a fact of cardinal importance, as will be shown below.

Upon this economic and military foundation, the United States created the political superstructure of the *Pax Americana.* [9] The political aspects of the *Pax Americana* have consisted of our security ties with Western Europe through the instrumentality of the North Atlantic Treaty Organization (NATO) and with Japan through the Japan-United States Security Treaty. These alliances were complemented by the

9. For a more detailed analysis see Robert Gilpin, "The Politics of Transnational Economic Relations" in Robert Keohane and Joseph Nye, eds., *Transnational Relations and World Politics* (Cambridge: Harvard University Press, 1972), pp. 48–69.

expansion of American political influence and/or military presence throughout Asia, the Middle East, Latin America and elsewhere.

The parallel expansion abroad of American political influence and of American multinational corporations raises the issue which is the concern of this essay. What *is* the relationship between these two global expansions? Most writings on this highly controversial question fall into two broad categories. The first is what I call the orthodox liberal view concerning the relationship of economics and politics. The second is the radical or Marxist position. After an analysis of both positions, I shall discuss my own view of the subject and its implications for the future of the multinational corporation.

The orthodox liberal view is the one held by most American economists, businessmen and government officials. The best statement of this view is made by Raymond Vernon in *Sovereignty at Bay*. This position argues that there is *no* relationship between the overseas expansion of American corporations and the overseas expansion of American power, that the rise of the multinational corporation can be explained essentially by the technological and economic factors mentioned earlier, that economics and politics are completely separate. Or, to use Vernon's phrase, the relationship between the American government and American multinational corporations is an "arm's length" one.

This position, I believe, runs counter to the available evidence. As has already been noted, there are a large number of American taxation and other policies, such as the creation of the Overseas Private Investment Corporation, whose purpose is to facilitate the foreign expansion of American corporations. Many other examples could be mentioned. Thus, the U.S. condition for the acceptance of the Rome Treaty creating the European Common Market was that the Europeans agree to treat American subsidiaries in Europe on the same basis as European corporations, that is, giving them the status of domestic corporations in Western Europe. And of course in Latin America and other less developed countries, the U.S. government has retaliated against foreign governments for actions against American corporations.

The second prevalent position on the relationship of American foreign policy and American multinational corporations is the radical/Marxist view. Although they are not Marxists, Richard Barnet and Ronald Müller in *Global Reach* best exemplify this position. This view argues that the American government and foreign policy have become the captive of the large multinational corporation and that the expansion of American power is due to the desire of American corporate leadership to expand throughout the world and into foreign economies. Marxists go further and argue that the foreign expansion of American corporations is due to the contradictions within the American economy, that the American corporation must expand or die, that capitalism will collapse unless new markets are obtained. According to this classical Leninist perspective, U.S. policy in Europe, Latin America and especially Vietnam can be explained by a corporate necessity to expand.[10] However, like the liberal perspective, this Marxist or radical critique represents a vast oversimplification of the relationship of American foreign policy and the American multinational corporation.

In specific cases, certainly in Latin America and especially in Chile, one can show corporate influence on U.S. policy; however, the Marxist or radical argument does not explain certain very important phenomena. Perhaps the best refutation of the Marxist argument is American policy toward Japan. American corporations have very much coveted the Japanese market. This market of 100 million people has been a prime target of American corporations. The Japanese gov-

---

10. Harry Magdoff presents a Marxist perspective in *The Age of Imperialism* (New York: Monthly Review Press, 1969).

ernment, however, has resisted the expansion of American corporations into the Japanese economy. Not only has the U.S. government failed to support American corporations in their bid for greater access to the Japanese economy, but it has even helped the Japanese resist American corporate expansion into Japan. In this case the larger U.S. security interests with respect to Japan and the Far East prevailed over the interests of American corporations.

The relationship between American foreign policy and American multinationals is far more complex than either the liberals or the Marxists make it out to be. My own view is that in effect a complementarity exists between the national interests of the United States as they have been perceived by American political leadership and the interests of the American corporations as they have been perceived by corporate leadership; there is a complementarity between the national political leadership and American corporate leadership with respect to the desirability of American corporate expansion.[11] Both believe that the foreign expansion of American corporations serves important national interests of the United States. American political leadership did not plan this; rather, American leaders came to realize it slowly as the consequences of corporate expansionism began to be appreciated.

In three principal areas the expansion of American corporations abroad has been judged to be in the national interest. The first is raw materials. American multinational corporations by and large have controlled the non-Communist world's access to raw materials, especially petroleum. American corporations have guaranteed security of access to raw materials and preference for American customers in times of shortages. They have also kept prices low during critical periods, such as the Korean and Vietnam Wars. American corporations have also been utilized by the United States government

11. For an elaboration of this view, see Gilpin, *U.S. Power and the Multinational Corporation*, ch. 6.

as a political weapon. The best example of this was the 1956 Suez crisis. The American threat to cut off petroleum from the British and the French forced them to withdraw from their invasion. This is something, incidentally, that the French have not forgotten; it is one factor that helps explain the French energy policy of the middle 1970s.

The second area in which American national interest has been judged to be served by the foreign expansion of American corporations is manufacturing. American official opinion has been that the appropriate way for the United States to maintain its relative position in the world market is through the multinational corporation.[12] The expansion abroad of multinational corporations has been regarded as a means to maintain America's dominant world economic position. This has been considered to be true because at the same time the corporations gain access to foreign economies, the real locus of corporate power—finance, research and development and managerial control—remains in the American economy. Also, the multinational corporations has been seen as an instrument of global economic development which would help contain communism and would spread the gospel of free enterprise to developing economies.

The third area where the interests of the United States have been seen to be served by American multinationals is in balance of payments. This appreciation came late to the government, only in the late 1960s when America's trading and balance-of-payments position began to deteriorate very rapidly. The multinationals were then recognized as major earners of foreign exchange (and foreign exchange was needed to purchase goods as well as to maintain America's global military-political position). The earnings of these corporations

12. See, for example, U.S. Council on International Economic Policy, *The United States in the Changing World Economy: A Report to the President, 1:A, Foreign Economic Perspective,* The Peterson Report (Washington, D.C.: Government Printing Office, 1971).

became recognized as an important factor in American economic welfare and global diplomatic position.[13]

This perception that "what was good for the multinational was good for the country" prevailed unchallenged until the early 1970s. The dominant motif of most writings on the multinational corporation (leaving out the Marxists, of course) was that the United States would and should become more dependent upon foreign investment. A number of economists at the Harvard Business School and the Brookings Institution in fact argued that the United States should become a service economy and live off its foreign investment income.[14] They advocated the exporting of capital, technology and management via the multinational corporations and the importing of manufactured goods from other countries.

For both economic and political reasons, organized labor and a few academic critics challenged this "service economy" doctrine. Labor's attack took the form of the Trade Reform Act of 1972 or the so-called Burke-Hartke Bill. This highly protectionist piece of legislation embodied organized labor's primary concern over "runaway plants" and the export of jobs. Academic critics were more concerned over the long-term costs of foreign direct investment for American economic development and the political dangers inherent in overdependence upon foreign investment.[15] They argued that foreign investment by American multinational corporations was to the long-term detriment of the American economy, and that excessive foreign investment would build up the industrial base of other economies at a cost to the industrial development of the United States.

13. Ibid.
14. See, for example, Lawrence Krause, "Why Exports are Becoming Irrelevant," *Foreign Policy* No. 3 (Summer 1971), pp. 62–70.
15. See Musgrave, *United States Taxation*, and Gilpin, *U.S. Power and the Multinational Corporation*, pp. 113–137.

My own position is that American multinational corporations have *accelerated* a shift in the global distribution of industrial and economic power to the disadvantage of the United States. I am not arguing that multinationals have *caused* this shift, but that they have accelerated the global redistribution of industrial and economic power away from the United States. Of far greater importance is the fact that Europe and Japan have recovered from the consequences of war and defeat. Yet, the shift is nevertheless real and poses major challenges for the United States in that it has weakened the political and economic base of the contemporary international order.

In Marxist terminology the inherent contradiction of capitalism is that it exploits the world. This writer suggests instead that the inherent contradiction of capitalism is that it *develops* the world. A capitalist world economy plants the seeds of its own destruction by diffusing industry and technology and by spurring economic growth in other economies. Capitalism undermines the distribution of power upon which it has rested and which has enabled it to expand. Such was the fate of British-centered world capitalism in the nineteenth century; it is the challenge that faces the American-centered capitalist world economy in the last quarter of the twentieth century.

A major shift has taken place in the world distribution of economic power, partly as a result of foreign investment by American corporations and partly because of the general growth of foreign economies. American economic hegemony is being challenged by the revival of other developed economies and by the emergence of important new centers of economic power among developing countries such as Brazil, Venezuela, Iran, Nigeria and Indonesia. Except for agriculture and a few high technology industries, the American trading position has deteriorated. The position of the dollar has been greatly weakened. The United States no longer controls the non-Communist world's supply of petroleum; the balance of power with respect to petroleum has shifted from the Texas Railroad Commission to the King of Saudi Arabia. One could also mention that the United States no longer has a monopoly on nuclear weapons. In short, the political order upon which the foreign expansion of American corporations has rested has been seriously eroded.

The issue that is raised as a consequence of this major shift in the global distribution of power is whether Americans will continue to perceive a complementarity of corporate interests and national interests. Will the American public continue to believe that what is good for the multinationals is good for the country? My own view is that it is highly doubtful that such a perception will remain unchallenged. The growing divergence of national and corporate interests will become increasingly apparent. While the divergence of interests has always been there, it will become sharper because of the effects of the global shift of power upon the United States in general and American multinationals in particular.

In the first place, the bargaining position of many host governments has greatly increased in terms of both manufacturing investment and raw material investment. Host countries are using their increased bargaining power to shift the terms of investment in their favor. They quite naturally want a bigger slice of the pie. At the same time, changes have occurred within the American economy which will force the American public and the American government to put increasing pressure on the multinational corporation. The American government has already moved toward seeking a higher fraction of foreign earnings in order to finance energy imports. Recently, in the Tax Reduction Act of 1974, a change was made in American tax policy which reduced the benefits of tax deferral. Though little noticed, this is a major shift in American policy; it will certainly increase the disincentive for foreign investment. Other changes in tax laws and other policies will surely follow. The country is sensing an immense gap between the supply and demand for investment capital to meet national needs in energy, urban development and increased industrial productivity. The incentive to export capital has, of course, decreased due to the devaluations of the dollar. Exporting is now easier; foreign assets are more expensive. Additionally, there is the problem of domestic unemployment. If the United States has an unemployment rate of six or seven percent over the next decade, one can imagine the increasing pressures to prevent foreign investment. Labor will intensify its attack. These domestic pressures will lead to policy changes directed against foreign investment.

Not only will the host country exert pressure on the multinational corporation, but so will the American government. Problems of balance of payments, domestic capital formation and unemployment will increasingly create pressures to restrict capital outflow. Both the host and the home governments will close in on the multinational corporation. It will become a question of who will milk the cow. The multinational corporation *is* a highly successful productive institution. The real question for the future is going to be to whom the benefits of that immense productivity will go. There will be increasing conflict over the distribution of benefits, with the host and home countries contending. Thus, with the decline in American power and the rise of foreign economies, we will increasingly see the multinational corporations caught between home and host governments.

The oil boycott of the winter of 1973-1974 was truly a turning point. Host governments, in this case the oil-producing states, particularly Saudi Arabia, were able to turn the tables on the multinational corporations. They not only changed the distribution of benefits to their advantage, but they were also able to make the oil multinational corporations serve their political interests as against the national interests of the corporations' home governments. In response, the U.S. government asserted greater control over its oil multinationals, relieving them, for example, of the responsibility for negotiations over price with the oil-producing states. While the oil industry is undoubtedly unique, this example is certainly a harbinger of things to come.

Three Challenges and the Future of the Multinational Corporation

The future role of multinational corporations will be determined by what happens to them during this transition period in world politics through which the world is passing. Their future role will be determined by the way the United States and the American economy adjust to the decline of American hegemony. Specifically, in the middle 1970s, the United States faces three challenges. The first is to decide whether Americans should hold fast to past political commitments or whether they should retrench. To what extent should the United States try to maintain the world political order that it created in its interests and to what extent should it retrench? Should the dominant hegemonic power hold fast to its commitments or should it fall back onto a more secure position? Britain faced the same question in the latter part of the nineteenth century. As pressures grew on her, and as she was no longer able to maintain her world position, she did retrench— although not enough—and thereby brought her resources and commitments into balance.[16]

Due to the redistribution of power in the world today, the United States faces much the same challenge that Great Britain, the declining hegemonic power, faced in the latter part of the nineteenth century. On the one hand, it has become increasingly costly for the United States to maintain its foreign commitments and its dominant world position; on the

16. Correlli Barnett, *The Collapse of British Power* (London: Eyre, Methuen, 1972).

other hand, it is difficult for the United States to retrench
without incurring the danger that its entire position may collapse. One of the reasons that the United States decided in
March 1968 to negotiate its way out of Vietnam was that the
costs of Vietnam were becoming too great; the position of
the dollar in particular was under attack. At the heart of the
recent debate over Vietnam was the question of strategic
retrenchment without suffering a total collapse of the international position of the United States. Whereas the president
and the secretary of state feared a global collapse of American credibility if the United States failed to support Saigon
and Cambodia, their critics believed that defeat and retrenchment in Southeast Asia would not influence America's global
position.

Behind this debate were two views concerning the meaning
of retrenchment. For President Ford and Secretary Kissinger,
retrenchment meant a falling back into isolationism. Once
you retreat in the face of defeat, there is no other stopping
point. For their critics, retrenchment meant a falling back to
a more secure position, that is, the giving up of untenable
positions in Southeast Asia and elsewhere, and the revitaliz-
ing of America's basic alliances with Europe and Japan.

In short, the first major issue we face is what type of international political order can and should the United States seek
to create in the wake of the weakening of the *Pax Americana.*
While this is an important issue in itself, it is of particular importance for the future of the American multinational corporation. Foreign investment, we have argued, follows the flag.
The retrenchment of American power will inevitably bring
about at least a partial retreat of American multinationals.
What therefore will be the nature of the new international
political order to which the American multinationals must
adjust?

The second challenge we face, a challenge which Great Britain also faced in the latter part of the nineteenth century, is

the future of the international economy itself. Will the United States attempt to maintain the open, liberal system it created in the postwar world, or will it accept some fragmentation of the world economy into regional blocs? For Great Britain the question was one of maintaining a free trade system or of creating a system of imperial preferences. Initially, when faced with this choice the British opted to continue free trade. Not until the Great Depression of the 1930s did the British finally move to the system of imperial preferences. A liberal international economy was not recreated until the United States emerged as the world's dominant power after World War II.

At the present time, the American-centered world economy is threatening to fragment due to the redistribution of power that has been taking place over the last decade. The question which arises is whether the United States still has the *power* to continue to manage the international economy. Does it still have the *will* to do so? Will the dollar continue to be the basis of the international monetary system, or will the system break up into monetary blocs—the Deutschmark bloc, the Yen bloc, the dollar bloc, and so on? Will the United States continue to champion liberal trade, or will it become increasingly protectionist? Will it continue to encourage the free movement of capital and foreign investment, or will it restrict both the outflow of investment capital and the inflow as well? What kind of world energy regime will it have now that it no longer controls the non-Communist world's supply of energy? Will the United States retreat into Project Independence, or will it be able to negotiate a new world energy system with the producers?

In economic matters the United States seems to be confronted by the same choices as in the case of political-strategic retrenchment. Americans are told that they must maintain a universal open system or else the world economy will collapse into economic nationalism and protectionism. There is said to be no middle course. However, another view has been suggested by certain economists. This is the idea of a negotiated system which would stabilize the world economy through a series of bargains over money, trade and investment. Such a system could be established, for example, by the three major centers of economic power: the United States, West Germany and Japan. These three powers have a common interest in the preservation of a liberal multinational system. All three have relatively strong economies, and they are tied together by security alliances. If these three economies could agree on trade, money, investment and energy, they could establish a basis for the survival of the world economy. They could prevent its fragmentation into regional blocs and exclusive alliances which threaten to unsettle the world economy.

Unfortunately, this kind of tripartite economic alliance runs counter to certain trends in the world economy. It runs counter to what has been called "world populism," that is, the notion that all the nations of the world economy should have an equal say in the reordering of the world economy, the notion that is embodied in the U.N. General Assembly effort to create a new international economic order, the notion that decisions about the future of the world economy should be reached by some sort of international democratic process and not by the great economic powers. We see here a clash between elitism and world populism.[17]

Another obstacle in the way of the tripartite arrangement is that it would probably mean the end of the European Common Market, as the French would never tolerate such an arrangement. It would strengthen Germany's position and would reduce the French to a second-class status in the world economy. A third problem with the tripartite arrangement is

17. Fouad Ajami, "The Global Populists: Third World Nations and World-Order Crises" (mimeographed) Center of International Studies, Princeton University (May 1974).

whether the economic interests of the United States, West Germany and Japan are sufficiently alike to sustain a cooperative effort over the long run. The three have become increasingly competitive over markets, resources and investment outlets in recent years.

Thus, the United States faces a major challenge with respect to the future of the world economy. The United States can no longer manage the world's monetary, trading and investment system as it has over the past several decades. As a consequence, it is faced with the choice of withdrawing into protectionism or else seeking to renegotiate a new set of rules. If it chooses the latter, it either must come to terms with the new centers of economic power emerging throughout the world, or else it must seek a more limited working arrangement with West Germany and Japan. None of these arrangements are attractive possibilities.

The third problem that the United States faces, as did Great Britain in the latter part of the nineteenth century, is whether to emphasize foreign or domestic investment, that is, whether to continue the export of capital or to channel the flow of capital back into the domestic economy.[18] From the 1890s on, this was a major issue for Great Britain as the British began to sense their relative industrial decline. The owners of capital and British political leadership were both favorable to the continued heavy export of capital. They saw British foreign investments both as a weapon to use against other powers and as a means to secure higher earnings and other economic benefits than could be secured at home. In effect, there was an alliance between the owners of capital and the managers of British foreign policy. The export of capital abroad was judged to be simultaneously in the British national interest and in the interest of the owners of capital. Those who opposed a policy of continued export of capital—

18. Michael Brown, *After Imperialism* (New York: Humanities Press, 1963), ch. 3.

social reformers such as the Webbs, industrialists such as
Joseph Chamberlain (who was also a proponent of Common-
wealth preference), political realists such as Halford
Mackinder (who was concerned that British industry was
falling behind its German rival)—argued for a greater emphasis
on domestic investment. Unfortunately, the group that
favored continued investment abroad won; Britain continued
to export capital in great amounts and her industry continued to decline. Britain is still paying the price for this
atrophy of her industrial base.

In a less acute, but nevertheless real form, the same issue
faces the United States today. Should the United States continue to encourage the overseas expansion of American corporations, or should it encourage a greater emphasis on
domestic investment? This has already become an issue in
American politics, as I indicated above, and there is a perceptible shift toward emphasizing domestic investment and
discouraging foreign investment. However, the full significance of this issue is appreciated only when it is placed in a
larger historical context. There is a relationship between foreign investment and the historical tendency for advanced
industrial economies to decline relative to their foreign
competitors.

Foreign investment is both a cause of and a response to this
historical tendency. With the spread of technology, the industrial leader over a period of time loses more and more of its
initial advantage to rising competitors. A gradual shift takes
place in the locus of industrial and economic activity as a result of this process. The locus of economic activity shifts
from the leader to the rising economies in the system. One
can observe this phenomenon throughout history. The distinguished classicist R. W. Walbank observed with respect to
the decline of the Roman Empire: "Modern investigation has
revealed in the Roman Empire the operation of an economic
law which finds its application equally in our society—the

centrifugal tendency of an industry to export itself instead of its products and of trades to migrate from the older areas of the economy to the new."[19] The consequences of this tendency are the gradual redistribution of wealth and power in the international system and a shift in the international balance of power.

As American technology has diffused to foreign economies, as American exports have become increasingly noncompetitive, and as other economies have begun to grow faster and provide better profit opportunities, American industry in response has also moved abroad. In effect, foreign investment has become a strategy by which a declining economy seeks to come to terms with its declining position. At the same time foreign investment accelerates that decline. As the dominant economy declines, the owners and managers of capital migrate to the more rapidly developing foreign economies. The logical consequence of this process is that the once dominant industrial economy becomes a *rentier* economy, living off its foreign earnings. This is precisely what happened to Great Britain. The United States fortunately has not gone as far in this direction as Great Britain did, but it has gone farther than it is in the interests of the United States to go.

Foreign investment may be said to be the second-best solution to the problem of economic and political decline; it is one way to come to terms with relative decline. The best solution, however, is the rejuvenation of the declining economy: the development of new technology, the generation of new industry and the redirecting of capital into the neglected sectors of the economy. It means increased investment in research and development related to civilian industry rather than defense. In terms of foreign economic policy, it means a strategy of foreign trade, not foreign investment. An argu-

19. R. W. Walbank, *The Awful Revolution: The Decline of the Roman Empire in the West* (Liverpool: Liverpool University Press, 1969), p. 47.

ment can be made that a greater emphasis on this kind of strategy on the part of Great Britain in the latter part of the nineteenth century would have been to her long-term advantage. A similar argument can be made for the United States today.

What this essay recommends, therefore, is a deemphasis of the current commitment to a foreign investment strategy. It proposes a greater emphasis on domestic investment and foreign trade. While such a reorientation of American policy would allow foreign investment, it would mean the elimination of taxation and other policies which create an incentive to overinvest abroad to the detriment of the American domestic economy.

There is, however, a third possible response to relative economic decline. The more appropriate term to describe it is "reaction." The declining economy draws in upon itself. As other economies advance, as competition increases, and as the terms of trade shift to its disadvantage, the declining economy retreats into protectionism and some form of restricted preference system. It throws up barriers to the export of capital and to the import of foreign goods. It begins to favor preferential commercial arrangements. Little is done to reinvigorate the industrial base. This tendency was long at work in the case of Great Britain; it is increasingly at work in the case of the United States.

We have, then, these three choices: the foreign investment strategy, the rejuvenation strategy and the protectionist strategy. Rejuvenation is obviously the best choice, but the problem here is that industrial economies tend to be highly conservative and resistant to change. The creation of new products and new industrial processes is an expensive one for industrial firms that have heavy investments in the existing plants. Labor can be equally resistant to reform. More likely, corporations will continue to invest in particular industrial sectors and product lines even though these may be declining sectors of investment. This conservatism plagued the British after the rise of foreign competitors in the latter decades of the last century. Rather than pioneering in new areas such as chemical and electrical products, they concentrated their efforts on finding new markets for old products, especially textiles. In short, the capacity of an advanced economy to transform itself is limited.

The rejuvenation of an economy and a shift of resources to new promising sectors would appear to come about only as a consequence of a catastrophe, such as defeat in war. It required a near defeat in World War I before Great Britain even began to move toward restructuring her economy. Even then she did not go far enough. It is not surprising that the three most dynamic industrial powers today are the two defeated nations of the last world war—Germany (East and West) and Japan. The three victors—the United States, Great Britain and the Soviet Union—are falling behind industrially. It may be true, as Peter Drucker and others have argued, that the United States has largely exhausted the innovative possibilities of its existing industries.[20] American economic power, foreign investment and the immense industrial growth of the last several decades have rested on such innovations in technology as the internal combustion engine, man-made fibers, electronics and steel; but the growth curves for these industries appear to have flattened out. It appears that they have ceased to be major fields of innovation and future industrial expansion, at least for the United States.

In the contemporary world the diffusion of technology from the United States to other economies has intensified. As industry has migrated from the United States to other countries, profits have declined; growth has slackened. Short-term economic conflict has been intensified by various economic crises—shortages in raw materials and world-wide economic

20. Peter Drucker, *The Age of Discontinuity* (New York: Harper and Row, 1969).

inflation. Yet, in the larger perspective, the crises faced in the middle 1970s in terms of resources, environment and inflation could have a beneficial effect. They could constitute the catastrophe which will stimulate the rejuvenation of the American economy. The search for the solution to these problems could force the United States to increase its economic efficiency and innovate a new order of industrial technology. If this search leads to technological breakthroughs and the creation of a new international division of labor, the United States may yet escape the economic conflict and relative economic decline with which it is now threatened.

10

Economic Tensions: America versus the Third World

C. FRED BERGSTEN

I. Introduction

Canada will now permit new foreign direct investments only when they bring "significant benefit" to Canada. The determination of "significant benefit" is explicitly to be a policy decision of the cabinet, based on five criteria: the contribution of the proposed investment to "the level and nature of economic activity in Canada," including employment, use of Canadian components, and exports; the degree and significance of Canadian participation in the enterprise; the effect on productivity, technological development and innovation in Canada; the effect on industrial competition; and the compatibility of the investment with the economic and industrial policies of the national and provincial governments.

The following scenario thus becomes almost inevitable. The Canadian cabinet will approve a large and controversial U.S. investment. Nationalist opposition will charge a sellout of Canadian interests. The government will respond that the investment brings "significant benefit" to Canada.

But Canadian politics will not permit the simple assertion of "national interest" by the governing party. Opponents of

This chapter is a slightly revised and updated version of an article that appeared in *Foreign Affairs* in October 1974. Copyright 1974 by Council on Foreign Relations, Inc., and reprinted by permission.

the investment (and of the governing party) will enumerate the alleged injury it brings to Canada. The government will be forced to counter by specifying the benefits which, in its view, outweigh the disadvantages. It will thus publicly reveal, for example, that the investment will bring x thousand additional jobs and y million dollars of additional exports to Canada.

International conflict becomes certain at this point. The AFL-CIO will charge that the x thousand jobs have been exported from the United States to Canada, validating its case against foreign investment by U.S. firms. The Treasury Department will charge that Canada has diverted the y million dollars of exports from the United States, weakening the U.S. balance of payments and the dollar. One virtually certain result is intensified U.S.-Canadian hostility. Another, which is a theme of this chapter, is an intensification of political pressure in the United States against all foreign investment by American firms.

Such overt efforts by Canada to capture an increasing share of the benefits of foreign investment would by themselves have a significant impact on U.S. policy, because Canada remains by far the largest single recipient of U.S. investment and because the rapid flow of communications between the two countries assures that adversely affected American interests will become aware of the situation. But the new Canadian policy is only illustrative of one of the basic global trends of the 1970s. Virtually every country in the world which receives direct investment—which means virtually every country in the world, big or small, industrialized or developing, Communist or non-Communist, left or right—is levying increasingly stringent requirements on foreign firms.

The objective of these policies of host countries is to tilt the benefits brought by multinational companies as far as possible in their favor and to minimize the costs to them which can be associated with such investments. Few countries any longer ask the simplistic question: "Do we want foreign investment?" The issue is how to get foreign investment on the terms which are best for them, and indeed to use the power of the firms to promote their own national goals.

Host countries are adopting a variety of strategies to achieve this objective. Most are applying much more sensible general economic policies, and thus removing such sources of windfall profits for the firms—and losses for the countries—as overvalued exchange rates and undervalued interest rates. In addition, most are seeking to position themselves as strongly as possible to negotiate better deals on the whole range of relevant issues with applicant firms. They list broad criteria for judging specific applications, require detailed statements from applicant firms on the effects of their proposals, and then seek the best mix of benefits they can achieve without deterring the investor. This effort of host countries to negotiate maximum benefits and minimum costs from foreign investors will shortly become the focus of the entire international debate about multinational firms.

II. Host Country Policies

Efforts by host countries to maximize their returns from foreign investors are, of course, nothing new. There are four features, however, which differentiate the present markedly from the past. First, virtually all host countries are now adopting such policies, whereas only a few did so before. Second, the policies themselves are becoming more evident and explicit and hence will attract increasing attention in the home countries of the firms, particularly the United States.

Third, host-country objectives are now much broader and deeper. Governments throughout the world are accepting responsibility for an increasing number of economic and social objectives—such as regional equity, better income distribution and the development of indigenous high-technology industries—in addition to the traditional macroeconomic goals of full employment, growth and price stability. Developing countries are also seeking to reduce unemployment directly rather than assuming that it will fall automatically with economic growth.

Thus governments are seeking additional policy instruments, to meet an increased number of policy targets. With the explosive acceleration of international economic interpenetration, external forces can hinder—or assist—the successful use of traditional domestic policy instruments. Multinational firms, as the chief engine of interpenetration, represent both a major threat to the success of internal policies and a major opportunity for help. Host countries are thus virtually compelled by their own political imperatives to seek to exert a maximum impact on the detailed behavior of almost all incoming direct investments.

Fourth, host-country efforts are now far more likely to succeed because of fundamental shifts in the world economic and political environment that have put many host countries in a far stronger position than before. They have large and rapidly growing markets, especially when they are members of regional arrangements, such as the European Community or the Andean Pact, which discriminate against imports from outsiders. Many represent highly productive, lower-cost "export platforms" from which multinational firms can substantially improve their global competitive positions. Those possessing key raw materials are in a particularly strong position, both with companies in the extractive industries themselves and with companies which use the materials;[1] producers of raw materials have now demonstrated the ability to get together to promote their common interests, rather than compete with each other to the benefit of outsiders. And the indigenous talent that has emerged in even the least developed, as the result of a generation of economic growth with heavy

1. See C. Fred Bergsten, "The New Era in World Commodity Markets," *Challenge*, 17 (September-October 1974).

emphasis on advanced education, enables host countries both to perceive their national interests accurately and take maximum advantage of their stronger positions. Outside help in negotiating with the firms is also increasingly available for those countries which still need it. So the firms can no longer dictate, or even heavily influence, host-country policies as they may have done in the past; the *dependencia* syndrome, under which foreign and domestic elites collude against the national interests of host countries, is rapidly disappearing.

In addition, host countries now have a far wider array of options in pursuing their objectives. Not long ago the multinational firm was the only source of large-scale capital, advanced technology and superior management. Not long ago the United States was virtually the sole source of large chunks of investment capital, technological know-how and marketing skills. Not long ago security considerations devolving from the Cold War enabled the United States to dominate its allies, most small countries, and the international rules and institutions which governed world economic relations.

Now, however, the multinationals have lost much of their power because the attributes which they once monopolized, and which could only be obtained in package form, can be increasingly "unbundled"—capital obtained in the private markets, technology licensed from a variety of sources, management hired directly. Increasing numbers of European and Japanese companies offer formidable competition for American multinationals—and are often willing to invest on terms more generous to host countries, to make up for their delayed emergence on the world scene. Capital, technology and other skills can be bought in Europe and elsewhere, as well as in America. With the onset of *détente*, host countries large and small no longer fear to cross the United States by challenging U.S.-based firms and the international economic environment which helped them flourish in the 1950s and 1960s. Multinational firms based in the United States, recognizing these basic changes and with their own international exposure greatly increased by virtue of their rapid global expansion, complete the circle by seeking in virtually all cases to accommodate to the new leverage of host countries and by eschewing the backing of the U.S. government.

In short, sovereignty is no longer at bay in host countries. To be sure, the degree of this shift in power differs from country to country, and from industry to industry. It is virtually complete in most industrial host countries and some developing countries as well, and is well under way in many other developing countries. Only in a few countries—industrial as well as developing, and indeed including the United States itself—have new host-country policies on foreign investment not yet begun to emerge.

The shift in power and resulting policy is further along in extractive than in manufacturing industries. Within manufacturing, it is further advanced for low-technology investments and those aimed at the local market than for high-technology investments and those which use the country as an "export platform." But the trend appears inexorable.

III. Effects on Home Countries

What about the effects of this trend on home countries —that is, the countries from which investment comes, via multinational firms based there—in particular the United States? Before addressing that question, we need to take a closer look at the specific requirements being levied on the multinational firms.

These requirements derive from the policy objectives of the host countries. They differ in degree from country to country, but fall into three broad categories: domestic economic objectives, foreign economic policy objectives, and national control over the local subsidiaries of the foreign-based firms.

In the first category, the most direct requirement is job

quotas for nationals. This has both a quantitative and a qualitative aspect. Developing countries with high rates of aggregate unemployment simply impose overall job requirements. Indonesia requires that 75 percent of all employees of foreign-based firms be Indonesian within five to eight years; Nigeria and Morocco sharply limit the access to alien labor of such firms. In both industrial and developing countries, such job requirements are often part of "regional policies": Canada, France, Iran, the Netherlands, and the United Kingdom, among others, offer major incentives to enterprises to bring jobs to "depressed areas." (In some countries, regional authorities themselves add to the list of requirements.) In addition, layoffs may be forbidden (Italy, some recent cases in France) or made very costly (Germany, Belgium), so that the firm is locked tightly into any level of employment which it initially recruits.

Qualitative job requirements are prevalent in both industrial countries and the new middle class of semideveloped countries. Argentina requires at least 85 percent of management, scientific, technical and administrative personnel to be Argentine. Singapore judges investment applications partly by the ratio of skilled and technical workers to be included in the work force. An increasing number of industrialized countries, particularly in Europe, are requiring the firms to carry out locally both a significant share of their total research and development and some of their most advanced research. Training of local workers is another requirement, aimed at both more and better jobs.

Two measures used to pursue both domestic and foreign economic objectives are "value-added" and "anticoncentration" requirements. To avoid becoming mere entrepôts for foreign firms, developing countries will now often require domestic production of a certain share of final output. This promotes the employment objective, both in the new industry itself and in those local industries which supply it; and furthers its balance-of-payments objective by raising the net foreign exchange return from the investment.

To avoid excessive industrial concentration, which can lead both to higher prices at home and to an impaired competitive position in world markets, some countries—particularly more developed ones—either reject foreign investments (especially take-overs) which would create excessive market power or let them proceed only if steps are taken to guard against such an outcome. Germany, the United States and Canada are particularly concerned with this issue.

Many developing countries are pursuing a similar aim through different means. Some multinational firms have traditionally limited or excluded competition among their own subsidiaries (and the parent) by dividing up world markets for each of their products. One result is that subsidiaries in particular countries are barred completely from the export market, or limited to a particular region. Global competition may be reduced as a result, and the export (and hence total production) opportunities of the country hosting the hobbled subsidiary are certainly reduced. Led by the Andean Pact, developing host countries are banning any such limitations on the distribution of local production by the subsidiaries (and any other tie-in clauses that would restrict the subsidiaries' use of the parents' technology).

Host countries are now promoting balance-of-payments objectives in several ways. A special target has been the trend in most multinational firms toward local financing, a practice which both limits the inflow of capital and diverts scarce local capital.

From 1957 to 1965, for example, only 17 percent of the investments of U.S.-based firms in Latin America originated outside the host country.[2] From 1965 until early 1974, U.S.

2. Ronald Müller, "Poverty Is the Product," *Foreign Policy*, Winter 1973–74, pp. 85–88.

policy actually promoted the trend toward local financing by limiting (first voluntarily, then mandatorily from 1968) the capital outflows of U.S. firms—but not their actual investments. Now a reaction has set in. Australia was one of the first countries to require external capital to come with the firm, largely in retaliation against the U.S. capital controls. Many hosts now require external financing for foreign investments, and others achieve the same purpose by limiting subsidiaries' access to domestic capital. On the other side of the capital account, a widening array of countries (e.g., Brazil, India, the Andean Pact) limit tightly the repatriation of capital investment and even profits.

Requirements that the investing firm export a sizable share of output are even more important, because they go directly to the location of world production, jobs and the most sensitive aspects of each country's external position. Andean Pact countries will permit foreign investors to avoid divestiture only if they export more than 80 percent of their output outside the group. Mexico permits 100 percent foreign ownership only if the firm exports 100 percent of its output. India requires foreign investors to export 60 percent of output within three years. Practically every host developing country —and many host developed countries—attach very high priority to the export criterion.

As with jobs, the export requirement is qualitative as well as quantitative. Many countries are seeking to upgrade and diversify their export base, and so require foreign investors to push the processing of raw materials or the assembly of components a stage or two further than might otherwise occur. A particular objective is building high-technology exports.[3]

Some efforts are still being made to get foreign firms to re-

3. This emphasis on high-technology exports may affect a country's balance of payments less than its industrial structure. In a country whose exchange rate is floating, such as Canada, any increase in the exports of the promoted sector will produce upward movement in the currency, which will tend to limit exports (and increase imports) in other sectors.

place imports as well. Canada recently barred a major U.S. computer company from competing for government contracts unless it helped Canada achieve balanced trade in that sector, by replacing imports as well as exporting. However, host countries are increasingly emphasizing exports because such a focus permits larger-scale production, greater efficiency, and more jobs and growth for the longer run. The shift requires more explicit policies toward the foreign investor and more affirmative action by the firms (especially if the host country is to avoid the costs to its wider objectives of excessive export subsidies and undervalued exchange rates). In addition, larger production runs by the subsidiaries mean greater potential conflict with the economic interests of the home country. This issue well illustrates the increasing clashes among countries which may arise.

Finally, virtually all host countries are seeking majority (if not complete) ownership of local subsidiaries of foreign firms. Many are seeking a major share in day-to-day management as well. The objective is to increase the likelihood that the subsidiary will respond positively to the national policies of the host country rather than to the global strategy of the corporate family, headquartered in the United States or another home country, and perhaps to the global strategy of the government of the home country as well.

Some of these host-country policies treat the multinational firm differently from local companies, though many do not. The main point, however, is not whether the policies are discriminatory. The significance is their clear intent to shift toward the host country the package of benefits brought by the foreign firms. To the extent that they do so successfully to an important degree, they trigger a potentially important new source of international conflict. To the extent that they do so through measures which produce results different from market-determined outcomes, there is increased justification for such clashes and even greater likelihood that they will occur.

IV. The Alliance between Host Countries and Multinational Corporations

The firms themselves may have little or no objection to these host-country policies. They may be relatively indifferent, within fairly broad limits, as to where to locate sizable portions of their production and how to finance it.[4] They may quite easily accommodate to host-country requirements on a majority, if not all, of the issues raised. The alacrity with which many firms have accepted the exceptionally detailed and far-reaching conditions imposed by Communist host countries is the most dramatic example, but the phenomenon is common. If too many firms do not play, a host country will sense that it has pushed too hard and retreat on the least important of its concerns, until it finds the mix that will maximize its interests.

The cooperativeness of the firms is promoted by the newly powerful positions of the host countries, as outlined above. It is often further accelerated by specific inducements. Some of the most frequent are favored tax treatment, export subsidies, "location grants" within the context of regional policies, subsidized training of local labor, prohibitions of strikes, preferred access to local credit, and protection against imports.

These considerations round out the strategies of the host countries. To maximize their returns, they must not only harness the activities of the firms but assure that the investments actually proceed. Thus they utilize the traditional mix

4. For an excellent analysis of this range see Paul Streeten, "The Multinational Enterprise and the Theory of Development Policy," *World Development*, 1 (October 1973). He counsels host developing countries to marry cost-benefit analysis of their own needs to bargaining-power analysis of how far they can push. However, he views many host countries as weaker in their relations with multinationals than do I.

of carrot and stick. The greater the incentives, the further the firms will, of course, tilt toward complying with the requests of their hosts.

Thus, a second broad trend is toward collaboration between the multinational firms and their hosts, and greater distance between the firms and their home governments. Few firms any longer appeal to their home government for support against host governments even in cases of outright nationalization, let alone to deal with the growing array of economic and political requirements which they face. Some firms, particularly in the natural resources industries, seek to limit the leverage of host countries by blending together capital from a variety of countries and selling their output forward to buyers in a variety of countries, to increase the problems for the host if it takes extreme action.[5] But even this strategy does not deter the achievement of the host's primary objectives; indeed, it may promote them by enhancing the inflow of external capital and assuring a diversified export market. And most firms, in recognition of the current balance of power, are in fact cooperating fully with their hosts. The oil industry is the most obvious recent case in point, but the trend is certainly widespread.

This analysis differs sharply from the picture painted in the recent debates in the United Nations and elsewhere, where the developing countries (and even some developed countries) continue to attack the alleged alliance against them of multinational firms and home-country governments. The difference can be explained partly by the usual lag in perceptions of overall bargaining power by the bargainer who is catching up step by step; partly by the dominance of the rhetoric by politicians whose perceptions are shaped by images, rather

5. See Theodore H. Moran, "Transnational Strategies of Protection and Defense by Multinational Corporations: Spreading the Risk and Raising the Cost for Nationalization in Natural Resources," *International Organization*, 27 (Spring 1973).

than by the technocrats who are implementing the new policies; partly by the zeal of the developing countries to stick together, which requires them to adopt the position of the weakest among them; and perhaps mainly by the overwhelming tactical advantage of keeping the home countries tagged as defenders of the multinationals and aggressors against host-country interests. As in the case of raw material prices, some of the traditionally have-not countries suffer from intellectual lag and others find it highly convenient to maintain the rhetoric of the past though it no longer bears much relation to reality. Their tactics can succeed as long as the home countries fail to recognize what is really happening. But reality in the field of foreign direct investment cannot be submerged much longer.

V. Impact on the United States

The main impact of these new global trends is on the home countries of the multinational firms. It falls most heavily on the United States, the largest home country by far.

If host countries are achieving an increasing share of the benefits brought by multinational firms, someone else is receiving a decreasing share. As just outlined, this "loser" is seldom the firms themselves; indeed, they may gain more from the incentives than they lose from the requirements. In some cases, countries which are neither home nor host to the company may lose—as when a Brazilian subsidiary of a U.S. firm competes with German sales in the world automobile market.

But the United States, as the home country, may frequently be on the losing side of the new balance in two senses. Host-country inducements to American firms may attract economic activity and jobs away from the United States, in some cases without economic justification. Traditionally, the United States has forcefully opposed policies which discriminated against foreign investors; now it increasingly finds its national interests threatened by policies which discriminate in favor of those firms. And host-country requirements may skew the results of U.S. investments against the overall U.S. national interest.

To be sure, many foreign direct investments represent non-zero-sum games: as in all classical market behavior, world welfare improves. It is also conceivable that all parties benefit from some of those investments. Some host-country measures may also help home countries, such as the United States; if a host country breaks up the global allocation of markets by a multinational firm, the home country may benefit more from lower prices than it loses in oligopoly rents. And some host-country policies (such as placing a few directors on the boards of subsidiaries) essentially bring them psychic rather than financial income, and have no adverse impact on anyone.

However, there is always the issue of how to divide the benefits even when all parties do gain. Indeed, there may be losses to the United States (through the firms) even when more economically sensible host-country policies increase world welfare by eliminating or reducing market imperfections which profited the firms in the past. Most important, many investments are largely indifferent to location and hence are close to zero-sum games; in such cases a decision that is one party's gain *is* another party's loss. Furthermore, world welfare may actually decline as a result of some foreign investments, such as those induced primarily by host-country tax preferences and those which increase global market concentration, even though host countries gain from them. So there is great latitude for home countries to lose when host countries successfully tilt the benefits of the investment package in their own direction.

The balance-of-payments aspects are the clearest case in point. Existing world demand for a product may often be relatively fixed in the short run, especially for the processed goods and high-technology items which countries are avid to produce. Thus there is a limit to world exports. If Brazil requires General Motors to export a certain share of its production in order to remain in business (or to retain its favored tax treatment), U.S. automotive exports may decline even though no such shift was dictated by purely economic considerations. Similarly, the U.S. capital which Brazil requires General Motors to use to construct its plant may not be automatically offset by other capital inflows into the United States. Similar shifts in benefits can occur with respect to jobs, technology or other economic aspects of investment whose outcome is altered by host-country policies.

The effects of shifts in ownership and management control imposed by host countries are more subtle, and more difficult to trace. In the past, control of foreign natural resources by U.S. companies generally increased the likelihood that those resources would be available to the United States in a crisis; now, however, the seizure of effective control by most host countries has rendered the United States as uncertain as all other countries in this area. Increased host-country control renders the firms less susceptible to the extraterritorial reach of the U.S. government. And shifts in effective control reduce the likelihood that the United States will derive monopoly rents or other benefits from the overseas activities of U.S. firms.

Such shifts of investment-induced benefits from the United States to host countries may, from many points of view, be desirable. They may distribute world income more equitably. They may reduce some of the tensions which have clouded interstate relations heretofore, because host governments felt inferior to the firms and hence susceptible to ill treatment by them.

However, these shifts may not always be so benign from the standpoint of the home country. Indeed, the United States now finds itself in a most peculiar position. Negotiations between U.S.-based multinational firms and host countries are having an increasingly important bearing on the national interests of the United States. The interests of the host countries are represented through their governments. The interests of the firms are represented directly. But the third major actor in the drama is at present wholly unrepresented.

In the past, some observers would have brushed off this apparent asymmetry on three counts: the U.S.-based firms could be counted on to represent U.S. national interests explicitly, or at least advance them inadvertently; that the United States was so powerful economically that any costs to its economy would be easily absorbed (and perhaps welcomed officially in view of U.S. support for economic development elsewhere); and that any such costs would be quite small anyway in view of the insensitivity of the U.S. economy to external events and the marginal economic importance of foreign investment.

Each of these considerations has now changed dramatically, as part of the change in the overall economic and political environment noted in Section III.[6] Many "U.S.-based firms have become truly multinational and thus, quite logically and defensibly from their standpoints, pursue a set of interests which may not coincide closely with any of several concepts of U.S. national interests. Indeed, as discussed above, many firms now respond much more clearly to host-country interests, because those host countries have both achieved a much stronger position vis-à-vis the firms and articulated far more clearly than home countries what they expect the firms to do.[7] In their constant quest for legitimacy and acceptance,

6. And elaborated in C. Fred Bergsten, *The Future of the International Economic Order: An Agenda for Research* (Lexington, Mass.: D. C. Heath, 1973), esp. pp. 1–8.

7. This in turn reflects a far clearer appreciation by host than home countries of the effects on them of multinational firms, and thus a far clearer idea of the ends to which they might want to harness foreign investors. There has been much more extensive analysis of the effects of foreign investment on host countries than of

the firms will naturally slide toward those who care most about their activities and who direct policies at them most explicitly.

And it is obvious that the U.S. economy is not so healthy that it can blithely ignore the effects of a phenomenon as large as direct investment. Such investment now accounts for more than 20 percent of the annual plant and equipment expenditures and profits of U.S.-based firms, and both numbers are rising rapidly. The corporations and the AFL-CIO agree that the phenomenon has an important impact on U.S. jobs and the balance of payments (though they disagree whether that impact is positive or negative). The United States is increasingly affected by world commodity arrangements, the structure of world markets and changes in exchange rates, all of which are influenced importantly by multinational firms.

It is thus both undesirable and completely unrealistic, in both economic and political terms, to anticipate continued abstention by the U.S. government from involvement in the foreign direct investment activities of U.S.-based enterprises. The British government has for several years made foreign exchange available to U.K.-based firms only if they can demonstrate that their foreign investments will benefit Britain's balance of payments, through exports and profit remittances. The Swedish government has had similar restrictions, and has just passed legislation which will also enable it to block foreign investments by Swedish firms which hurt its economy or foreign policy. Japan and, to a lesser extent, France have also traditionally used a variety of government levers to try to assure benefits to the home country from the foreign activities of their firms. So the United States is virtually alone, among home countries, in not playing an active role toward foreign investment by national enterprises.

---

the effects on home countries, a situation which a forthcoming book on U.S policy toward such investment by the present author, Thomas Horst and Theodore Moran seeks to help balance.

As in host countries, the issue will not be whether or not to permit foreign investment as a general rule. Nor will it primarily focus on the simplistic U.S. concerns of the past: "prompt, effective and adequate" compensation for nationalized properties, avoidance of barriers to U.S. investment or discrimination against it, codes of conduct to legitimize the firms. The issue will sometimes be whether to permit a specific investment. But it will primarily be the terms on which investments proceed, and the equitable sharing of the resulting impact on the national economies involved.

VI. The Risk of International Economic Conflict

As the United States seeks to fill the empty chair which currently marks most international discussion of its foreign direct investment, the likelihood of international conflict will rise sharply. For at stake is nothing less than the international division of production and the fruits thereof. Indeed, "the kinds of techniques used by governments both to attract and to constrain multinational firms sometimes look like the largest nontariff barriers of all."[8] Unless host countries cease their efforts to tilt the benefits of investment in their own direction, which is unlikely (and undesirable unless accompanied by other steps to help them achieve their legitimate objectives), the clash of these particular national interests could become a central problem of world economics and politics.

Over the coming decade, international investment policy could therefore replicate to an unfortunate degree the evolution of international trade policy in the interwar period. At that time, trade was the dominant source of international economic exchange. As governments accepted increasing responsibility for the economic and social welfare of their

8. A. E. Safarian and Joel Bell, "Issues Raised by National Control of the Multinational Corporation," *Columbia Journal of World Business*, 8 (Winter 1973) p. 16.

populations, particularly with the onset of the Depression, many sought to increase their national shares of the international benefits which resulted from trade. Other governments would not accept such diversion, and either emulated the moves of the initiators of controls or retaliated against them. There were no international rules and institutions to deter and channel such conflict. The result was trade warfare, and the deepening and broadening of the Depression.

Some observers fear that another depression looms on our contemporary horizon. Others wonder whether a Great Inflation, which in my view is more likely, will similarly lead countries desperately to pursue nationalistic measures in an effort to export their problems and insulate themselves from external pressures. Either cataclysm would greatly intensify the problem under discussion. Indeed, the national clashes outlined here might already have arisen much more frequently had not the postwar world economy progressed so successfully until recently.

Even without such extreme underlying conditions, however, the struggle for the international location of production will almost certainly continue to grow in both magnitude and impact on all countries concerned. Foreign direct investment and multinational enterprises have now replaced traditional, arms-length trade as the primary source of international economic exchange. As indicated throughout, host countries are increasingly adopting explicit policies to tilt in their directions the benefits generated by those enterprises. The impact of these efforts may turn out to be even greater than their trade predecessors of the 1930s, both because the economic interpenetration of nations is now more advanced than in the 1920s and because governments now pursue so many more policy targets.

Indeed, the U.S. government has already begun to voice opposition in international forums to the tax subsidies and other incentives which artifically lure U.S. firms to invest abroad, and the changes in U.S. taxation of foreign income proposed by the Treasury Department in April 1973 were largely aimed at countervailing such practices. Much stronger U.S. reactions can be envisaged over the next few years. The original AFL-CIO attack against foreign investment by American firms, as embodied in the Burke-Hartke bill, was based on ambiguous aggregate data and a handful of unrepresentative individual cases. Hence it made little headway. The efforts of the Treasury Department to limit direct investment outflows in the middle 1960s were similarly stymied by ambiguities over the effect of the outflows on the balance of payments.

But now labor, those concerned with the balance of payments, and the many other opponents of multinational enterprises will have a much stronger case: the shifting of benefits from the United States to host countries *through the overt policy steps* of those host countries. Such groups will ask how the U.S. government can sit idly by and let such shifts occur, just as similar American groups have since the 1930s—correctly and usually successfully—insisted that the U.S. government retaliate against the efforts of other countries to tilt the benefits of trade through subsidizing exports to the United States, blocking imports from the United States, or other measures of commercial policy which injured U.S. economic interests. And there are no domestic or international rules and procedures through which to channel such protests, like those developed for trade after World War II to avoid a repetition of the interwar experience.

The problem is further exacerbated by the subtlety and variety of inducements offered, and requirements levied, by host countries. A tariff or import quota is easy to see, and is usually known publicly. But a regional investment grant can be negotiated privately with a firm, and portrayed as "purely domestic" in any event if exposed. Export or job quotas, which are by their nature negotiated on a case-by-case basis, are even less obvious. The universal call for "transparency" of the operations of multinational firms must be joined by a call for transparency of the policies of many host countries toward those firms.

VII. The Need for a New International Economic Order

The scenario envisaged at the outset of this chapter can thus be concluded as follows. After the Canadian government approves the proposed investment, because it transferred x thousand jobs and y million dollars of exports from the United States to Canada, the U.S. government—under intense domestic political pressure—decides to retaliate. It seeks to bar the particular investment, either directly or by declaring that the foreign tax credit will not apply to its profits.

Either approach, however, requires legislation. Congress, probably supported by any administration in power, properly decides that such legislation should cover the overall issue of foreign investment rather than a single case or even a single country. The legislation clearly derives from a foreign action to pull jobs and exports away from the United States, and more examples of such actions, by a growing list of host countries, are added to the debate each day. The whole discussion may even take place with unemployment rising and the trade balance slipping. Thus the new legislation slaps a licensing requirement on all foreign investment and eliminates the tax credit altogether, except perhaps for investments where host countries avoid levying any requirements on U.S.-based firms.

Canada and most other host countries of course stick to their guns, being unable politically to back down in favor of multinational firms and at the dictates of the U.S. government. Foreign-based multinationals quickly begin to fill the void, and the United States begins to lose the many advantages conferred on it by the foreign investments of U.S.-based firms. Many of these firms then seek to "leave the United States," but the Treasury pursues them. In the end, as in the trade wars of the interwar period, the results include open political hostility among nations, a severe blow to the world economy, and a shattering of investor confidence.

Hopefully, the world will learn from its past mistakes and prevent this scenario from ever occurring. To do so, host countries should limit their efforts to skew the activities of multinational firms, perhaps by following the Australian example of insisting on "no adverse effects" rather than the Canadian example of requiring "significant benefit." But many will not do so unless some other power countervails the power of the firms. Nor will many of them, particularly the developing countries, do so unless they find other ways to meet their legitimate national aspirations.

It follows that home countries, particularly the United States, should take steps to help developing host countries achieve their goals in less disruptive ways. Such measures should encompass trade policy, commodity arrangements, and foreign assistance.[9]

More narrowly, home countries will also need tools that can be used to counter efforts of host countries that go beyond reasonable norms. For example, legislation increasing taxation of the foreign income of American corporations to offset tax inducements offered by host countries would be a precise analogy to present laws, in the trade field, that provide for countervailing duties against export subsidies by foreign governments. And a mechanism is needed to deal with individual cases where problems arise, analogous to the present escape clause in the trade area providing for temporary protection where U.S. interests are injured by particular import flows.

But such measures by home countries could simply lead to a series of retaliatory and counter-retaliatory steps between them and host countries. Thus international investment wars

9. See C. Fred Bergsten, "The Threat From The Third World," *Foreign Policy*, Summer 1973.

will be prevented only by the adoption of a truly new international economic order, just as the trade wars of the 1930s were prevented from recurring in the postwar period only by the creation of a new international order based on the GATT, the IMF, the World Bank and American leadership.

The new order will have to include international rules governing investment itself, to limit the jousting for benefits between home and host countries and to provide a channel for the disputes that will inevitably arise among them, however ambitious the preventive rules. It will have to limit the power of the firms in ways acceptable to host countries, and provide alternative means for the latter to reduce domestic unemployment and expand exports. Multinational enterprises have a vital interest in the creation of such a new order, because they will otherwise be caught increasingly in the struggle between host and home countries; it will no longer be possible for them to side with home countries because of the weakness of the hosts, as in the 1950s and early 1960s, nor with hosts because of the inattention of the home countries, as in the late 1960s and early 1970s.

There are already many reasons to begin the construction of a new international economic order to replace the order of the first postwar generation, which has collapsed: the globalization of inflation, international monetary instability, the growing use of export controls, the scrambles for oil and other natural resources, the dire needs of the resource-poor countries of the "Fourth World" and the abilities of the new "middle class" of semideveloped countries to help in assisting them.

The threat of investment wars adds another crucial issue to the list for global economic reform. Fortunately, this particular threat has not yet become acute. There is time to deal with it carefully and constructively, instead of waiting for a series of crises to force hasty reaction. To begin to do so would both defuse the emotional issues raised by the existence and spread of multinational enterprises, and begin to apply the tested principles of international rules and cooperation to one of the major new features of the postwar world economy.

VIII. Epilogue

Trends of the past several years, very likely to be projected into the future, make it clear that host countries, including those in the Third World, will drive an increasingly hard bargain in their negotiations with multinationals. Multinationals in turn will be tempted to accept host-country requirements in preference to those of home countries like the United States. This development means that economists who stress the *dependencia* phenomenon—the dependence of the Third World on multinational corporations and their parent countries—are wide of the mark. Whatever may have been true in the past, the trend is not toward *dependencia*, but in the opposite direction. The relevant question is whether the existing and probable future imbalance in favor of the host countries, and perhaps the firms themselves, can be redressed. As a result of these trends, will home countries like the United States require that a larger portion of their firms' investments be made at home?

The answer to this question is not yet clear. Some preliminary indicators suggest that even without any such direct control, investment in the United States may be more attractive in the future than it has been in the recent past. First, the depreciation of the dollar has made investment in America more attractive relative to industrialized countries such as Germany, France and Japan. Second, Congress is reconsidering the U.S. tax treatment of multinational companies. It has already tightened the treatment of the oil companies, and may well provide incentives or requirements that will produce a greater repatriation of profits earned abroad. The House Ways and Means Committee has initiated study of the current deferral of U.S. taxation of foreign earnings until they are repatriated, and may also again consider changes in the foreign tax credit. Changes in this direction would increase the U.S. tax burden on foreign earnings and make investment in the United States relatively more attractive. Such changes would also represent a more active engagement by the United States in the jousting for the benefits generated by multinational enterprises. Hence they would heighten the potential for conflict among home and host countries and add urgency to the need for the creation of new international rules and institutional arrangements to govern foreign direct investments.

11

American Influence in World Politics

RICHARD ROSECRANCE

Plus ça change; plus ce n'est pas la même chose.

The world is changing, and it is *not* ever more the same. American policy will have to change with it. The question of the future is whether we can adjust to altered circumstances.

In order to sketch the outlines of the "new world" which lies before us, it may be best to compare it to the past. International relations in the aftermath of World War II were essentially simple. Enemies were clearly denominated; allies were known and trusted; the tasks of American foreign policy were direct and largely uncomplicated: to build a strong Western coalition to stop what was then believed to be a united Communist conspiracy from taking over the rest of the world. Communist intentions were quite straightforward, or so at least it was thought: to threaten or to attack other states. An international threat could have the effect of weakening Western nations internally or externally. Without the means to resist external attack, nations could be vulnerable to internal subversion as it was then called. If, however, tolerable external security and adequate living standards were provided, internal Communist parties could not come to power. In the end, therefore, strong states with the economic and military means of defending themselves externally would not be prey to communism from within or without.

The task of American foreign policy, then, was to provide external support and internal aid. No other nation possessed the economic or military strength to stem the Communist challenge. Europe was weak and divided; Japan and Germany were in ruins; the rest of the world was either hostile or impotent. America came to the center of the world stage at a time when other leaders had left it. This placed the United States in an almost unparalleled position of strength and influence, a position of far greater power than even Great Britain enjoyed during the peak of her nineteenth-century primacy. For Britain had never held untrammeled sway. She not only had important enemies: France, then later Russia and Germany; she had strong associates: first Austria, Russia, Prussia, and later, France. For the period 1815–1890 British strength on the continent was never *the* major element in the balance of European power. She merely added her strength to scales which were already heavily weighted. The British contribution was important, but it was not decisive.

American power in 1950, however, was paramount. Americans would conceal their essentially imperial position in the trappings of alliance rhetoric. But the U.S. contribution was crucial. Britain, France and Germany were not strong; they were strong only so long as America supported them. Thus the fundamental premises of American commitment to Europe were twofold: unchallenged American strength, and marked European weakness.

Even though U.S. policy makers may not have been fully aware of it, these twin presuppositions greatly conditioned American diplomacy, and produced a particular set of expectations. Weak Europe should do the bidding of the strong United States. It could not be expected to pursue a course of international action different from America's. Basic American perceptions were fixed at a time when no other conclusion was possible. It thus became feasible to try to build a "situation of strength" in Europe to resist Soviet encroachment, without fearing a clash of interests between Europe and the United States. With the perspective of hindsight it is difficult to understand how those who strongly propounded the Marshall Plan and European integration to make the use of Marshall monies more efficient could not have seen that they were laying the foundations of a European-American rivalry. In the eyes of American policy makers, Europe should be an economic giant, but a political dwarf. She should be militarily capable of resisting Soviet attack, but she should not pursue an independent diplomacy.

In part this conviction may have stemmed from American rejection of discredited European balance-of-power policies. Cordell Hull ceaselessly inveighed against such disastrous practices. American candor would replace European subtlety and deviousness. The notion that international politics could not be conducted on balance-of-power assumptions comported well with the ideological character of the post–World War II age. Communists were irrevocable enemies; democrats were permanent friends. To balance between them was to slight the moral issues. It was inconceivable that one could interchange allies and foes, as the balance of power occasionally demanded. Thus, Europeans as friends would always remain friends; Communists as enemies would remain enemies. One did not have to worry about European fidelity.

One of the surprising evolutions, of course, is that Europe has not been more independent of the United States. To an amazing degree the American assumptions have been accepted by European countries. The feeling of political and military impotence has tended to stifle European diplomacy. Politically, Europe has sought a measure of continental solidarity but has pursued no Great Power role externally. Significantly, Europe's major diplomatic effort outside her borders has been to mute the conflict with the Soviet Union. Her response is that of a worried nation striving to reach a compromise with a potential foe. She has not taken a major role in the Far East, Southeast Asia or the Middle East. She is not a diplomatic force in Latin America.

There are a number of reasons for Europe's relative inactivity and uncertainty. First, the avoidance of a major world power role has permitted European states to concentrate on economic development, trade and welfare. The protection offered by the United States has made it unnecessary for Europe to spend large amounts on arms. Broadly speaking, European nations have devoted just enough money to defense to assure continuity in the American alliance, to make sure that American efforts would not flag because Europe was not doing her part. Thus the restricted diplomatic role has been in part consciously chosen.

Second, given the political movement toward integration, a wider diplomatic focus was difficult to sustain. Political and economic differences among European states were so significant that diplomats could do little more than try to harmonize national policies in an intra-European context. No time or energy was left over for broader tasks. But almost as important as these considerations is acceptance by many if not all Western European states that a wider role might cause conflict with the United States. Habituated to American leadership, Europe has largely accepted U.S. presuppositions and left the major initiatives to Washington. (The relative decline in American power has not yet generated new foreign policy lines in Brussels, Bonn or London. Only Paris has followed an independent tack, and even Gaullist separatism was merely a marginal departure from the course of Western cooperation.)

The two propositions of America's 1950 diplomacy had other consequences. If America was so powerful relative to weak Europe, she could also afford to be generous in her relations with allies. The Marshall Plan was only one of many indications of American willingness to transfer resources to Europe. The U.S. international financial position was such that with very large reserves and a favorable balance of payments, the surplus could be ploughed back. Even when the United States ceased to run a surplus, she was still willing to transfer funds in the form of military and other investments in Europe to continue the process of European reconstruction, economically as well as militarily.

The American role in the world monetary system reflected similar assumptions. In the nineteenth century Britain maintained the international financial system and provided the standard of value, the pound sterling. She did this largely without cost to her own internal economy through manipulations of the London bank rate, regulating the inflow and outflow of gold. She did not at the same time, however, have to maintain the European balance of power. During the final quarter of the nineteenth century, Britain did not have a continental ally. Her energies were devoted to the tasks of empire. Her military strength was used against the much weaker and less organized nations of Africa, the Middle and Far East. Only in seapower did she dominate her continental colleagues; she did not have a role in the intracontinental balance. British foreign policy, therefore, had an easier task in the later nineteenth century than American policy in the twentieth. London was able to assume for thirty years that the continental balance did not require British intervention, or a British alliance. The ability to remain spendidly isolated, then, allowed her to concentrate upon international financial and imperial roles. This result was both fortuitous and favorable. Her economic and military power would never have allowed her to dominate the world if her major rivals had not canceled one another out in the continental balance. Thus, Britain, a much weaker nation than America, could appear far stronger than she was.

The American role in the early 1950s, however, was much more critical than Britain's in the nineteenth century. There was no continental balance; there was no worldwide balance; there was no international financial system without American power. In each area the American contribution was decisive. Hajo Holborn was right when he talked of "the political collapse of Europe." Never before had Europe's fate depended so completely on outside powers, the United States and the Soviet Union. American policy toward Europe was therefore unprecedented. It rested on a "collapse" of European power the like of which had never previously occurred. The United States had to become the makeweight where none naturally existed.

This definition of the U.S. role, however, continued even after the conditions producing it had passed. Both Europe and the United States, but particularly the United States, continued to assume European political and military weaknesses when her economic strength no longer justified such conclusions. The United States went on thinking of herself as the leader of a coalition of weak nations; she continued to try to manage European political affairs when her own strength had begun to decline relatively, if not absolutely. The political, economic and military commitments which the United States has made to Europe are now anachronistic. Given European economic and even military strength, the United States should not expect or feel obliged to bear such a large proportion of future burdens.

The American position at the end of the 1940s not only provided American dominance in Western Europe; it offered an unparalleled position of world primacy. American GNP was approximately 40 percent of world GNP. Soviet GNP, contrastingly, was only 15 percent of American. The Western system of states plus Japan were economically dominant over the remaining states, with Europe and Japan having a preponderance over Soviet allies similar to that the United States had over the Soviet Union. The term "bipolarity" in these circumstances was a misnomer. The world was not divided into two "poles" of equal attractive or magnetic power; one pole was far stronger than the other. It therefore followed that as the Cold War became more intense the greater was the pressure on the Soviet Union and her colleagues. The only case in which the term "bipolarity" could have been even roughly descriptive was a situation in which the USSR mobilized her forces to the maximum while the United States and Europe did not. The greatest Soviet losses in influence thus occurred after Korea when Western nations began to mobilize, economically and militarily. Premier Khrushchev's attempts to continue a policy of confrontation with the West were finally given up when his efforts were seen to be self-defeating.

Outside of Europe the absence of a worldwide balance led the United States to fashion an artificial one by committing American power in every situation of local weakness. When this policy was initiated, it was not entirely unrealistic. The United States was very powerful; the Soviet Union was relatively weak, and local balances were not to be found. This could be only a temporary situation, however. European power would revive. New nations would develop their own resources and capabilities. Soviet power would recover and increase. But even more fundamentally, in a system of states, no single power can expect to have dominion in every context. The European powers of the nineteenth century managed to create episodic balances by matching interests and capabilities. Since no power's interests were unlimited, since powers had denominated separate spheres of influence and operation, encroachment could not go too far. At some point an expanding power encountered another whose interests and capabilities were even stronger than its own in a particular geographic locale. Power alone, therefore, did not create a balance; it was the careful direction of power by interest that helped to do so.

After 1950, however, the United States at least briefly entertained two notions. The first was that she could afford a policy of unlimited generosity toward Western Europe. The second was that she could afford a policy of unlimited hostility to Communist regimes and movements elsewhere in the world. America's contours of interest thus became analytical, not geographic. It was not conceived that other states would be able to nibble around the confines of the American empire; their power would not allow them to compete with America's. What was not recognized, however, was that influence and control were as much a function of interest as strength. When America, on behalf of a theoretical policy of containment and commitment, outran the geographic limits of her real interests, some other power's interest and resolve would be greater than her own in particular theaters. This more than any particular military weakness is the explanation for American failure in a number of recent contexts. Despite her great strength, America's interests are not primary in every region of the globe. In a number of places the combination of local strength and resolve is bound to be greater than that of the United States.

If it was an error to commit the United States to a theoretical policy when its interests were fundamentally geographic, it was an equivalent error to think that the interests of Communist states were theoretical and worldwide. The Union of Soviet Socialist Republics is a single state, not even a fully organized and coordinated nation-state. It is situated in a particular part of the world, and its interests are also in large part geographical. If the United States does not dominate local international outcomes in every region of the globe, it does not follow that the Soviet Union's position must automatically have improved. The Soviet ability to force its own policies on distant regimes is as limited as America's. In some ways the international communist movement is even a disadvantage to Russian national interests. Communist parties have to be helped even though their policies may be at some variance with Soviet interests. Communist regimes have to be assisted even though they may balance between Moscow and

Peking. Thus the apparatus of international communism may force the Soviet Union to make commitments without actually securing control. The communist movement in this sense represents the same kind of overcommitment as has been justly criticized in John Foster Dulles's pathological "pactomania."

There is a difference, however. Since America's anticommunist commitments were starkly drawn and clearly defined, any government benefiting from U.S. commitments which was not militantly pro-Western and pro-United States represented *ipso facto* a case of the failure of such commitments. Regimes uninterested in the global struggle between capitalism and communism were bad. Countries whose interests were regional and who did not wish to define their policies in terms of the worldwide rivalry were evil. Even worse were national Communist regimes—governments which did not do Moscow's bidding internationally but which adopted a communist social system. The movement of such regimes to power was everywhere described as a failure of American power or diplomacy. The Democratic party "lost" China and could thereby be impugned for twenty years of treason. Each time the United States did not prevail unconditionally, as in Korea, the result could be described as a loss for America.

But the Russians have had a much more subtle policy. They have tried to manage national communism without regarding each defection as a "loss" for Russian interests. Essentially and with a few exceptions their policy has been that if the regime does not adopt a militantly anti-Soviet stance it can still be regarded to be within the Communist fold. It thus appears that the fissures within communism are less deep than in fact they are. It also appears that the fissures in the American position are much greater than in fact they are. The Soviets have normally tried to plaster over differences; we have exaggerated them. By some paradox of international reasoning it thus becomes possible to regard the triumph of a nationally-oriented Communist regime in South Vietnam as a "triumph" for Moscow and a "loss" for the United States. With time, however, it may turn out that Moscow's gain has been greatly exaggerated, and so also America's loss. Moscow's influence in Hanoi and Ho Chi Minh City may decline as China's increases. And China, it should be recognized, is one Communist country with whom we should seek to be on the best of terms. In short, America's definitions of gain and loss may be overly precise, inaccurate and too short-run in character. Does the "loss" of China in 1949 now look like a great setback to American interests?

I am arguing thus that the American position in world affairs in the early 1950s was unique. The collapse of other powers artificially inflated the American role. It made us think we could do anything. American power temporarily sustained American moralism—the pursuit of a policy based on "right" against "wrong"—an analytical policy divorced from geographic limits. But that policy could not last. It was founded on assumptions of both physical power and transgeographical interests that no nation has ever maintained successfully. The revival of other states has now occurred. In Europe, the Middle East, southern and eastern Asia, the interests and strength of local states will largely determine political outcomes. The U.S. role, like that of Britain in the nineteenth century, will be to add strength to that balance. But the American contribution will not be the sine qua non of stability everywhere in the world. American or other efforts will not produce internal stability in a world in flux.

There is a critique here of both Right and Left in American foreign policy. The Right err because they assume with John Foster Dulles that America must be heavily involved, creating a balance of superiority of strength in every area of the globe. The Left err because they tend to assume that if only our moral position were more firmly grounded we could not fail.

But the failure, if that is what it is, is not due to moral error, but to a misunderstanding of what is possible in international politics. And the conclusion of the Left, or some of the Left, that having failed to prevail morally we should withdraw, is also in error. It represents an erroneous retraction of our interests just as the Right espouses an erroneous expansion of our interests. We should not try to do too much; but we should try to do what we can to advance American concerns. Not to do so leaves the field to others whose interests are at least partly different from our own.

This is not the place to talk in specific terms about the definition of the U.S. national interest. But one should note that some regions and some countries are more important than others. Our connections with Western Europe and Japan are well sustained by basic economic and political solidarities. Latin American countries are a concern for many historical as well as geographical reasons. Some countries in the Middle East and the southern Pacific would probably be defended by the United States if their existence were threatened by regional imbalance. But in all but a few cases American deterrents are not the only pressures making for stability and independence.

Certainly we should not place ourselves in the position of trying to determine internal political evolutions in a host of countries, even if we were able to do so. The best we can do is to fashion, with others, an external balance that allows internal politics to develop without bending to some external threat.

Many believe that the carrying out of even such a reduced list of obligations will be difficult. The United States is still the leading power in the world, but it is not supreme. The Soviet Union, European nations, China, Japan, Canada, rising states like Iran, Brazil and the other oil producers, and perhaps India have come to participate in the worldwide balance. But a more multipolar world can be viewed as an opportunity as well as a problem. From cold war and American hegemonical perspectives, it is unquestionably a problem. If America's international function is to produce a global balance by participating directly in every local balance, stronger powers perhaps endowed with nuclear weapons are certainly a challenge to the United States. Their behavior cannot be governed, but only influenced. If, on the other hand, a more traditional veiw of foreign policy prevails, there is less for America to do.

One of the reasons for American misunderstanding of its role has been the misuse of foreign policy instruments. U.S. foreign policy has been *en bloc,* insufficiently nuanced. Economic policy has been used to reward allies; military policy has been used to threaten or punish enemies. Reward has been applied to one group, sanction to the other. But the United States is no longer strong enough to perform both tasks. Western Europe and Japan are in some ways economically stronger than the United States, though they are vulnerable to raw material shortages. They can no longer be rewarded out of the stock of American reserves or capital, because they now possess these more abundantly than the United States. After August 15, 1971 the United States ceased such policies and now seeks a return flow of economic strength. In the military field, the United States is not superior to the Soviet Union in strategic nuclear weapons, or if it is, it is not sufficiently superior to be able to use its strategic power to threaten the escalation of conventional conflicts around the globe. In Europe it is conventionally weaker; on the high seas it is still stronger, like the British in their heyday. But in areas near the Soviet periphery like the Eastern Mediterranean and the Persian Gulf, the balance is becoming more equal. The United States can no longer police the world militarily. If it undertakes to do so, and conflicts escalate, the consequences for the American people will be as severe as for other peoples.

What has been neglected until the past few years is diplomatic policy. Diplomacy seeks to persuade states to create balances of strength where military force fails. It strives, in short, to use national interests of others to provide an equilibrium where purely American capabilities may be lacking. It is in this sense a cost-effective policy. Taken as a critique of past U.S. policy, it suggests that more benefit is attainable at less cost. In this respect it harks back to nineteenth-century presumptions where no Great Power sought to fashion balances entirely by its own strength. U.S. containment partly inhibited the development of well-defined national interests on the part of European and other nations after World War II. Europe did not have to restrain the aggressive ambitions of the Soviet Union if America would do it for her. A variety of smaller powers also rested on their oars: American commitment made it unnecessary to develop purely *national* security policies. Reliance upon America was the *prima ratio* as well as the *ultima ratio.* Links between Western Europe and China, however, might help provide a greater balance against the Soviet Union than that offered by American efforts alone. U.S. links with the USSR might provide a reason for less reliance upon Western Europe as the pivot of American policy. Diplomacy now offers two new possibilities: it provides a basis for greater pressure on possible opponents than was available before; it provides a basis for greater cooperation with opponents than previously has seemed possible. Diplomacy thus makes possible the creation of a *mixed* system of international relations, a system in which relations with major powers consist of an amalgam of cooperation *and* conflict. A mixed international system is of great importance because it tends to defuse hostilities that remain from the cold war and bipolar period. Because allies are not all on one side and enemies on the other, the cooperation among camps can be much greater. No final pattern of accentuating opposition can emerge, as occurred before

World War I. The relationships between camps may be almost as significant as relations within camps. The polarization of the system can greatly decline.

In the aftermath of World War II and the Korean War, however, it was difficult for American policy makers to see initially that it was not in their interest to adopt a policy of irrevocable opposition to the Soviet Union. Any rapprochement with an enemy, it was initially reasoned, was a repetition of Munich. If one power gained, the other could only lose. This, of course, was true if the bargain took place when one party had no alternative to agreement on the other's terms but war. If one state had no alternatives to compromise, and the other possessed many, the bargain could only be one-sided. Chamberlain failed at Munich because there was no means short of war of putting pressure on Hitler. The attempt to draw the Italians into an anti-German stance had failed, and Chamberlain was not willing to effect an anti-Nazi rapprochement with Moscow. The British cabinet declined the only working relationship that might have made Hitler pause.

The options today, however, are much more numerous and powerful. First, and probably least significant, the United States might decide to put much greater military pressure on the Soviet Union than she has sought to do in recent years. While American economic and productive strength has relatively declined, American technology can still put the Soviet strategic and tactical systems under great stress. Conventional rearmament (which is now beginning to take place), particularly if accompanied by even a modest effort in Japan and Western Europe, could have a dynamic effect on the tactical balance. It could reverse the trend of events since 1968. Such conclusions operate on the assumption that Western productivity if effectively harnessed could more than compete with that of the central Communist power.

This option, however, is not of critical importance. Second, and perhaps of the greatest significance is the U.S. connection with China. The rapprochement with Peking is crucial in two respects aside from the manifest importance of ending a futile and nonproductive dispute on both sides. First, closer ties make it less necessary for the United States to tailor its policies to Western Europe. The European connection has been a frustrating and partly unsuccessful one for both parties. Europe has never developed the political or military will to assert itself in negotiations with the Soviet Union. It has remained all too dependent militarily on the United States. Besides, despite all American assumptions of the 1950s, European nations have not developed enough internal political or economic cohesion to serve as a reliable balance against Soviet pressure. Politically Europe has been paralyzed since 1965. Economically, it has been so since the late 1960s. It does not represent, in short, a cohesive "situation of strength." American connections with China thus make it less necessary for the United States to depend upon such an irresolute group of states. China is a logical associate of the United States. She exerts considerable military pressure on her northern frontiers, affecting indirectly even the European balance. She can decide policy affirmatively. She is not normally paralyzed by indecision or internal disputes. Her policy toward the Soviet Union is not likely to shift greatly in the next few years. As her military potential increases, both tactically and strategically, she will be an even more potent force for the Soviet Union to reckon with. Thus, the link with China creates uncertainty in Moscow. From Peking's point of view, the link with Washington at least reduces her major enemies from two to one, and conceivably it even adds a major associate to her side. At minimum, the rapprochement has made any precipitate Soviet move on the frontier or against Chinese nuclear capabilities much more unlikely. The major difficulty with American diplomacy in the past few years, however, has been that the initial breakthrough in relations with Peking has *not* been effectively followed up.

The Sino-American tie has an additional advantage in that Moscow has had difficulty in trying to outflank it. A possible Soviet response to the Peking-U.S. connection might be to foster a special relationship with Tokyo. Japan has not been drawn by Soviet offers of cooperation, however, and seems likely in the long run to follow the American path to Peking, on both economic and power grounds. The U.S. link with Japan is thus probably strengthened by our rapprochement with China. Only in regard to India has some Soviet outflanking been accomplished, and this is not of decisive importance. Indian nuclear threats against China add little to those Moscow already poses. They do not change the conventional balance on China's northern or southern frontiers. It is ludicrous to think that Indian pressure in the south could be used by the Soviet Union to offset presumed Chinese pressure in the north.

The third American option is, of course, Europe. For reasons we have already given, U.S. policy has not been entirely successful in this area. But if a united Europe has not been created, several powerful European states have emerged. Germany and France are measurably stronger militarily than they were at the end of the war. They are dynamically stronger economically. Their technology is desired by Russia. Their political structures are relatively stable. While their governments are interested in productive relations with Moscow in trade and arms reduction, no European regime is willing to pay the Soviet price for mutual balanced force reductions. While trade, raw materials and technology agreements will certainly continue, some European leaders appear to have become disenchanted with the movement in Soviet policy on crucial issues. *Ostpolitik* is not likely to produce any marvelous new gains in relations with Moscow, though the process of opening up Eastern Europe will continue.

There is an additional advantage for the United States in close ties with Europe. The *détente* between Russia and America has generated something of a counter-reaction in European attitudes toward the Soviet Union. In arms negotiations the United States is sometimes accused of acting precipitately in reaching premature accords with Russia. In certain respects therefore, the Western Europeans have sought to hold America back. This, as was proved in the Vladivostok accords, is a very useful pressure, and may bring more Soviet concessions than otherwise could be obtained.

A fourth very important pressure on the Soviet Union is American domestic opinion. Though Kissinger has not said this publicly (and though he may occasionally bemoan the fact), if Senator Jackson did not exist, he would have to be invented. Sometimes the Right may press too hard, and agreements like the trade agreement be lost in consequence. But the alternative of greater military spending, diminished trade and technology deals, and a more pro-NATO, pro-Israeli position is surely not attractive to Moscow. The Vietnam imbroglio in 1975 should not mislead the Kremlin on the general tenor of American domestic opinion and policy. Many influential leaders in the Republican and Democratic parties are to the right of President Ford and Kissinger in foreign policy. Vietnam was one of the few episodes in American foreign relations when almost as many right as left and center spokesmen were in favor of withdrawal and disentanglement. This is not true in other areas. It is probably not lost on the USSR, moreover, that next to Joseph Alsop, Senator Jackson is one of the most pro-Chinese leaders in public life. This domestic firmness is very useful in negotiation, particularly in the aftermath of Vietnam. Many will insist that the advantages of *détente* to American interests be more fully demonstrated before new agreements are made. Far from weakening the American position in Europe, Japan or the Middle East, this requirement will tend to strengthen it. The

Soviet Union will have to pay more to get less. The specter of right-wing Republican dissent will force President Ford in this direction even prior to 1977.

Under these circumstances of appropriate degrees of pressure and alternative options, another productive course is *détente* with the Soviet Union. If pressure is present, cooperation can often be quite significant. *Détente* may even be cost-effective if it brings a reliable lessening of tension among nations. No military or deterrence policy can provide against all the possible threats that might imaginably be ranged against it. Soviet and American defense budgets could escalate geometrically if the worst case assumptions of defense planners were allowed free rein. Any realistic estimate of probable opponent action, therefore, must be an amalgam of capabilities and intentions. To rely only on intentions is to abandon pressure altogether; to rely only on capabilities is to spend far more than is realistically needed. If *détente* brings a scaling down of the American and Soviet defense efforts, it is more than justified. This is true even if all that it does is reduce spending below what it would otherwise have been. SALT agreements should be evaluated in these terms and not just in terms of actual reductions in forces.

Détente is valuable in other respects. It reduces the polarization of the international system, and it also probably makes the management of international crisis easier. This is not a negligible advantage. The basic and most far-reaching polarizations in future international politics are likely to be found in regional rivalries outside Europe. In the absence of some measure of crisis avoidance or control, the Soviet Union and the United States could find themselves on opposing sides of such disputes. This issue becomes more important with the spread of nuclear technology and weapons, further stimulated by the oil crisis. Even aside from overt military nuclear programs, the rapid development of nuclear power will place bomb capabilities in the hands of fifteen to twenty states. In the developing world alone current plans call for nuclear power programs producing enough plutonium for some 1,000 bombs a year by 1980, and thirty times as much by the year 2000. If even a small portion of this output is used for bombs or options on a bomb, stability in the developing world may be much harder to achieve. Of absolutely first importance, then, are superpower arrangements to defuse local crises where this is possible, or to dissociate from them when it is not.

The likely spread of nuclear weapons or capabilities might seem to warrant a Herculean attempt on the part of the United States to prevent such a dispersion from occurring. It has been argued by many that only American nuclear guarantees will stop the process of nuclear diffusion. But for a variety of reasons an attempt to use such guarantees to prevent the spread of nuclear weapons would not be successful. They would not be credible to the recipient or faithfully applied by the donor. Such guarantees would represent a unilateral extension of American interests that could not be justified or sustained, domestically or internationally. If such guarantees are not to be given, the most reliable means of coping with local crises seems to be an understanding with the Soviet Union.

The further spread of nuclear capacities then, with its malignant implications, at least makes the *détente* more durable and dependable. In fact, it is striking that superpower ties have become much closer as other powers joined the nuclear club. Such joint arrangements would not themselves prevent acquisition of weapons, but they might so discourage provocative threats that the incentives to nuclear status could decline. Guarantees by one superpower to protect a potential nuclear state may not be credible. But guarantees by both superpowers to prevent local claimants from resorting to drastic threats could be much more so.

This possibility deserves much more examination than it

has received. If nuclear weapons spread, it seems unlikely that each pair of opponents will automatically attain a condition of mutual deterrence. Because of vulnerabilities, one state may be able to attack another without reprisal. In the absence of superpower agreement, such attacks could actually take place. They would be less likely, however, if the two major powers were prepared to enforce a common policy in the local crisis. Superpower involvement could provide an element of deterrence otherwise lacking.

Today there is a pervasive malaise concerning the American role in world affairs. I believe that pessimism is premature. If the nation is once again asked, as it was by President Kennedy, to "pay any price, bear any burden, meet any hardship, support any friend or oppose any foe" to achieve its objectives, our resources will not be adequate to the task. But if our ambitions are more limited, they may not be difficult to achieve. During the last thirty years of the nineteenth century Germany was the dominant continental power with a much less marked advantage over its rivals than the United States presently enjoys. Britain, for most of the period was informally associated with Germany and capitalized on the stability produced by German efforts. France was contained by Germany, and other powers were linked with Germany in one or more understandings. Both Great Britain and Germany tended to assume that local balances either would naturally exist or could be created without necessitating draining commitments. Russia would contain Austria, a Mediterranean *entente* Russia. France could not move, initially because she had no ally, and afterward because Russia would not support her in an offensive war against Germany. Thus neither Germany nor Britain had to do much to keep the peace.

Today and for the foreseeable future, the United States has equivalent, and perhaps even greater advantages. Russia is hemmed in between China and Europe; China between

Russia and India. Neither Japan nor the European states would remotely think of using military means to advance their positions. The United States, therefore, is in a position to make limited, not unlimited, contributions. It does not have to solve the world's energy crisis, the food crisis or the financial crisis by itself; the interests and capabilities of other important states are equally involved in helping with such efforts. Today the United States has returned to a position of being the world's greatest power, not the world's dominant power. The recognition of this new role in a new and more multipolar environment could provide a much more enduring pattern of world equilibrium and peace than we have known since World War II, making our present discontents somewhat easier to bear.

New Directions?

12

RICHARD ROSECRANCE

The World Political System

The evolving international system requires a new American role. New trends can now be discerned that will bring change in American foreign policy. Among other developments, the trend toward regional political, economic and military solutions of problems seems to have been slowed or even reversed. In Europe, the EEC (European Economic Community) cannot solve monetary, energy, economic or defense problems without the help of other countries. New monetary arrangements depend upon the agreement of the United States as well as that of the developing world. Regional solutions cannot be devised for worldwide problems like the economic recession. Outside of Europe, regional efforts to provide security or economic welfare on a local basis have not succeeded. In the future, the primary trend will almost certainly be away from regional responses and toward particular forms of international cooperation on most issues.

These tendencies mean that the United States cannot hope that the world can be run on the basis of regional "clock-universes." Previously many people in and out of government believed that if a fully developed regionalism could take hold in several areas of the world, providing economic, political and military strength on a local basis, the United States would be left with little to do. After "winding up the clocks," it could watch them run, safe and secure in its North American redoubt. The failure of this conception means a new form of American involvement in world politics, but not the one imagined by policy makers in the 1950s and 1960s. The United States may participate more actively in a future international system than it has in the past, but the form of its involvement will not be to reinforce patterns of alliance and opposition, commitment and deterrence. Nor will America's own role be decisive. Rather its efforts will be added to those of like-minded nations performing similar functions.

The erroneous cold war conception of the past was that American military power conjoined with economic aid could determine the future in one geographic context after another. U.S. intervention in the domestic affairs of other countries as well as internationally would be both necessary and sufficient to safeguard American interests. Not only would European societies remain dependably anti-Communist, and perhaps also desirably Christian Democratic, but other less developed societies could also be ensured against left-leaning tendencies by U.S. aid. The extension of this reasoning to Vietnam led to the most notable failure in American foreign policy since 1945. It is now clear in contrast that the United States neither can nor should try to determine the domestic evolution of friendly states. It can affect certain international power relationships, but it has neither the right nor the ability to chart internal outcomes for other peoples.

Generalizing upon America's failure in Vietnam, one can observe a growing intransigence in the domestic politics of many countries, making internal change essentially unpredictable. This is the second characteristic of present and likely future world politics. European Communist parties obtain funds from Moscow, and their leadership is often Moscow-trained. But the French and Italian Communist parties are far more latin than they are Soviet. They are much more likely to be servants of French and Italian national interests than they are of Russian. If Communists should play a role in a coalition government in either country, the result would not necessarily redound to the benefit of Soviet interests; it would correspondingly not jeopardize American interests. They would not be likely to force their countries out of the Western alliance, nor would they seek to leave the Common Market. The fundamental point is that the French and Italian Communist movements are genuine projections of their own national societies, not instruments of Soviet power. They are not likely to be truly more subject to Russian control than they are to American.

In Angola as in other African societies, this conclusion is likely to hold with equal force. Current U.S. concern with developments in that country is just as misplaced as are Soviet concerns. Whatever the short term result, Moscow will not be able to count upon an Angolan satellite, nor will the United States have to face an implacable or permanent foe. African politics is so fluid and so largely determined by domestic impulses that it is not a fit subject for the great power rivalry which it has occasionally evoked.

If longer term domestic evolutions pose problems, they are far more likely to do so for Communist rulers in Eastern Europe and the Soviet Union than for leaders in the West or the developing world. The processes of economic growth and the demands of consumers may well have set certain limits upon regime policy and posture, at least in the European Communist countries. Governments there have little positive support and might be undermined by sudden political events, such as the revolutionary disturbances in Czechoslovakia, Poland, and Hungary of recent years. The opening up of those societies to Western influence, both economically and culturally, could gradually erode their regimes, or it could force regimes to follow certain minimum policies. Certainly the development of Eastern European nationalism now makes it much more difficult for the USSR to get its way even with those regimes it supports. The relative placidity of relations between bloc countries then owes more to Soviet forebearance than to Eastern European flexibility.

These trends underscore a third feature of present and likely future international politics: the renaissance of stronger national interest dimensions in government-to-government bargaining. Two kinds of social situations produce this result. First, there are plural societies with weak governments. Where there is little national support for government action, cabinets may have to pursue their interests ever more assertively in international relations, seeking to prove that they are deserving of domestic loyalty and trust. Second, there are more or less nationally unified societies that will support their governments in demanding concessions from other countries. Britain is an example of the first; France and West Germany of the second. The result in either case, however, is increasing obduracy and assertiveness at the international level. Bargaining becomes more difficult because major states no longer adhere to common interests.

Part of the more intransigent atmosphere results from the failure of international ideologies and institutional remedies to take root. The great ideological currents that reached the height of their force after World War II have now abated: democracy, socialism, communism and international integration no longer inspire exclusive loyalties. Economic development is no longer seen as a panacea. National sentiment emerges because it is familiar. But even where a nationalist orientation succumbs to ethnic or cultural pluralism, the pressures on a government are largely the same: it must demonstrate competence and effectiveness in dealings with others. Thus, the British, with basic ethnic cleavages, have to bargain harder, but the Germans, with greater national consciousness, are less willing to make concessions. It goes without saying that in the developing world, nationalism is the *sine qua non* of even a modicum of social stability and coherence. Government could not exist without it.

The renaissance of specifically "national" as opposed to "international" interests is partly responsible for U.S. and Soviet discomfiture in recent years. The United States can no longer inspire devotion with appeals to Atlantic unity or an anti-Communist crusade; equally, the Soviet attempt to get Communist parties to put loyalty to Moscow ahead of national Communist interests has persistently failed. Nationalism has thus strengthened an already growing intransigence in domestic politics. As more than one observer has noted, there is a rising cost to intervention in the domestic affairs of other peoples. Interveners achieve less and pay more for it and, even then, the long term results are by no means guaranteed.

A fourth trait of world politics that is likely to be accentuated in the future is the intermeshing of issues. Previously, economic, resource and security arenas were largely differentiated and distinct. It was presumed that the major world economic questions—currency, investment, aid and technological expertise—fell in the exclusive preserve of Western and highly developed nations. A "Group of Ten" could in effect handle all such questions because other states did not have the resources to gain admission to the game, nor could they greatly affect it. One could form a "Paris Club" that could determine the distribution of the world economic product in relative privacy.

Security questions were the preserve of the United States and the Soviet Union. Other states were either economically weak or too devoted to their own internal economic development to allocate resources to security tasks. The spread of nuclear weapons initially reflected this pattern and the bipolar dominance that it represented. Britain and France acquired weapons, but, it appeared, only to reinsure the American guarantee. The basic superpower preeminence in the field was unquestioned. But the Chinese and Indian development of weapons, and Israel's acquisition of them mean a decisive shift away from superpower control. China and India did not acquire their nuclear capability under the umbrella of superpower alliances, and neither would use its weapons conjointly with a superpower strategy. Israeli weapons are an insurance policy, but if Washington and Tel Aviv move apart, they could become purely an instrument of national policy. The development of production reactors by Brazil, Iran and many other nations will lead to a further erosion of superpower influence over and control of the strategic environment.

The provision of world resources was never fully controlled by the West, but the economic incentives to sell cheap oil and raw materials were supposed to be so overwhelming that Western capitals never questioned their abundant availability. Multinational corporations and a few developed governments were conceded the ability to drive tough and effective bargains with producing states. Once again, the previously operative assumption has been challenged, and the number of major participants involved in resource decisions has greatly increased.

In each of the formerly closed political environments a host of new and important participants has appeared. International negotiation has become much more complex, and the range of interests that has to be accommodated has grown proportionately. Trade-offs between issues are now a typical means of reaching agreements. "Linkage" in this sense has become the name of the game. This situation contrasts with that of a past period, in which the United States could keep its policy compartments separate and nearly watertight. In those days it would not have had to modify its policy on the Middle East to ensure access to oil supplies. The International Monetary Fund did not represent an important pressure on Washington to alter its Vietnam position.

The increasing intermeshing of issues and the broadening of the scope of interdependence do not necessarily make peaceful agreements easier to achieve. They mean that several issues must be handled at once in a kind of international "package deal" before any one can be settled. A breakdown in one phase of the negotiations imperils others, as it would not have done in years past. At the same time, because of the linkage of issues, governments that were previously denied participation in international decision making now possess an important share in it. Though agreements are harder to reach, when they do emerge, they command greater support, and the subcomponents of the overall package are held more firmly in control by the negotiators. If these agreements are strongly supported by major powers, it is even possible that local participants, for example in the Middle East, may lose the "freedom" to make war on their own. Considering the effect of such crises on other, linked issues, superpowers may exert great pressure to prevent local initiation of hostilities. Equally important, superpowers now strive much harder than they have in the past to reach regional accords that obviate a recourse to force.

A fifth characteristic of future world politics is the increasing obsolescence of military solutions to international problems. Obviously, force cannot solve environmental or raw material problems, but is it any more useful in economics, or in winning prestige and influence? In the nineteenth century the way to gain diplomatic power and honor was to win battles. Power in war translated itself into power in peace. Both Britain and Germany illustrated this rule. In the late 1970s, however, the use of force may not compel assent, given greater nationalism and the declining malleability of domestic politics. But perhaps even more important, the use of force, even if successful, raises serious questions about its user. Can an aggressive nation be trusted in the diplomatic and political bargaining which is necessary to wrap up the "package deals" that are more and more characteristic of world politics? Even if the United States could have seized and held major oil producing facilities on the Persian Gulf, it would have completely undermined its credibility in negotiations to end the Arab-Israeli conflict.

It follows that the next decade will be, par excellence, an

era emphasizing and depending upon diplomacy and diplomatic skills. As issues become more interlinked, the use of force at a particular point can more easily disrupt the overall system of agreements, but it can offer nothing in its place. For force to be successful in grappling with all the issues it would in practice have to achieve a world monopoly. But in military, strategic, political and economic terms, world domination is now harder to achieve than ever. Not only are societies resistant to outside control, but the spread of nuclear and conventional capabilities reduces both great and middle power leverage.

What remains of superpower influence and control is primarily in the economic, diplomatic and technological fields. The ability to offer and withhold rewards and to do so impartially—these are the negotiating credentials of the future. Too great a commitment to one side is a disadvantage, not an asset. The recognition of this reality constitutes another new feature of world politics, and it contrasts markedly with past eras. For a generation after World War II, the *modus operandi* of the United States in international affairs was "commitment and deterrence": to define a line or area of commitment and then to deter all attacks upon the protected region. Under Secretary of State John Foster Dulles it was a commonplace that the firmer the commitment, the greater the deterrence. In the late 1970s too one-sided a commitment is paradoxically a handicap; it means that all one's associations are with one side, and that the other side has no reason to offer its trust. American diplomatic capabilities in the Arab world have depended upon loosening the tie with Tel Aviv. With China they have rested upon an increasingly remote connection with Taipeh. U.S. negotiations with the Soviet Union have become more profitable as the United States began to feel somewhat less tightly bound to its alliance with Western Europe. The same result holds for other powers. China has been able to approach the United States only since she severed the link with Moscow. Diplomatic autonomy and impartiality, then, take precedence over past commitment.

The United States: General Orientations

The changed international system implies a number of differences in the U.S. role. Most importantly, success for American policy will almost certainly depend upon an ability to retain diplomatic contact and also leverage with opposing sides in each political confrontation. This means that America will do less *ex parte* defending of specifically American and Western interests, but this should not present a major problem, for U.S. interests are no longer so specifically and rigidly defined that they require primary defense by American efforts alone. Even though European defense was considered in the past to be a primary American responsibility, others can now make important, even decisive contributions to it. As the Angolan imbroglio shows, Congress may refuse to finance a policy that puts the United States "out front" of allies and other interested parties in defense of sectarian political or regional interests. This does not mean that there are no special American interests which would be defended with force by the United States alone, if need be. Certain confrontations in the Western Hemisphere or on the high seas could see the United States act independently. It is most likely however, that U.S. force would be used jointly with others and after a regional conflict had begun.

But a major and decisive resort to force, conventional or nuclear, may be less likely in the future. The USSR could not solve its conflict with China by a conventional attack on Europe, nor help itself in Europe by striking at China. Furthermore, an attack on China would not neutralize Japan. A Soviet move into South Asia could only jeopardize its diplomacy and would probably produce a Sino-Indian rapprochement. A Soviet thrust into the Middle East would propel the

Arabs into the arms of the United States. In sum, there are now too many important participants in international diplomacy to permit a superpower to think that the kind of limited, conventional struggle that is within its abilities could resolve its quarrels with others. As things now stand, a sudden conventional thrust could only exacerbate them, and a nuclear attack could wipe out gains of the past two hundred years.

What remains is diplomatic influence and leverage, and it is in this realm that the United States will be if anything more active than it has been in the past. Indeed, it might even be argued that at the point of maximum U.S. physical involvement in world politics (at the peak of the Vietnam conflict) U.S. diplomatic influence was surprisingly low. A lessening physical presence, therefore, will not prevent an increase in American diplomatic leverage. Indeed, the growing interrelationship of issues provides a further reason for an enhanced American role. No other country, not even the Soviet Union, is a pivotal member of all international environments: military, economic, technological and political. The USSR is not and will not for a very long period be an important participant in international financial or currency negotiations. Despite its ability to give economic assistance to developing countries, the Soviet Union cannot solve their problems in a larger sense. Only access to Western consumer markets and financial resources can do that. Here American help is critical.

Despite its developed economy and the progress of its heavy industry, the USSR is not usually in a position to offer the most appropriate technology to the less developed countries. The required technical inputs and industrial skill seem to come from American, Western, and Japanese multinational corporations. Even in resource and raw material negotiations the Soviet Union has had a muted role. The Arab producers must find a reliable means of protecting the profits they gain from oil. Ultimately this requires a stable relationship with Western economies, so that longer term commitments can be made. When Arabs rapidly transfer funds between money markets to benefit from short term currency fluctuations, Western central banks become less and less willing to take Arab monies. If a larger agreement with the West and Japan is not obtained, the Arabs may find that their revenues are a depreciating asset: unable to make long term gains through investment, they may discover that banks do not want their short term funds. Even here, therefore, the key to a solution of the problem of primary and secondary recycling of funds lies in the hands of Western economies, particularly that of the United States. The Soviet Union has little or nothing to contribute.

Here we see a distinction between positive and negative power: the ability to find a solution to a problem as opposed to the ability to veto a solution. Military power, commitment and deterrence are elements in negative power; they provide the wherewithal to say no. As long as the greatest problems and challenges in world politics were military, and as the threat of war increased, negative power was very important. But negative power does not foster solutions. Solutions depend not upon military threats but upon political good faith and trust. They also require sophisticated economic capacities and financial systems that are flexible enough to accommodate considerable shifts of resources from one actor to another. In 1976 Western economies tended to display resilience and toughness that were unimagined in the initial stages of the oil crisis three years earlier. The system did not collapse; Arab surpluses did not build up as rapidly as had been foretold; Arab imports from the West were higher than had been forecast. Western and Japanese central banks and credit facilities were much more capable of dealing with the crisis than had been believed. It was a measure of the buoyancy of Western economies that finance ministers could turn to the problems of the developing states, instead of concentrating on their own.

A future policy environment, then, is likely to see, as Pierre

Hassner has noted, a series of interlinked issue and regional contexts with the United States as a participant in each. It will be the only superpower thus involved. Because the United States will have important friends or associates on both sides of a given issue, it will be a kind of crucial intermediary. If it is to attain and keep this position, America cannot risk individual adventures or unilateral policies. It is essential that the United States remain at the hub of the network of multilateral diplomacy.

The United States: Individual Policies

The trauma of Vietnam and Congressional fears of involvement in Angola have delayed the formulation of a new American foreign policy. Secretary of State Kissinger appears to vacillate between strong support of *détente* on the one hand, and, on the other, a rather ill considered and hasty opposition to Soviet and local Communist projects in several areas of the world. U.S. national interests are not likely to be permanently affected by particular outcomes in Portugal or Angola. But to seek to intervene in such contexts, where local forces dominate, harms American diplomacy in two respects. It shows America to be ineffective in the first place, and in the second it poisons relations with a successor government. Domestic balances in other countries should not be on the American foreign policy agenda.

There are, however, three international balances that the United States should strive to bring about. The first is a balance between the Soviet empire and the Western and developed world. The second is a balance between Arab oil producers and the world's consuming nations. The third is a balance between the developed and the developing nations. The United States should be an important participant in these balances, but as a balancer or intermediary; its influence should not be wholly on one side.

First, the Western-Soviet equipoise. It remains true that the

United States is the guarantor of the Western alliance and would immediately be involved should there be an attack on Germany or the flanks of NATO. The establishment of a strategic and a conventional balance of forces, however, should not be sought as it was in the 1950s and 1960s. Military preparations with American forces in Germany and elsewhere, together with a cohesive North Atlantic Alliance, are not necessarily the only recipes for European security. It should be accepted that in foreign policy, and ultimately even in defense, Western European states will begin to chart their own courses. Thus, British and French deterrents have to be taken into account as independent factors. British and French tactical nuclear weapons compound the uncertainty in Soviet calculations and reinforce deterrence. West Germany has emerged as a powerful conventionally armed state with technological capacities second to none.

More important, however, is the China factor. Despite the diplomatically-timed release of Soviet helicopter crews in 1975, China's tensions with the USSR are not likely to abate in the next few years. The new Chinese leadership will probably reflect traditional military as well as ideological hostilities toward the Soviet Union. It is clear that the Chinese wish to improve relations with Western countries, particularly the United States. The United States responded to Chinese overtures in 1971 and 1972 but has since let its ties languish. Western European states neglected Chinese initiatives in the early 1970s but are now beginning to take them up, economically and politically. There is a particular merit in such ties because Europe and China lie on opposite flanks of a common enemy, the USSR.

China's position, therefore, has important implications for Western defense. The one million Soviet troops that China's armies tie up in Siberia and Central Asia, could, if released, undercut the Western defense position in Europe. Secretary of Defense James Schlesinger noted in 1974 that NATO armies could, under some circumstances, cope with 80–90 Warsaw Pact divisions in Europe. But they could not hope to withstand the more than 130 divisions that would result if China permitted the Russians to move forces from the Chinese border. China's stance at the time of a conflict in Europe, therefore, would be critical to its outcome. Even a Chinese mobilization could put great pressure on the Russians.

It is, therefore, difficult to understand why the United States has been so laggard in implementing its rapprochement with Peking. The Chinese remain interested in a much enhanced trading relationship, covering the exchange of oil and other minerals for Western industrial goods. U.S. defense ties with Taiwan are an impediment to full recognition, but there is no reason why the United States might not move to formal relations with Peking and still keep close economic links with Taipeh. Japan has already done so. The special problem of the U.S. defense treaty might be solved by a Chinese pledge not to use force in bringing about an eventual reunion with Taiwan. In the short term, in any event, the Taiwanese defense forces could repulse a mainland attack on their own, so Peking has no alternative to diplomatic persuasion. A stronger formal relationship with China would also strengthen U.S. ties with Japan. Japan has now abandoned its "even-handed" stance between Peking and Moscow and is moving toward Peking. It is very important that the United States not appear to favor a more pro-Moscow orientation, which in East Asia would not be in its own interest.

It is not enough, however, merely to oppose the Soviet Union and assume that hardline policies will produce maximum Russian concessions. Improving relations with China should be designed to permit, indeed encourage, better relations with the USSR. *Détente* cannot be productive without some diplomatic leverage on the Western side; but neither is leverage without *détente* likely to be productive. If Russian leaders are to be able to restrain their own cold warriors and military leaders, they must be convinced that Washington is genuinely interested in an accommodation. SALT bargaining may now be the only way in which either side can limit its military budget. Western countries as a group have important negotiating cards to play in their dealings with Moscow. Strategically, the United States has an overall technological superiority of great magnitude, and if the strategic arms race were to be pressed, it would redound to the disadvantage of the Soviet Union. Economically and industrially, the Russians are far behind Western societies. They have not been able to reach a high and dependable level of agricultural productivity, and they have not been able to produce a highly sophisticated industrial and computer technology on their own. Some observers believe that the USSR cannot make the transition to a modern industrial economy without Western help. To have this help made available, the Soviets must sacrifice certain time-worn options. In the Middle East they have already largely restrained their Arab clients and have given America diplomatic scope. In Europe they have been required to implement some of the Helsinki accords that they did not like. Their temporary euphoria about Portugal has been greatly moderated, and their temporary success in Angola, if that is what it is, means that they must find other means of demonstrating their good will and belief in the *détente.*

If the United States was merely to seek to capitalize upon Russian weaknesses, economically and militarily, however, it would succeed neither in limiting the defense budget nor in persuading Congress to permit greater U.S. intervention in troubled areas of the world. The world would be redefined in cold war terms, but without a U.S. political will to carry on cold war policies. Perhaps the major benefit of *détente* to this point, therefore, is that it has permitted America to make do with policies of limited commitment and involvement. A measure of Soviet restraint is implicit in this recognition.

Détente is important for still another reason. Just as superior technology is possessed by the West and Japan, so the USSR has great untapped natural resources. It is difficult to imagine very long term solutions to the world's energy and raw materials problems without eventually drawing Soviet production into the world economy. The availability of these resources will, of course, partly depend upon Russian estimates of their future relationship with Western countries. It is beneficial to both sides, therefore, that political relations provide a good basis for closer economic contacts.

The U.S. role in *détente* is two-sided. In one respect America must defend Western interests against Soviet moves. In another way, however, the United States must also see that she does not become so tied down by relations with her Western European colleagues that the chance for a fruitful accord with the USSR is lost. She must be on both sides of the fence and cannot afford to mortgage her future to any one primary connection.

A second balance in which the United States must play a major role is that between the OPEC oil producers and the world's consuming nations. In the immediate aftermath of the oil crisis in late 1973 and early 1974, many economists favored breaking the OPEC cartel and its unilateral ability to set prices. Only a united front by the consuming countries, it was argued, would prevent a toppling of the international finance system. Since then, however, OPEC has had to countenance an informal softening of export prices, and much higher prices for industrial and food imports. The build-up of surplus funds has been much slower than was forecast. Arab countries' need for money has left all but Saudi Arabia and Kuwait in fairly tight circumstances. OPEC's imports have been higher than estimated.

At the same time, the consuming nations have found reasons to oppose a sharp cut in oil prices. A cut would not only inhibit the production of energy from alternative sources, but it would probably, through the mechanism of an elastic demand, lead to even higher total expenditures on oil than occur at the moment. High oil prices serve to cut down the consumption of energy and make alternative sources more economic. Thus there are more common interests linking consuming nations and OPEC than was previously supposed. These common interests may ultimately see agreement on investment policies and greater stability in currency markets. Arab economists have come to recognize that a major depression in the industrial world would harm not only consuming nations but also their own investments in currency, real estate and industrial property. They have an interest in the recycling of petro-dollars that is second only to that of the consuming nations themselves.

Common interests in monetary and economic arrangements partly extend to political questions. If there is another Arab-Israeli war, followed by another embargo, both sides will be greatly hurt. It is unlikely that OPEC could absorb all the effects of production cutbacks that an embargo would involve without experiencing an internal crisis. Only Saudi Arabia could take severe cutbacks without having her development plans affected. If other OPEC members had to retrench as well, they would have to draw on Saudi funds. Whether the Saudi government would be willing or able to sustain other Arab economies is not clear. Furthermore, Arab investments in embargoed countries might be sequestered, their funds impounded until a settlement was reached. Thus Arab portfolio managers must either decline to invest long term funds in Western economies or run considerable risks. For their part, Western countries surely do not want another embargo. Thus there is strong pressure from both sides for a settlement of the Arab-Israeli conflict. Whether this pressure will be suffi-

cient to bring about an agreement cannot be said, but an accord is now an international necessity.

The U.S. role in Middle East negotiations reflects America's
position as an essential intermediary. On the one hand, Washington has been Israel's leading supporter in the international
community and sought initially to bring down the price of
oil. On the other, its connections with Egypt and Saudi
Arabia in addition to Iran have made Washington understand
the Arab and Moslem political case and the oil producers'
economic argument. A solution to the quarrel depends upon
Arab as well as Israeli trust in the United States. The Arabs
will look to the United States to produce Israeli territorial
concessions. Tel Aviv will demand American guarantees and
Arab recognition of Israel's right to exist within reduced
frontiers. If negotiations came to a halt, the parties might
take up arms once again. Without the U.S. facilitative role, a
compromise could be beyond reach.

The third and perhaps ultimately the most important balance which the United States must seek to maintain is that
between the developed and the less developed parts of the
world. This involves much more than helping poorer countries which cannot pay for oil imports. It means, finally, providing a fairer share of the world economic product than
these countries have yet received. What is at issue is not
merely an increasing share of new wealth, but a transfer of
some part of existing wealth from the Northern Hemisphere
to the Southern. The economic activities of multinational
corporations, operating under new political constraints, have
commenced this process. But more concessions, including
greater access to developed country markets, are required.

What is necessary is a broadening of the Lomé Agreement
to include generalized tariff preferences for African, Asian,
Latin American and Pacific goods in developed country markets—not only those of Europe, but also North American and
Japanese. The exports of such countries would be admitted

freely, but their own economies would not be expected to withstand the full blast of competition from developed country imports. These would continue to be restricted by tariff barriers. The developing nations have pressed very hard for commodity agreements to sustain prices in adverse economic conditions. The United States has agreed to consider these "on a case by case basis" but prefers arrangements that would stabilize Third World income. Whatever the exact formula, a greater share of the wealth derived from bauxite, coffee, cocoa, tin and other products should be funneled into the less developed world. Long term economic planning becomes impossible when uncertain market conditions lead to vast swings in export revenues from one year to the next. Indeed, it appears likely that the cartelization of such commodities will occur in the absence of satisfactory commodity agreements.

A more radical proposal involves providing new monetary units like the SDR (Special Drawing Rights) to poorer countries on preferential terms. At the moment, the international monetary system operates according to the biblical maxim, "To him that hath shall be given." SDRs are now allocated according to the shares countries hold in the International Monetary Fund. If developing countries were given an extra quota of SDRs, more than in proportion to their existing shares, they would have a redistributive claim on purchasing power that would facilitate economic development as well as providing a basis for coping with high oil and Western manufacturing and food prices. Such a change would be an indirect tax on Western and Arab production, but it could do more to integrate the world economy politically than all the foreign aid since World War II. It would give the developing nations a basis for believing that their poverty need not be permanent, that they need not become poorer as the developed world becomes richer.

Free enterprise economists in the United States, Europe

and Japan will resist these proposals, and they may not be implemented. At the same time, the prospects for the developing world are now relatively brighter than they have been. But if the United States does not make a major effort on their behalf in the short term, the long term will see a gradual and irreversible alienation not only from the international economy and Western economic systems, but also from Western political systems. While the EEC has taken important initiatives to tie some of the developing countries more closely to Western markets, only the United States can offer possibilities that make a general solution of the problem possible.

Conclusions

In light of the future U.S. role, it is important to understand in what American "ordinariness" consists. America is and should be "an ordinary country" in foreign relations in terms of burdens and commitments. She should not assume, nor should she ever have thought, that her efforts alone stood between anarchy and order in international relations. Her national interests should not be vastly larger than those of lesser powers. In other words she should not be prepared, on her own, and supported solely by her own means, to perform tasks that most other states would not undertake. This does not mean, however, that her participation in world politics will be that of an "ordinary nation." Indeed, her participation in the solutions of many international problems will, if anything, increase in the years ahead, and may do so in direct proportion to the decline in her physical and military presence.

U.S. alliance ties with more than forty other nations should, as Alastair Buchan argues, be seen more and more in terms of equal relationships within an overarching "coalition." The United States cannot be "proconsul" of the world. But coalitions vary greatly in membership depending upon the issue. The monetary coalition is not the same as the resource coalition. The political-security coalition is not the same as the development coalition. The critical point, however, is that the world's problems can no longer be approached from a single perspective. Security considerations do not provide a final answer any more than economic ones. What is true of issues is also true of nations. The power and relevance of one nation's solution to world problems is not only limited; it is more limited than it was. America, in this sense, is not the only country which has become "ordinary." The complexity of international issues has become so great that many nations and many points of view must be enlisted to find solutions.

As the problems in international relations have increased, the means for dealing with them has had to become more varied and complex. Simple support or opposition solves little. Nor is it sufficient to support a state on one issue and oppose it on another, for issues have become interlinked. Increasingly, on states and issues, qualified support and qualified opposition are the order of the day. Complete antinomies or polarizations create "negative power" without providing "positive power." If solutions are to be found at all, they will depend upon the creation and development of a mixed international system in which polarization declines and nations maintain contacts and relationships with states which hold a variety of other ideological, economic and issue perspectives.

This is a particularly important point to make at a time when some are calling for a new polarization and a return to cold war patterns. It is not sufficient merely to brand the Soviet or the OPEC camp as "enemy" and to proceed on another American "crusade" to eradicate evil in the world. As an "ordinary country," the United States is not nor should it be in a position to solve world problems by force of will, economic power or arms. It is not strong enough to do that, and world problems are far too complex to yield to such simplistic remedies. Rather, the United States should strive to create and to help maintain a world in which adversaries still remain in contact with one another and where compromises are still possible. Because of the interlinking of issues, many international problems will not be solved unless they can be solved ensemble. The role of the United States should be that of balancer, peacemaker and intermediary, not military leader or autocrat. This would be a more modest role than some Americans have been used to accepting, but in the final analysis it could be far more beneficial, for the United States itself and for the world at large.

Index

ABM, *see* Anti-ballistic missile
Acheson, Dean, 35
Adenauer, Konrad (Chancellor, German Federal Republic), 111, 112, 122
Africa, 13, 41, 82, 94, 100, 163, 170, 228, 247, 262
Agriculture, 89, 93, 186, 259; *see also* Food
Ajami, Fouad, 192n
Albania, 25, 41
Aliber, Robert, 179n
Allies and alliances, 12, 15, 25, 27, 31, 33–37, 42, 52, 59, 62, 66, 71, 77, 101–104, 114, 120, 126, 142, 143, 150, 153, 155, 156, 158, 160, 165, 172, 180, 190, 192, 193, 203, 210, 225, 226, 227, 228, 235, 236, 243, 246, 247, 250, 252, 253, 257, 260, 264; *see also* Coalition, Concert, North Atlantic Alliance, *and* North Atlantic Treaty Organization
Alsop, Joseph, 240
Andean Pact, 202, 206, 207
Angola, 17, 30, 49, 50, 73, 247, 253, 256, 259
Anti-ballistic missile (ABM), 53
Arab-Israeli conflict, 26, 37, 98, 251, 261; *see also* Middle East
Arab nations, 25, 77, 117, 149, 161, 252, 254, 255, 259; *see also* Middle East, *and* Oil-producing nations
Argentina, 205
Arms control, 39, 50, 55, 71; *see also*

Nuclear weapons, Strategic arms, *and* Strategic Arms Limitation Talks
Arms expenditures, 15, 31, 42, 52–53, 164, 227, 240, 241, 259; as proportion of GNP, 15, 53, 164
Arms, sale of, 79, 103, 111, 117, 149, 155, 157
Asia, 13, 25, 29, 43, 136, 138, 139, 140, 144, 153, 157, 158, 163, 181, 262; *see also* East Asia, Far East, *and* Southeast Asia
Asian Collective Security System, 140
Atlantic Charter, 68, 74, 101
Atlantic Community, 121, 128; *see also* North Atlantic Alliance, *and* North Atlantic Treaty Organization
Australia, 53, 59, 137, 155, 157, 207, 220
Austria, 24, 25, 92, 225, 243
Axis powers, 21

Balance of payments, 15, 16, 116, 168, 169, 178, 184, 188, 200, 206, 207n, 212, 218, 227
Balance of power, 22, 24, 43–45, 51–52, 67, 158, 210, 225, 226, 228, 230, 233, 234–236, 257; bipolar, 31, 64, 65, 67, 69, 72–73, 74, 158, 229–230, 236, multipolar, 64, 65, 74, 75, 168, 234, 244
Balance of trade, 15, 16; *see also* Trade, international
Ball, George (U.S. Undersecretary of State), 62, 87

Burke-Hartke Bill, *and* United States Trident missile and submarine system (U.S.), 55; *see also* Nuclear weapons, *and* Strategic arms
Truman Doctrine, 23; *see also* Containment, *and* United States
Truman, Harry, 28, 146
Turkey, 17, 25, 30, 36, 47, 60, 80, 83, 84, 99, 103, 106, 111, 127; *see also* Cyprus, *and* Greece

Unemployment, 77, 114, 160, 166, 167, 168, 172, 188, 202, 205, 219, 221; *see also* Depression, *and* Recession
Union of Soviet Socialist Republics, 12, 23, 24, 25, 26, 33, 37, 40, 43, 46-59, 67-75, 77, 78, 80-85, 93, 94, 102, 106, 107, 110, 122, 127, 138, 139-142, 147, 149, 150, 151, 152, 155, 156, 157, 163, 176, 225, 229-233, 234, 237-241, 243-244, 246-247, 253, 255, 256, 257, 259, 260, 265; expansion of, 14, 23, 24, 29, 51, 72, 85, 158, 224-226, 231; limited role in world bargaining, 74, 107, 239, 254-255; nuclear capability of, 15, 28, 32, 50, 51, 68, 139-140, 237, 259; vulnerabilities of, 51, 75, 197, 229-230, 240, 259; *see also* Cold War, Communist nations, *Détente*, Sino-Soviet split, *and* Superpower relations
United Nations, 22, 23, 26, 27, 29, 34, 145, 174-175, 192, 210; Security Council, 29
United States: commitments of, 17, 19, 23, 25, 26, 42, 62, 77, 78, 97, 116, 136-137, 138, 144-145, 146, 151, 155, 156, 189, 225, 229-231, 232, 234, 242, 246, 249, 252-253, 258, 260, 264; economic interests of, 16, 164, 195, 200, 211-212, 235; energy policy of (Project Independence), 191; flexibility of, 15, 27, 29, 62, 65, 67, 74-75, 79, 101, 156-157, 165, 173, 252, 262; geographical and functional interests of, 13, 231, 233, 234; leadership by, 11, 14, 21, 59, 60-61, 63, 66, 68, 74, 78,

104, 113, 119, 126, 129, 147, 158-159, 163, 180, 182, 183, 191, 221, 224, 227, 229, 233, 234, 244; national interests of, 12, 14, 20, 22, 24, 26, 29, 38-39, 55, 76-77, 81, 102, 106, 115, 122, 129, 148, 154, 155, 157, 158, 163-164, 167, 173, 183-189, 214, 234, 240, 242, 246, 247, 253, 256, 264; "ordinariness," 11, 264-266; role as intermediary, 69, 74, 85, 94, 233, 256-264, 266; security interests of, 22, 35, 55, 76, 116, 151, 154, 183, 192, 203, 231, 242; troops, 15, 16, 17, 25, 116, 117, 123, 124, 136-137, 143, 144-149, 257; *see also* Cold War, *Détente, and* Superpower relations
United States Congress, 17, 20, 28, 30, 62, 80, 83, 99, 103, 123, 144, 147, 160, 219, 222, 253, 256, 259
United States-Japan Security Treaty, *see* Japanese-American Security Treaty
USSR, *see* Union of Soviet Socialist Republics

Venezuela, 186
Vernon, Raymond, 174n, 179n, 181
Vietnam, 11, 13, 16, 26, 30, 42-45, 56, 63-65, 69, 73, 78, 82, 115, 136, 137, 141, 146, 147, 152, 155, 156, 159, 160, 165, 173, 182, 183, 190, 233, 240, 246, 250, 254, 256; North Vietnam, 14, 78, 140-141, 154, 156, 164
Vladivostok agreements, 32, 54, 240; *see also* Arms control, Nuclear weapons, Strategic arms, Strategic Arms Limitation Talks, Union of Soviet Socialist Republics, *and* United States States

Wallace, Henry (U.S. Secretary of Commerce), 23, 26
War, 25, 34, 39, 73, 138, 140, 144, 145, 147, 148, 158, 166, 186, 237, 243-244, 251, 253, 255, 262; nuclear, 73, 253
Warnecke, Steven, 90
Watergate (issue in U.S. politics), 30,

Library of Congress Cataloging in Publication Data

Main entry under title:

America as an ordinary country.

  Includes bibliographical references and index.
  1. United   States—Foreign   relations—1945-   —Addresses, essays, lectures.
I. Rosecrance, Richard N.
E744.A485   327.73   75-38427
ISBN 0-8014-1010-X